Get Better at Anything

ALSO BY SCOTT H. YOUNG

Ultralearning

12 Maxims for Mastery

Get Better at Anything

SCOTT H. YOUNG

HarperCollins*Publishers*

HarperCollins*Publishers*
1 London Bridge Street
London SE1 9GF

www.harpercollins.co.uk

HarperCollins*Publishers*
Macken House, 39/40 Mayor Street Upper
Dublin 1, D01 C9W8, Ireland

First published by HarperCollins*Publishers* 2024

1 3 5 7 9 10 8 6 4 2

Designed by Michele Cameron

A catalogue record of this book is
available from the British Library

ISBN 978-0-00-867946-0

Printed and bound in the UK using 100% renewable
electricity at CPI Group (UK) Ltd

This book contains FSC™ certified paper and other controlled
sources to ensure responsible forest management.

For more information visit: www.harpercollins.co.uk/green

To Thomas and Julia

CONTENTS

Part III   Feedback: Learning from Experience

Get
Better at
Anything

How Learning Works

L ife depends on learning. We spend decades in school, acquiring an education. We want to be good at our jobs, not just for the perks that come from being one of the best, but for the pride that comes from mastering a craft. Even the things we do for fun, we enjoy to a large extent because we feel we're capable of getting better at them.

Yet learning is often mysterious. Sometimes it comes effortlessly, as when we quickly find our way around a new neighborhood or pick up the routine at a new job. In other cases, it's a slog. We may spend hours in the library, with little to show for it on the final exam. We may want to switch companies, industries, or even professions, but not feel qualified to make the leap. We can spend decades driving a car, typing on a computer, or hitting a tennis serve without reliably getting better at any of them. Improvement is inconsistent, if it comes at all.

Whether your aim is eventual mastery or just to get a little bit better, it helps to understand how learning works. Simple principles can explain why progress comes easily in some situations, and can be frustratingly absent in others. To begin, let's look at an unlikely story of world-class skill development—how *Tetris* players suddenly became much better at the game, three decades after it first became popular.

The *Tetris* Enigma

As he does most days, Joseph Saelee fired up a game of *Tetris* on February 15, 2020. Immediately, the iconic, four-square multicolored bricks begin falling at a rate of roughly one every second. Despite a pace that would make most arcade buffs sweat, Saelee is barely paying attention. Instead, he's chatting with the handful of followers who have come to watch him play live on the online streaming platform Twitch. The conversation slows as he reaches level 19. Saelee must now find and maneuver each brick into the best possible spot in the two-thirds of a second it takes for them to reach the bottom. Before it lands, he is already glancing at the display indicating the next piece—the only reprieve from the otherwise completely unpredictable sequence of shapes. After nine levels at this blistering pace, the speed doubles once more. The bricks barely blink into existence before they are already at the bottom of the screen. As he completes this stage, the level counter glitches, changing from displaying "29" to "00"—a clear sign that the game designers thought nobody would make it this far. Seemingly in a trance, Saelee jiggles his fingers to tap the buttons on his controller more than ten times per second. He is able to perfectly place each brick, clearing space fast enough to prevent new ones from overwhelming the screen. After a few minutes, he makes his first mistake—a single misplaced brick stands tall above the otherwise neatly arranged rows. In the blink of an eye, it is all over, a deluge of squares filling the screen. Despite this, Saelee is smiling. Defeat may have been inevitable, but Saelee had managed to reach level 34, a feat that had never been accomplished in the thirty-year history of one of the most popular video games of all time. Saelee was just eighteen years old.

Joseph Saelee is obviously skilled at *Tetris*. But what is more remarkable is how much better he is than the first generation of players who were obsessed with the game. Playing on level 29 was long thought impossible. Bricks dropped so fast that simply holding left or right, a player couldn't move them all the way to the edge of the screen before they became locked in place at the bottom. Since a complete, horizontal row of blocks is needed for them to disappear in the satisfying *Tetris* click, fans regarded the level unplayable, nicknaming it the "killscreen." Another feat, achieving a maximum score of 999,999 points in a single session, was long sought by early players. But the first documented "max-out" didn't occur until two decades after the game's release, when Harry Hong reached the top score. In contrast, over the span of a single tournament in 2020, Saelee maxed out twelve separate times. Nor is Saelee unique in his *Tetris* proficiency. During the same tournament, forty different players reached the maximum possible score. How does a game, long past its prime, produce much better players?

Tetris, Then and Now

Tetris feels dated today, so it's easy to forget the sensation it caused when it debuted. Invented by Russian computer scientist Alexey Pajitnov in 1984, the game spread via floppy disc through the twilight years of the Soviet Union. Pajitnov, like many an office employee after him, was hooked by his own creation, playing *Tetris* instead of working. Vladimir Pokhilko, a psychologist and friend of Pajitnov, thought the game was so enticing it could be used to study addiction. Eventually he had to destroy all his copies when it became clear that his research staff weren't getting any work done. After it was stumbled upon by software broker Robert Stein during a trip to Hungary, the game set off a ferocious battle for distribution rights in the West. Eventually Nintendo emerged victorious, creating the definitive edition for its Nintendo Entertainment System (NES), selling millions of copies and creating a generation of devoted fans.

While for most players, *Tetris* was just an amusing pastime, others became obsessed. Ben Mullen, an early record holder, kept detailed statistics on his play to try to find hidden patterns to optimize his performance. "I found out that, actually, exactly one half hour after you have some coffee, you play the best *Tetris*," he reports. Harry Hong played so much he had to place a shirt between his thumb and the controller to keep from getting blisters. Others played until they began to hallucinate falling blocks, in what would later be called the "*Tetris* effect." But devoted as they were, none came close to the performance effortlessly displayed by modern players like Saelee.

Resolving the Enigma

A clue to understanding the stark change in proficiency comes from observing how players made their achievements known. In the earliest days, official records were managed by Twin Galaxies, a video game record database. Players submitted their high scores, along with some form of verification. If deemed legitimate, referees would post the scores to a central leaderboard on their website. But the process was cumbersome. Players might fail to sufficiently document an attempt, resulting in a record that was ultimately unsubmittable. This was the fate of Jonas Neubauer and Thor Aackerlund, who had claimed to have reached a max-out before Harry Hong, but couldn't prove it. But for years, there was no other option. If you wanted to be seen as the best, you had to go through Twin Galaxies.

This started to change after YouTube. Freely uploading videos, players could share their world records directly, rather than going through an intermediary. While this made it easier to submit a new top score, it had an important side effect: if you posted a video of a world record performance, everyone could see how you did it. Before that, Twin Galaxies had only posted the top score, not the evidence itself used to verify it. Players could now not only marvel at the skill of elite *Tetris* players, but see how they did it.

While early YouTube provided greater transparency, the informal nature of the records also created temptations to cheat. Older games like *Tetris* could be run on an emulator, a piece of software that allows you to play console games on a personal computer. This specialized software lets players slow down the gameplay or rewind to undo mistakes. While careful sleuthing can often spot telltale signs of a fraudulent record, genuine players started investing in ways to authenticate their performance. Recording not just the screen but also video of the players' hands became common. Livestreaming further increased authenticity, as the best players could be watched playing the game in real time, making cheating nearly impossible.

Observing hand movements, innovations in button pressing could be widely replicated. A method known as hypertapping, where players vibrate their thumb to hit the direction buttons more than ten times per second, was key to breaking through the level 29 barrier. Thor Aackerlund, the best player of the early era, had invented the technique. But as few could witness and emulate his approach, it remained unused for nearly two decades. Livestreaming also created an incentive for commentary. Great players, pushed to communicate with an audience, shared their thinking behind the game in real time. Discussion ran in both directions, as top players not only shared their strategies, but viewers could immediately scrutinize potential mistakes. While an earlier era of game masters might have jealously coveted a secret strategy that gave them an edge, modern competitors were forced to be radically transparent, with every button press exposed for all the world to see.

Online forums greatly expanded the network of potential players to learn from. In the 1990s, your resources for improvement were limited to your circle of friends. If you happened to know a very good *Tetris* player, you might learn a few tricks. But if you didn't, some of the subtler aspects of the game might be invisible to you, despite years of experience. Harry Hong revealed in a 2010 documentary that his preferred strategy was building his blocks on the right, leaving a gap on the left side of the screen. This strategy is considered inferior today. A quirk in the game's rotation algorithm makes the all-important bar-shaped block easier to rotate and shift to the opposite side. Dana Wilcox, another former top player, wasn't even aware that you could rotate the pieces in both directions. Such a gap in knowledge meant she couldn't execute a few tricky maneuvers, such as a "T spin," where the T-shaped block is twisted at the last possible moment to hook into an otherwise unreachable position. Today a new player can easily find the best strategies, even if they take considerable practice to master.

Tetris players are better today because their environment enables it. Video hosting allows detailed demonstrations of the best play to be broadcast widely. Online forums transform informal conversations into permanent reservoirs of knowledge. Livestreaming encourages extensive practice, including near-instantaneous feedback from an audience increasingly knowledgeable about the top techniques. Ultimately, the story of *Tetris* is not about any individual, although players such as Joseph Saelee certainly merit distinction. Instead, it's a story about the game itself, and how the way it was played accelerated progress.

The Three Factors for Getting Better at Anything

As the story of *Tetris* illustrates, improvement depends on more than just talent or tenacity. There are three factors that determine how much we learn:

1. **See.** Most of what we know comes from other people. The ease of learning from others determines, to a large extent, how quickly we can improve.

2. **Do.** Mastery requires practice. But not just any practice will do. Our brains our fantastic effort-saving machines, which can be both a tremendous advantage and a curse.

3. **Feedback.** Progress requires iterative adjustment. Not just the red stroke of a teacher's pen, but contact with the reality we're trying to influence.

When we're able to learn from the example of other people, practice extensively ourselves, and get reliable feedback, rapid progress results. Yet, when one or all of these factors are inhibited, improvement often becomes impossible.

More often, we find ourselves in a situation between the extremes that maximize learnability or prevent it entirely. Instead, there are both obstacles and opportunities, ways we can accelerate progress by finding the right environments, mentors, practice regimens, and projects to work on. The difficulty is often in knowing exactly what to look for.

See: The Power of Examples

We learn best through other people. Our ability to learn from each other greatly exceeds our ability to solve problems on our own. *Tetris* performance accelerated once the methods for high-level play became widely accessible. "The secret of our species' success lies not in our raw, innate intelligence or in any specialized mental abilities," writes Harvard anthropologist Joseph Henrich. Instead, he argues it's the ability to learn easily from the innovations of others that makes us uniquely capable as a species.

In some cases, intelligent animals can beat us in displays of problem-solving ability. Researchers have shown that crows can solve the problem of getting food out of a narrow bottle by fashioning a hook with a metal wire. Yet if a modified version of the same task is given to five-year-olds, fewer than a tenth figure out the trick. But if our problem-solving capacities are only modestly greater than some of our animal cousins, our imitative abilities are second to none. In an experiment, researchers compared two-and-a-half-year-old children to chimpanzees and orangutans on a battery of cognitive tests. Contrary to our species' presumed superiority, the researchers found that children and apes performed similarly on puzzles involving spatial, quantitative and causal reasoning, with the chimps even edging out the children on some tasks. The clear exception was in social learning, where the toddlers were easily able to solve a problem when given a demonstration, but virtually none of the apes could. Young children may not compare favorably to crows and chimps in raw problem-solving ability, but they regularly learn to read, write, talk, add, multiply, draw, sing, and use a television remote—something no other animal can even attempt. The cliché of mindless learning, "monkey see, monkey do," has it exactly backward. Imitation is the foundation for human ingenuity.

Yet the ability to learn from others has its drawbacks. When we lack access to people we can learn from, we struggle to make progress. The early devotees of *Tetris* were essentially isolated from one another. They played alone, or with a handful of close friends. Techniques for best play couldn't be transmitted, so each person had to evolve their own methods. In rare cases, such as with the video game prodigy Thor Aackerlund, this could go quite far. But in most cases, the result was play far below human potential. New technologies such as video uploading, livestreaming, and online forums greatly accelerated the dissemination of best practices. Even if *Tetris* is no longer the most popular game in the world, today's generation of players is far more interconnected.

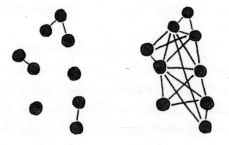

Figure 1

More connections between players means more chances for innovations to spread. Members of the network on the right have more opportunities to learn from peers than those on the left.

The quality of examples we learn from also matters greatly. The transition to scientific chemistry from its origins in alchemical practice serves as a useful illustration. Early alchemists may have been wrong about the possibility of turning base metals into gold, but they did possess some reliable chemical knowledge. Many alchemists worked to develop a theory of matter and others even conducted controlled experiments. Yet they chose to deliberately obfuscate their findings out of a desire to keep esoteric techniques out of less experienced hands. As historian and chemist Lawrence Principe writes, "Alchemy's primary sources present a forbidding tangle of intentional secrecy, bizarre language, obscure ideas, and strange imagery. The alchemists did not make it easy for others to understand what they were doing." Alchemists used code names, or *Decknamen*, to conceal the identity of certain substances. They wrapped recipes inside fantastical allegories that had to be deciphered to be understood. They omitted, swapped, or added unnecessary steps to confuse unskilled readers. While this certainly had the intended effect of limiting knowledge to a privileged few, it also prevented the accumulation of reliable knowledge. Would-be alchemists had to repeat predecessor's experiments dozens of times. A failed attempt didn't prove the recipe was incorrect, as it was always possible that it hadn't been properly decoded. Even a brilliant thinker such as Isaac Newton spent much of his life chasing down alchemical lore without realizing it was a dead end. In contrast, Robert Boyle's experiments with his air pump—which led to the formulation of Boyle's Law still taught in chemistry classes today—were meticulously documented, with dozens of illustrations of his experimental setup and the measurements he obtained. Confusing explanations and omitted steps in a process aren't limited to alchemical texts. We often struggle to learn when materials are poorly designed and force us to do more work than is necessary to understand a concept or master a procedure.

Knowledge is not evenly distributed. Despite the promise of the internet age, the majority of the world's knowledge isn't written down and freely available. Instead, it's locked away in the minds of experts, many of whom would struggle to articulate what they know. Knowledge is often not inside the head of any individual at all, but embodied in practices spread over groups. In a 1980 documentary, economist Milton Friedman, channeling an earlier essay by Leonard Read, used the example of a wooden pencil. "There's not a single person in the world who could make this pencil. Remarkable statement? Not at all." Friedman goes on to explain that the wood chopped down requires saws, which requires steel, which requires iron ore. The rubber, paint, glue, and graphite all involve enormously complicated supply chains to manufacture. The knowledge of building something as simple as a pencil isn't held by any individual, but groups who work together toward a common purpose. As our science and technology develop further, individual achievements may become increasingly rare as distributed groups become necessary to bring together all the knowledge required to solve hard problems. New advances in artificial intelligence may accelerate this trend, as the world of book knowledge becomes increasingly accessible, but the tacit understanding of unspoken practice remains within cloistered communities of experts. Access to the environments where knowledge resides is often a bigger hurdle to mastery than learning itself.

Do: The Necessity of Practice

Being able to learn from others is only the first step. Skill requires practice, not just observation. Practice plays a number of important roles in learning. The first is that repeated practice reduces the mental effort to perform tasks. Using functional magnetic resonance imaging (fMRI), researchers observed the brain activity of *Tetris* players as they gained experience with the game. Contrary to the expectation that using more of your brain equals greater performance, players' neuronal activity decreased as they played more. This broadly supports the idea that, through repeated play, the players had become more efficient in using their nervous system. If you've driven a car for years, you have probably noticed something similar. What was previously an effortful task that required your full attention now can be done unthinkingly. Your mind wanders elsewhere while your hands and feet go through the motions. The ability to automate component skills is a key factor in the performance of many complex tasks, and is one of the reasons why we can't simply perform at an expert level merely from watching someone else do it.

Another reason for practice is the importance of memory retrieval. Watching someone perform a skill is often necessary to figure out how to do it. But if the answer is always available when we practice for ourselves, we may not remember it deeply. If you're old enough to remember an era before cell phones, you probably memorized a few dozen phone numbers you called regularly. Today, despite seeing the number every time you hit the dial button, you may struggle to recall a single phone number other than your own. The difference is that, before contacts were saved directly on our phones, every call forced you to retrieve the number from memory. Retrieval beats review for strengthening your memory.

Finally, while we're fantastic imitators, many parts of a skill cannot be emulated. How the arm moves in a tennis serve or how the wrist flicks in a brushstroke can certainly be observed. But everyone's musculature is unique, so these observations are only approximations of how you must perform the skill yourself. Perceptual skills like discriminating patterns in an X-ray or predicting the path of a golf ball rolling down a green have large tacit components that can't be easily communicated, even with a patient teacher. Hands-on practice is essential to master the aspects of skills that can't be taught in a book.

The necessity of action in learning creates its own obstacles. It's more effortful to actively practice than to passively watch a video, so it's easy to lean toward consumption rather than action. Access to the real environment for performing the skill may be limited. It's hard to get good as a pilot without a plane or as a filmmaker without a camera. Finally, the balance between learning from others and doing it for yourself can be tricky to find with complex skills. Too little support, and learning is frustrating trial and error. Yet too much can be harmful too, as when seeing a pattern preempts our ability to retrieve it. We don't always make this choice correctly. Researchers have found that low-ability students benefit from more structured environments, so they can learn problem-solving patterns they don't yet have in memory, while high-ability students benefit more from less structured environments, where they can get more realistic practice and are forced to retrieve knowledge they already possess. Yet students prefer the method of learning that works worse for them! An explanation for this perverse tendency is that learning is effortful and we try to conserve effort. Low-ability students find the demands made by the structured approach taxing, and so opt for the flexibility to avoid meeting a rigorous standard. In contrast, high-ability students find the added structure easier and so prefer following the recipe rather than generating the right answer on their own. Fine-tuning the difficulty matters greatly for learning, and we don't always get it right.

Feedback: Adapting with Experience

Repeated practice isn't enough. Without feedback, improvement is often impossible. As early as 1931, psychologist Edward Thorndike had subjects practice drawing lines of a particular length. Despite performing the skill three thousand times (in what must have been a riveting experiment), subjects failed to make any progress. The expert of expertise, psychologist Anders Ericsson, developed the concept of deliberate practice to explain how elite performers in music, chess, athletics, and medicine were able to reach peak levels. The presence of immediate feedback was central to this conception. Just as high-quality, immediate feedback underlies the progressively deepening skill of elite athletes and musicians, its absence can also explain deteriorating performance. In a systematic review, researchers found that the quality of medical care tended to decline as doctors spent more time on the job. Patient outcomes only depend partly on doctor's interventions, and the difference between best practices and outdated techniques is often only possible to spot in carefully controlled trials. This spotty feedback means it can be difficult to engage in the kind of deliberate practice Ericsson argued is central to continuing mastery.

We can accelerate our progress by creating better systems for feedback. During the Vietnam War, both the Navy and Air Force were losing a fighter plane for every two enemy planes taken down. To improve this, the Navy created the Navy Fighter Weapons School, also known as the Top Gun program. This involved simulated sorties where trainees flew against the best possible pilots. After each encounter, their performance was reviewed in depth, with each decision discussed in an after-action report. The result was that while the Air

Force's success in taking down enemy fighters continued to be two-to-one, the Navy jumped up to twelve-to-one, a sixfold improvement. Ericsson reported an experiment run with foreign exchange traders in a European bank that experienced similar performance improvements from the competitive simulations with after-action feedback. Being able to design more valid, informative feedback into your improvement efforts can be the difference between progress and stagnation.

Why Learning Still Matters

Separate from the worry about whether improvement is possible is the worry that learning may soon be obsolete. As I write this, sophisticated computer programs can now write poems, explain quantum mechanics, and illustrate pictures in any artistic style, on demand. Assuming such technological progress continues, what will be the point of mastering skills that can be performed effortlessly through silicon chips? But the rise of technological change is just as likely to create a demand for new learning as it is to undermine old abilities. The invention of paper was decried by Socrates for degrading the faculty of memory, but the outcome was an explosion of knowledge that no individual could hope to memorize in a single lifetime. Information technology has rendered some jobs nearly obsolete, even as it has invented new ones that did not exist before. In a paper authored by Massachusetts Institute of Technology economist David Autor and colleagues, the researchers found that roughly 60 percent of the jobs people had in 2018 didn't exist in 1940. While technology may have reduced the demand for typists and telephone operators, it also created an explosion of software developers and business analysts. A reasonable extrapolation of past technological trends would suggest that advances in artificial intelligence will result in greater demands for learning, not less. Predictions are hard, especially about the future.[*]

---

[*]   A paraphrase of a famous saying, attributed to (depending on whom you ask) Nobel Prize–winning physicist Niels Bohr or baseballer Yogi Berra.

And so I will avoid speculating on which exact skills and knowledge will end up as essential for future generations. However, insights into the process of learning, and how we can make it more successful, are likely to become more relevant, not less.

A Curious Quest

I've long been fascinated by learning. In 2019, I published my book *Ultralearning*, diving into the strange world of obsessive autodidacts, and drawing upon some of my own experiences learning languages, programming, and art. But curiosity is a strange drive. Unlike hunger or thirst, curiosity is stoked, not sated, when we learn more. And so, despite spending years both striving to learn new skills, and trying to make sense of the academic research behind skill development, I ended up embarking on a new quest to try to resolve questions my previous efforts left unanswered. A couple hundred books and several hundred academic papers later, I've found satisfying explanations for some of my earlier puzzles. But, in keeping with all quests of curiosity, new questions have multiplied in their place. This book is, in many ways, an effort to make sense of what I've found.

I wrote this book with two audiences in mind. First, I wanted to write from the learner's perspective. If you want to get better at anything, how should you do it? What kinds of examples should you seek? What kind of practice works best? What influences whether you'll attain mastery or plateau early on? Secondarily, I wanted to examine how teachers, coaches, parents, and those responsible for shaping learning within an organization can cultivate improvement. Since the birth of my two curious learners, I've become keenly interested in what I can do as a father to guide them in becoming the best they can be. Good teachers are precious, and the science underlying successfully fostering skill development is not widely known. Above all, I wrote this book for people like me—those interested in getting better, but not always sure the best way to proceed.

What to Expect from This Book

Over the next twelve chapters, we'll dive deeper into the three themes of seeing, doing, and feedback. Improvement may not always come easily, but we can all think more intelligently about how we learn. Each chapter is expressed as a simple maxim. My hope is that long after the details of the research explored in each chapter have faded, these rules of thumb will serve as both a reminder and a useful—if imperfect— summary of the key principles.

Maxims one through four are about the power of examples:

1. **Problem Solving Is Search.** We'll begin with a mathematical mystery that lasted for over three centuries, and the groundbreaking theory of problem solving that can help us understand its resolution. We'll explore the difference between routine and creative thinking, and how what we learn from others greatly shapes the complexity of problems we can solve.

2. **Creativity Begins with Copying.** Next, we'll dive into artistic training during the Renaissance. Imitation—far from being opposed to creativity—is the seed for original work. We'll explore the mind's bottleneck, and how the best strategies for acquiring knowledge often differ from the processes used to generate new ideas.

3. **Success Is the Best Teacher.** Sophisticated skills depend on having the proper foundation. When the building blocks are missing, learning is slow and frustrating. Experiencing genuine successes early in the learning process can make motivation self-reinforcing.

4. **Knowledge Becomes Invisible with Experience.** Finally, we'll explore the curse of knowledge, or how expertise leads

to a receding awareness of the basis of our own proficiency. Expert intuition, while powerful, often makes it more difficult to acquire complex skills, as capable performers lose the ability to explain how they do it. To remedy this difficulty, we'll explore a family of tools to extract the knowledge experts take for granted.

Maxims five through eight deal with improving our practice:

5.   **The Difficulty Sweet Spot.** Progress depends on finding a delicate balance between making practice too hard or too easy. We'll explore research showing when difficulties can be desirable . . . as well as when they are not. We'll look at the writer's paradox—or, why the best writers seem to suffer from the most writer's block. We'll examine several tools for fine-tuning the difficulty level of your improvement efforts, from progressive problem solving to constructing a practice loop.

6.   **The Mind Is Not a Muscle.** What improves when we practice a skill? Despite its enduring appeal as an analogy, the metaphor that the mind is like a muscle is highly flawed, as shown by over a century of research. Research on the transfer of learning will help us understand when strengthening one ability will lead to improved performance in another.

7.   **Variability Over Repetition.** Next, we'll dig into the development of improvisational abilities among jazz musicians. How do players create complex performances without repeating themselves? In answering this question, we'll explore the science showing how practice variability can lead to more flexible skills.

8.   **Quality Comes from Quantity.** Genius is prolific. In this chapter, I'll explore research showing how, to a surprising

extent, creativity simply *is* productivity. Those who produce the best work are almost invariably those who produce the most work. We'll look at the implications of this for your own efforts to make an impact.

Maxims nine through twelve revolve around the role of feedback:

9. **Experience Doesn't Reliably Ensure Expertise.** Practice doesn't make perfect. Indeed, without the right kind of feedback, practice often doesn't even make us very good. In this chapter, we'll look at learning in environments of uncertainty. We'll compare poker players, who manage to master a complex game despite wild swings of luck, with the more typical case where decades of professional experience lead to mediocre predictions. Drawing on these differences, I'll offer suggestions on how we might tame unfriendly learning environments.

10. **Practice Must Meet Reality.** In this chapter, we'll explore the reckoning from the worst aviation disaster in history. What we learn in a classroom has a complex relationship to what is practiced in the field. True proficiency requires contact with the physical and social settings where a skill will be used.

11. **Improvement Is Not a Straight Line.** Getting better often first requires getting worse. In many subjects, we come equipped with intuitions that bear little resemblance to proven scientific theories. As we progress, improvement comes to depend on rooting out misconceptions, inefficiencies, and mistakes.

12. **Fears Fade with Exposure.** Finally, I'll shift from learning skills to the anxieties that often surround them. We'll look at the surprising effectiveness of exposure therapy in

overcoming fear, and why many of the intuitive strategies we develop to cope with our anxieties backfire. Courage, not just cleverness, is essential for mastery.

Finally, in the conclusion, I'll step back from the research and discuss how you can integrate these ideas in your own practice. Whether you're studying for an exam, needing to learn a new skill at work, or just want to get better at something you're interested in, I hope these suggestions will provide a starting point for thinking about how you might do it better.

To start, let's look at the science of problem solving, by looking at the story of a puzzle that took over three hundred and fifty years to resolve.

PART I

SEE

LEARNING FROM OTHERS

CHAPTER 1

Problem Solving Is Search

Whenever one cannot go from the given situation to the desired situation simply by action, then there has to be recourse to thinking.

—*Psychologist Karl Duncker*

- How do people solve hard problems?
- Are there generic methods that work on *all* kinds of problems?
- How do we solve problems that no one has ever solved before?

have a truly marvelous proof of this, which this margin is too narrow to contain." In that one sentence, Pierre de Fermat created a mystery that would perplex mathematicians for over three centuries. It stumped the great Leonhard Euler. Almost a century after the enigmatic mathematician's death, Euler begged a friend to rummage around his old house, hoping some scrap of a proof remained. It fooled the mathematicians Augustin Cauchy and Gabriel Lamé, who briefly claimed to have discovered a proof, before a fatal flaw in their logic was uncovered. German industrialist Paul Wolfskehl put up a prize of one hundred thousand marks to anyone who could resolve the riddle. Yet despite their best efforts, the proof of Fermat's Last Theorem remained a mystery.

Fermat's claim is easy to understand, even if it isn't easy to prove. Pythagoras tells us that in a right-angled triangle, the square of the hypotenuse is the sum of the square of the lengths of the other two sides: $a^2 + b^2 = c^2$. If you play around with it, you can find whole numbers that fit the equation. The numbers 3, 4, and 5 do the trick $(9 + 16 = 25)$; so do 5, 12, and 13 $(25 + 144 = 169)$. In fact, there are an infinite number of these Pythagorean triples, so called because the ancient Greek himself showed they were limitless. But what if you changed the equation, adding cubes instead of squares? Could you find any three whole numbers that fit the pattern? Fermat said you couldn't. In fact, he argued, if you took any exponent higher than two, you would always fail. Stated mathematically, Fermat argued the equation $a^n + b^n = c^n$ had no whole number solutions for n greater than two.

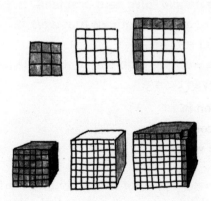

Figure 2

Two squares can be added up to make another square:
$3^2 + 4^2 = 5^2$. But two cubes will never make a perfect cube. Here, for instance, $6^3 + 8^3 = 9^3 - 1$.

Andrew Wiles first heard of the enigma of Fermat's Last Theorem when he was ten years old. "It looked so simple yet all the great mathematicians in history couldn't solve it," he reflected upon his first encounter. "I knew from that moment I would never let it go." Wiles went to school, graduated from Cambridge University, and specialized in a branch of mathematics known as elliptic curves. Fermat's final puzzle never strayed far from Wiles's thoughts as he established his career. Still, having bested mathematicians for centuries, he could see no path forward to finding a proof.

This changed in 1984. Mathematician Gerhard Frey suggested an unexpected link between Fermat's Last Theorem and a famous conjecture made by a duo in Japan. Yutaka Taniyama and Goro Shimura had argued that two seemingly distant branches of the mathematical tree were actually twisted together. Every modular form, they argued, had a counterpart in an elliptic curve. The conjecture had been a workhorse for mathematicians, with many papers tentatively assuming it for their conclusion. Still, it was no more than a suspicion. Frey's contribution was an even more surprising connection: if the Taniyama-Shimura conjecture was true, so was Fermat's Last Theorem. Wiles, already a specialist in elliptic curves, had finally found a path to realizing his childhood dream. All he had to do was prove Taniyama and Shimura's hunch was correct.

Wiles chose to work in total secrecy. Having accumulated some publishable work, he decided to drip it out in a series of papers, creating the impression he was still actively working on old projects. He stopped going to conferences and cut his teaching duties to the bone. Every moment he wasn't at work or with family, he was working on the proof. Adopting a risky strategy, he was isolating himself from the help of colleagues. He claimed the solitude increased his focus. Still, it probably didn't escape his notice that if he worked on the problem alone, he wouldn't have to compete for glory if he uncovered the proof.

Wiles's first eighteen months were spent at the library, learning every piece of mathematics related to modular forms and elliptic curves. An adventurer wandering into an uncharted jungle, he needed to equip his toolkit for any possibility. After mastering the essentials, he explored the math on his own, looking for patterns that might suggest a path to a proof. After two years of solitary work, he made his first breakthrough. He found a way to demonstrate that the first element of each modular form was linked to the first element of every elliptic curve. Now he had only an infinity of elements left to go.

Hitting an impasse, he probed his colleagues for help, careful not to reveal the nature of his project. Maybe they knew of some yet-unpublished mathematics that escaped Wiles's notice? His old advisor, John Coates, mentioned work done by one of his students, Matheus Flach, extending the technique of another mathematician, Victor Kolyvagin. "It seemed to be exactly what I needed," Wiles recalled, "although I knew I would still have to further develop this Kolyvagin-Flach method." Wiles was close, but "it involved a lot of sophisticated machinery that I wasn't really familiar with. There was a lot of hard algebra which required me to learn a lot of new mathematics." Wiles finally decided to break his silence. Confiding in his friend and fellow mathematician Nick Katz, he got the pointers to finish his proof. After seven years of effort, Wiles succeeded where no mathematician had in over three centuries. "It was the most important moment of my working life," Wiles reflected in a BBC documentary made about his triumph, "Nothing I ever do again will mean as much."

How People Solve Hard Problems

Few challenges are as tricky as Fermat's Last Theorem. Yet Wiles's story reveals much about the thinking behind solving hard problems. In 1972, the cognitive scientists Herbert Simon and Allen Newell published a landmark book, *Human Problem Solving*, investigating those mental processes. In their research, they asked participants to share what they were thinking about as they solved problems. Comparing their performance to a model, the duo made rigorous observations about how people work through tricky puzzles. Their discoveries kicked off decades of research and have been applied in domains as diverse as chess, writing, science, mathematics, and medicine.

Central to Simon and Newell's theory was the idea that problem solving is a search through a problem space. A problem space is like a maze: You know where you are now and you can tell whether or not you've reached the destination. Along the way, however, you're constrained by walls that limit how you can move. What makes a maze difficult is that you can't just walk straight to the finish, but need to search to find the twisted path that reaches the exit.

In a maze, the problem space is a physical one. But problem spaces are typically abstract. Consider trying to solve a Rubik's Cube. The starting position is the scrambled cube. The finished position has only one color on each side. The moves you can make are the twists and turns of the cube. The problem space here isn't a literal space, but a space of configurations. Each spin changes the state of the problem into an adjacent one. The goal, as with the maze, is to navigate this abstract space and get from the start to the finish.

Proving Fermat's Last Theorem was also a search through a problem space. In Wiles's case, he had to pick a starting point of previously proven mathematical theorems. His end goal was to write the statement that $a^n + b^n = c^n$ had no solutions for n greater than two. What made the task difficult was the requirement that each move in the problem space be a valid deduction from previous results. The constraints of logic worked like the walls of the maze preventing Wiles from writing down whatever he'd like. Wiles had to chart a path through the twisted corridors of mathematics to a statement confirming Fermat was right.

Once you get used to seeing them, it's easy to spot problem spaces everywhere. Scientists search through a problem space to discover new laws. The starting point is a confusing set of data. The ending point is a theory that explains the data. Solving a problem involves searching through both a space of hypotheses that might explain the data and a space of possible experiments that can test the theory. An architect designing a building is searching a problem space of possible designs, looking for one that fits the constraints of cost, space, and building codes, while trying to optimize its functional and aesthetic value. Writing this chapter was a problem-solving process. My starting point was a blank document. The end goal was a finished chapter, explaining the ideas I wanted to present.

The Tricky Thing About Hard Problems

Simon and Newell's formulation of problem solving has an immediate consequence: most problems are not solvable. The space of possibilities is too large to find a solution. Without a clever method, random guessing would never work. A Rubik's Cube has over forty-three quintillion configurations. Exploring them one by one, even for only one second each, would require five thousand times the age of the universe. Yet Wiles's task was to chart a course in waters incomparably vaster. While a computer program can be written to mechanically solve a Rubik's Cube, it is impossible, even in principle, to build such a device that can prove any piece of mathematics. The mathematician, armed with finite knowledge, must navigate an infinite sea with no guarantee of arriving safely on the other shore. Wiles himself was aware of the likelihood of failure: "Perhaps the methods I needed to complete the proof would not be invented for a hundred years. So even if I was on the right track, I could be living in the wrong century."

If most problem spaces are too big to search through, how do we cope? Simon's answer was that we "satisfice": instead of choosing the best possible solution, we go with one that is good enough. A manager doesn't explore every possibility and piece of information before making an urgent business decision. Instead, she searches until she finds a good enough option, given her limited time and attention. But satisficing has two major drawbacks. The first is that, in choosing the option that is good enough, we may never learn the better option. For unique problems this may not be an issue. But if we expect to face the same problem again and again, our tendency to go with whatever works in the moment may limit our eventual progress. The person who solves a typing problem by hunting and pecking on the keyboard with one finger will manage just fine, but that will also make it harder to learn the touch-typing method. The second drawback is that even finding an acceptable solution can be quite difficult. In Wiles's search, he may have been willing to satisfice on the elegance or length of the proof, but certainly not on its mathematical rigor. A proof that was somewhat clunky or verbose might have been good enough, but certainly not one that violated the rules of logic.

Beyond lowering our standards, another way that we reduce our problem-solving difficulty is by using knowledge to constrain our search to more fruitful directions. At an extreme, this eliminates problem solving entirely. I don't need to conduct a problem-solving search to figure out 5 + 7. I simply remember that the answer is 12. In a similar way, much of our daily life is problem-free because we have saved the solution in memory. Driving a car, making a doctor's appointment, or doing our laundry is not a problem for most adults because they remember the path to a solution. However, you might still remember a time when figuring out how to use a washing machine was a genuine puzzle. Where do you put the detergent? Which clothes go together and which need to be separated? Experience transforms problems into routines.

In some cases, memory can provide a method, even if it can't provide an answer. I can't recall the answer to 128 + 47 directly. However, by following the multi-digit addition algorithm I learned in grade school, I can easily arrive at the answer 175. Not all problems have such convenient algorithms. This fact came as a surprise to mathematicians. In 1900, the mathematician David Hilbert posed a list of twenty-three questions he hoped to see resolved in the coming century. One was an algorithm for figuring out whether equations like the one in Fermat's Last Theorem had whole-number solutions. Seventy years later, mathematicians proved that no such algorithm can exist! For other problems, there is a method that can be guaranteed to find a solution, but it isn't much better than the strategy of simply trying out every possibility. Sudoku, chess, and even *Tetris* can all be shown to belong to this class of problems. Our experience with classroom problems may be deceiving, therefore, as the vast majority of real-life problems have no method that ensures the right answer.

Even if a method can't promise a solution, it can still reduce the amount of searching. Heuristics are methods that offer no guarantees but may work decently in many cases. Facing tech troubles, one heuristic is simply to turn the device off and turn it back on again. This won't always work, but it does solve the problem in a surprising proportion of cases. Wiles had no textbook algorithm he could apply—the refutation of Hilbert's tenth problem showed there weren't any. Yet he had many heuristics he had acquired through years of study and practice doing math. Applying proof by induction, for instance, is a relatively general mathematical strategy whenever you want to prove that a property holds for an infinite number of things. All you need to do is show that it holds for the first thing, and then show that the property doesn't change as you move from one thing to the next. Like knocking over a row of dominos, this trick allows you to prove something is true for an infinite number of items without actually checking an infinite number of times. This heuristic was essential for linking each element of the elliptic curve in Wiles's proof with each element of a modular form.

Another common mathematical heuristic is to look for an invariant. If you can find something that doesn't change in a problem, no matter how you modify it, you can avoid a lengthy problem-solving search. Consider the problem of the mutilated chessboard. In this problem, you're asked whether you can lay dominos to perfectly cover a chessboard that has the top-left and bottom-right squares removed.

Given the sixty-two remaining squares, and each domino covering two squares, at first blush the problem would seem to involve a lot of searching. A lot of different combinations of thirty-one dominos might need to be attempted to decide, one way or another, whether they can fit. However, if you're clever you might look for an invariant. One such invariant is that each domino covers exactly one white and one black square, regardless of how it is placed. Once we recognize that the two squares deleted were both white, it now becomes clear why we can never tile the board—it would require a domino to go on two black squares, which we just showed was impossible. Applying the right heuristic just saved us a lengthy search.

Proof by induction and searching for an invariant are used throughout mathematics and logic. Still, they work only on a fairly narrow range of problems compared to those we might encounter in life. Understanding induction won't help much with painting a portrait or creating a marketing plan. Psychologists call these kinds of methods domain-specific, because they apply to a circumscribed range of problems. This raises an interesting question: Are there any heuristics or strategies that work on *many* different kinds of problems?

Figure 3

Is it possible to completely tile the mutilated chessboard with dominos?

Are There Strategies for Solving All Kinds of Problems?

In their study of problem solving, Simon and Newell observed a number of generic problem-solving strategies that people applied to a diverse set of problems. They argued that people use these strategies as a fallback when more specific methods are unavailable. Simon and Newell called these weak methods, to contrast with the strong methods of guaranteed algorithms or domain-specific heuristics that drastically cut down the problem-solving search. These weak methods include generate-and-test, means-ends analysis, planning, and hill-climbing.

Weak Method #1: Generate-and-Test

The most basic strategy Simon and Newell observed in participants was to simply try something and see if it worked. If I've forgotten my computer log-in for an old account, I might cycle through a half-dozen passwords I know I've used in the past. With luck, one of them will be correct and I won't need to go through a more extensive problem-solving attempt to reset the password. Similarly, if I can't find my keys, I might randomly guess a few likely spots, before trying to retrace my steps. When writing an essay, I might overcome my writer's block by simply writing anything and then editing it later. It's likely that a random utterance isn't going to be good prose, but the first thought generated from memory may not be half-bad, provided I already have a lot of experience with a topic. The obvious disadvantage of generate-and-test is that it is disastrous when the problem space becomes large. Generate-and-test only works when the problem is already constrained or familiar enough that guessing is likely to produce reasonable answers.

Weak Method #2: Means-Ends Analysis

Another near-universal strategy observed in problem solving is means-ends analysis. This is a back-and-forth reasoning strategy that starts by first identifying gaps and then finding moves that will reduce those gaps in the problem space. Consider this example presented by Simon and Newell:

> I want to take my son to nursery school. What's the difference between what I have and what I want? One of distance. What changes distance? My automobile. My automobile won't work. What is needed to make it work? A new battery. What has new batteries? An auto repair shop. I want the repair shop to put in a new battery; but the shop doesn't know I need one. What is the

difficulty? One of communication. What allows communication? A telephone . . . and so on.

Means-ends analysis works by alternating between a goal, observing a difference between the current state and the goal state, and then finding a suitable method to close the distance. This can repeat in a recursive fashion, as Simon and Newell's story illustrates.

Weak Method #3: Planning

Another general tool people use for solving problems is planning. Planning can be seen as reformulating a problem in a simpler problem space, solving it in the simpler space, and then trying to generalize that approach to the real problem space. For instance, when writing an essay I may start with an outline, which is a kind of simplified version of the essay, only including the main points I want to state and ignoring all the detail. Once I'm satisfied that I've solved the problem in the planning space, I can use that to guide my search in the larger space of writing the entire essay.

Weak Method #4: Hill-Climbing

Suppose you're in a large landscape, shrouded in mist, and you want to find the highest possible point. One strategy would be to simply walk in whatever direction is steepest. Hill-climbing applies this notion to problem solving. Start with a tentative solution to the problem, no matter how lousy, and then make small adjustments in the direction that improves your starting point the most. In certain classes of problems, simply following the direction of best improvement is sufficient to eventually reach the optimal point. Editing an essay is often a process of hill-climbing, as you make successive adjustments to the text in whatever way best improves the quality of the writing as a whole. Similarly, applying hill-climbing to solving a Rubik's Cube might involve trying to increase the number of colors segregated to each side with each move. This approach fails with Rubik's Cubes, but the fact that people often attempt it shows our built-in hill-climbing heuristic at work.

Why Weak Methods Frequently Fail

Weak methods apply broadly, but they often fail us. Generate-and-test fails with large problem spaces. Means-ends analysis multiplies goals, which can make it harder to keep track of the problem. Planning may oversimplify the problem, leading to a solution that works on paper, but fails in practice. Hill-climbing fails in exactly those situations where things first need to be made worse, in order to be made better. What we call puzzles may themselves be the category of problems where one of our weak methods conspicuously fails, so that the only way to solve the problem is to ignore a tempting heuristic. The Tower of Hanoi puzzle involves moving disks between pegs. The overall space of the problem has only twenty-seven states, so it shouldn't pose a serious problem even for generate-and-test. Yet the solution often takes a little practice, both because reaching the desired end state requires you to move disks away from the destination (violating hill-climbing) and necessitates many nested subgoals (making means-ends analysis more complicated).

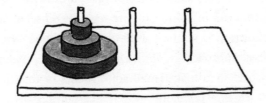

Figure 4

Tower of Hanoi: Goal is to move all disks from the left to right peg. Only one disk can be moved at a time. Larger disks cannot be placed on top of smaller disks.

A deeper question about weak methods is whether they are innate or acquired. Psychologists André Tricot and John Sweller argue that there is little evidence for the teachability of weak methods, showing that people tend to apply means-ends analysis or hill-climbing instinctively. In this view, general problem-solving ability is something that can be neither taught nor practiced. Accordingly, we can't learn better methods for dealing with problems in general, but only acquire a larger library of specific skills and methods that we apply to different situations. Wiles was able to prove Fermat's Last Theorem, not because he had extensive practice in weak methods, but because he possessed an enormous library of strong methods that drastically reduced the problem space. Yet that same knowledge would probably be of minimal use in helping him fix a car or file his taxes.

The Knowledge Frontier: The Two Types of Problems

This picture suggests we face two distinct types of difficulties in solving problems. The first kind of difficulty occurs when we face a problem that stumps us, but would be routine for someone else. This is a difficulty of learning from others. What are the strong methods experts use to solve those problems effortlessly? Without that knowledge, we're forced to engage in a potentially lengthy and failure-prone problem-solving search. If the problem isn't too far outside our zone of problem-solving ability, we may uncover the answer with some effort. But if the space is too large, we may never land on the best approach.

The second kind of difficulty occurs when we're venturing into the unknown frontier beyond any individual's problem-solving ability. This was Wiles's challenge as he searched for the proof for Fermat's Last Theorem. He had to find the solution to a problem that no mathematician had uncovered in over three centuries. Given his eventual path through huge swaths of the problem space that were utterly unknown to Fermat, it seems quite likely that the long-deceased Frenchman himself didn't have a correct proof. Perhaps

Fermat had uncovered a flawed proof, like Cauchy or Lamé. Or perhaps he had found an alternative route, so surprising and creative that it has gone untrodden by the best mathematical minds for hundreds of years. In either case, this knowledge died with Fermat, and so Wiles had to venture into the unknown when charting his mathematical course.

Most of us will not embark on a problem as difficult as Wiles's. Yet we'll never eliminate the need for problem solving because most situations are unique. You only have to type a sentence or two before you've written something that has never before been uttered in human history. Every essay written, song composed, or building designed is a novel problem, and thus can't merely be copied from solutions of the past. But even if many problems are new, the knowledge that is best served to solve them usually isn't. Seeing further into the problem space depends on standing on the strong methods of the giants that came before us.

Practical Takeaways of Problem-Solving Search

Many psychologists doubt that problem solving, as a general ability, can be taught or practiced. The weak methods appear universal. Instead, it appears the path to mastery is through acquiring the specific knowledge and methods of the expert. Even if we can't become better problem solvers in general, I'd nonetheless like to suggest a few practical takeaways suggested by this theory of problem solving.

Takeaway #1: Start with the Right Representation

Search is only half of the difficulty of solving problems. The other half is in finding the right way of representing the problem, so that you know the best problem space to work in. Prior to Newell and Simon's pathbreaking work, the Gestalt psychologists also explored problem solving, except their focus was on how experimental subjects perceived the problem and how those perceptions could inhibit or enable insightful solutions. As an example, consider the famous nine-dot puzzle. The aim is to draw four straight lines without lifting your pencil that intersect all nine dots.

Figure 5

Nine-Dot Puzzle: Draw four straight lines through all nine dots, without lifting your pencil between lines.

Can you do it? For those who haven't seen it before, they can view the answer on page 243. The key insight revolves not around how we search through the problem space, but how we represent it. If the successful answer is mistakenly excluded from the initial possibilities, we will miss it even in an exhaustive search. Problem solving in messy, real-life situations often involves switching back and forth between searching our problem space and trying to find new ways of representing the problem that may be more tractable.

Begin any new project by finding out how competent people think about the problem. What do they view as the problem space? The major moves you can make to solve it? While knowing how to think about a problem doesn't guarantee a solution, it is an essential first step.

Takeaway #2: Seek Out Promising Problems

The realization that many problems are impossible to solve suggests an immediate application: don't work on impossible problems. Unfortunately, the problem of figuring out which problems are solvable is also unsolvable! The solution may always be just around the corner, or it might result in a century of unrewarded effort. Despite our inability to know precisely which problems are genuinely impossible, we can, with experience, make better guesses. Wiles only began working on Fermat's Last Theorem when Gerhard Frey made the connection to the Taniyama-Shimura conjecture, as it suggested to him that the problem was ripe. Entrepreneurs, scientists, and inventors all make calculated bets on what levels of technological advances they predict in the near future, even if they cannot know exactly how far they will need to venture into uncharted regions of the problem space.

The best way to discover promising problems is to work with people who are actively pushing at the frontier. The advantage of working at firms, research labs, or in groups of people who are making new contributions is that you can get strong hints as to which aspects of the problem space are ripe for exploration and which are unlikely to immediately yield fruit.

Takeaway #3: Explore the Problem Space, One Room at a Time

To explain how he approaches mathematics, Wiles draws an instructive analogy:

> I could best describe my experience of doing mathematics in terms of entering a dark mansion. One goes into the first room, and it's dark, completely dark. One stumbles around bumping into the furniture, and gradually, you learn where each piece of furniture is, and finally, after six months or so, you find the light switch. You

turn it on, and suddenly, it's all illuminated. You can see exactly where you were.

As we'll discuss in more detail in the next chapter, when we have no one we can learn from and must find our way in an unfamiliar problem space, it helps to first explore the space rather than solve problems. Approaching an unfamiliar branch of mathematics, Wiles not only equipped himself with mathematical tools discovered by others, but spent considerable time applying them until they became a familiar part of his repertoire.

Exploring the problem space can proceed by trying things out and observing what happens, without deliberately trying to reach particular goals. The aim here is not to accomplish anything in particular, but to pay attention to patterns that may result in new strong methods. A painter trying out different techniques to "see what happens" rather than produce a saleable work will end up with a lot of lousy compositions. But occasionally he may stumble upon a technique that gives his work a unique look.

From Solving Problems to Learning How to Solve Them

Simon and Newell's early work focused on how people solve difficult problems. They believed that understanding how we solve problems was a prerequisite for understanding how we learn to solve problems. Only once you know how a person is performing a skill, they reasoned, do you have much hope in figuring out how they learn to perform it.* In the next chapter, we'll shift from how people solve problems to how they learn to solve problems. Along the way, we'll discover how a quirk of our psychology becomes one of the most important limits on this process.

---

* This emphasis on performance before learning is challenged by connectionist models, which tend to focus on relatively simple learning mechanisms—even if the actual performance algorithm is too complex to be easily stated and understood.

CHAPTER 2

Creativity Begins with Copying

Rules are not the fetters of genius. They are the fetters of men with no genius.

—Joshua Reynolds, painter

- Can you solve a problem without learning how to solve it?
- How much of creativity comes from borrowing others' ideas?
- Does imitation lead to a shallow understanding?

In November 2017, records were shattered when Leonardo da Vinci's *Salvator Mundi* sold for over $450 million. This more than doubled the previous record-high price for a painting, when Pablo Picasso's *Woman of Algiers* sold for slightly below $180 million in 2015. A Da Vinci selling for astronomical sums isn't surprising. The artist left few completed paintings in his lifetime. Those that exist are universally recognized as masterpieces, from the immense crowds drawn daily to the *Mona Lisa* at the Louvre, or his enigmatic depiction of *The Last Supper*. Nor is Da Vinci alone in veneration. Botticelli, Raphael, Titian, Caravaggio, and Michelangelo all rightfully deserve the status of master painters. Although we tend to fixate on their genius, I'd instead like to turn to their training.

Artistic training in the Renaissance followed an apprenticeship model. At twelve or thirteen, novices would submit themselves to a master's workshop. Italian painter Cennino Cennini describes the process at the turn of the fifteenth century:

> Know that there ought not to be less time spent in learning than this: to begin as a shopboy studying for one year, to get practice in drawing on the little panel; next, to serve in a shop under some master to learn how to work at all the branches which pertain to our profession . . . for the space of a good six years. Then to get experience in painting, embellishing with mordants, making cloths of gold, getting practice in working on the wall for six more years; drawing all the time, never leaving off, either on holidays or on workdays. And in this way your talent, through much practice, will develop into real ability.

Apprentices proceeded through a structured sequence of both subjects and media to slowly introduce themselves to the skills of the craft. First was copying masterworks. This enabled a novice to closely study how an adept translated light and form into marks on a panel. Next was drawing from plaster casts of sculptures. This added the difficulty of translating a three-dimensional object into a two-dimensional representation, but avoided the challenges of a live model who might move around during a sitting. By the time apprentices worked from life, their mastery of the fundamentals was secure enough that all their attention could be paid to subtleties such as posture or expression. Artistic media went through a similar progression, from charcoal drawings, to grisaille paintings done in shades of black and white, and finally to full color in oil or tempera paints.

Copying from masterworks formed the backbone of artistic instruction. Da Vinci himself argues for the proper sequence of study: "Of the order of learning to draw: first draw from drawings by masters done from works of art," only then, "having acquired that practice, under the criticism of his master, he should next practice drawing objects in relief of a good style." The idea of spending considerable time copying seems antithetical to modern perceptions of artistic training. Artists are supposed to be fountains of originality and drills are alleged to kill the creative spirit. Yet despite the imitativeness of the training, artists of the periods in which such methods were widespread often produced work of breathtaking originality. Even though the Renaissance-era training methods were apparently successful, they are largely out of fashion today. To understand why, we need to briefly review the history in the evolution of artistic training methods.

A Brief History of Artistic Training

The history of art education in the West begins in Greece. The ancient Greeks celebrated art, but not the artist. Visual arts were the province of an artisanal class that was barely above the slaves who upheld an aristocratic society. Poetry and philosophy were the proper study for a member of the elite; painting was not. This attitude persisted through the Middle Ages, when the artistic production was controlled by the guild system. Only in the Renaissance, with the arrival of painters like Da Vinci and Michelangelo, did the status of individual artists begin to rise above that of mere craftworkers. Instrumental to this shift in perception was Renaissance painter and art historian Giorgio Vasari. His major book, *Lives of the Most Excellent Painters, Sculptors and Architects*, created the image of the artist as an intellectual, on par with scholars and philosophers. To that end, Vasari convinced Cosimo de' Medici to found the first art academy in Florence in 1561.

Yet this elevation of the status of the artist had a paradoxical effect on the craft. As historian of art education Arthur Efland writes, "When the artist rose to the position of genius, new educational questions presented themselves, for how does one instruct a genius? Is it appropriate to train the potential genius like a lowly apprentice?" This tension grew during the Romantic movement. Philosopher Jean-Jacques Rousseau writes of his suggested artistic training regimen: "So I shall take good care not to provide him with a drawing master, who would only set him to copy copies and draw from drawings. Nature should be his only teacher, and things his only models." In the nineteenth century, this attitude would be further exaggerated by Viennese art educator and champion of the creative self-expression movement Franz Cižek. "Cižek has been compared to Rousseau in his insistence on avoiding all adult influence, but in some sense Cižek was more extreme," Efland writes. "Rousseau recognized some need for adult guidance, while Cižek's class was not taught at all in the usual sense of teaching." This tension between craftsmanship and creativity, which was largely absent in Da Vinci's time, persists today. "In our arts climate," artist and educator Juliette Aristides writes, "historical education and art training are often considered antithetical to genius. Rising artists are frequently expected to tap their knowledge directly from the ether, disconnected from history and labor. However, when the instincts of the individual are elevated above education, the artist can become stuck in a perpetual adolescence where his passion outstrips his ability to perform."

Patiently learning from examples, before creating original work, was central to a classical artistic education. Yet the power of examples is not limited to artistic skills. Somewhat surprisingly, cognitive psychologists have found that, in some situations, studying an example can lead to more useful skills than solving the same problem on your own.

Can You Solve a Problem Without Learning How to Solve It?

"A first principle not recognized by scientific methodologists," wrote the great psychologist B. F. Skinner, is, "when you run into something interesting, drop everything to study it." Such a maxim might have been on John Sweller's mind when, in the early 1980s, the psychologist encountered some odd results from his experiments. "[We were] running an experiment on problem solving, testing undergraduate students," Sweller reflected. "The problems required students to transform a given number into a goal number where the only two moves allowed were multiplying by 3 or subtracting 29." A puzzle might be to go from 15 to 16, for instance, which would require first multiplying by three to yield 45 and then subtracting 29 to get to 16. "Each problem had only one possible solution and that solution required an alternation of multiplying by 3 and subtracting 29 a specific number of times," Sweller explained. "My undergraduates found these problems relatively easy to solve with very few failures, but there was something strange about their solutions. While all problems had to be solved by this alternation sequence . . . very few students discovered the rule," Sweller wrote. "Whatever the problem solvers were doing to solve the problems, learning the alternating solution sequence rule did not play a part."

How could students solve a problem, but not learn the method they used for solving it? This was shortly after Herbert Simon and Allen Newell's treatise on problem solving, discussed in the previous chapter. Building on their work, Sweller's investigation found a potential culprit: means-ends analysis. This was one of the weak methods Simon and Newell had found in many of their studies, the back-and-forth spotting of gaps between your current position and the ends you'd like to reach, as well as finding means to close those gaps. This strategy works, but it requires you to keep many aspects of the problem in mind simultaneously. This mental overhead might not leave enough capacity for generalizing the procedures for solving similar problems in the future. "It seemed plausible to me that the same processes might apply when students were asked to solve problems in an educational context," Sweller reflected. "Perhaps we should be showing students how to solve problems rather than having them solve the problems themselves?"

This suggested to Sweller an experiment: if you could somehow suppress means-end analysis, students would have more cognitive capacity left over to learn from their actions. Sweller and his colleagues tested his hunch in a series of experiments, including one using trigonometry puzzles. These puzzles involving angles and line lengths typically have several unknown quantities. They're also mentally taxing for beginners. Finding the missing quantity requires a lot of means-ends analysis. Sweller split students up into two groups. One was given standard find-the-missing-angle problems. The other group was given the same puzzles but with the advice to find as many unknown quantities as they could. Without a distant goal, students no longer needed to engage in means-end analysis, and could freely explore the problem space. After a brief practice session, Sweller gave the students a novel problem. Instead of trying to find missing angles in a diagram, he asked them to draw a diagram, given a description of the values of the sines and cosines. This was done to test how well students understood the patterns within the trigonometry puzzles, rather than just memorizing a response. The results weren't even close—eight of the ten students in the goal-free condition managed to solve the novel geometry problem, while only three in the traditional problem-solving condition did.

Goal-free problems free up the heavy cognitive toll imposed by means-end analysis but they have an obvious drawback. When the problem space is too large, people easily get lost. Sweller found an alternative in the form of worked examples. A worked example is a problem with a solution, and all the intervening steps that the solver went through to reach the answer. Sweller again tested his hunch, this time with algebra problems. One group studied worked examples for algebra problems pairing a worked-out solution with an immediate problem of the same type. Another group solved the problems themselves, without the examples. Any student from the problem-solving group who failed to find the answer after five minutes was shown a worked example, just as in the first group. This ensured that members of the problem-solving group wouldn't underperform simply because they didn't figure out as many answers as the worked examples group. When a test of similar problems was presented, both groups performed about equally. Yet, when a novel question format was presented, 75 percent of the worked example group was able to solve it, while none of the problem-solving group could. This was despite the fact that the problem-solving group had spent three times as long in training.

The goal-free and worked-example effects showed up repeatedly in experiments, but they went against the prevailing intuitions at the time. "It was the worst possible time to be publishing papers calling into question the efficacy of using problem-solving as a learning device," Sweller recounted. Following Simon and Newell's work, the study of problem solving had reached new heights in psychology and artificial intelligence. "Most of the field leapt on the problem-solving bandwagon. The research on worked-examples was treated with hostility, or more commonly, ignored, a state of affairs that lasted about two decades."

While Sweller's research may have been initially controversial, the property of the mind he based his findings on was not. Researchers have known for the better part of a century that the mind is fantastically limited in the amount of information it can hold on to simultaneously. This history of our understanding of the mind's bottleneck begins with the number seven, plus or minus two.

The Magical Number Seven, Plus or Minus Two

"I have been persecuted by an integer," wrote the Harvard psychologist George Miller in the opening of his now-famous 1956 paper. "This number assumes a variety of disguises, being sometimes a little larger and sometimes a little smaller than usual, but never changing so much to be unrecognizable." Miller presented a variety of seemingly unrelated experiments revealing his magical number seven, plus or minus two. Ask people to distinguish tones based on pitch, for instance, and people do quite well when there are only two or three to separate. Beyond six, however, people increasingly make mistakes.

The same effect occurs for loudness, with only about five different volumes being distinguishable. Yet the magic number doesn't just show up when classifying sounds. It occurs when study participants are asked to judge the saltiness of water in a taste test, the area of squares perceived visually, or variations in hues. Nor is the number limited to perceptual discrimination. Memory experiments show the same falloff for performance when subjects have to remember more than seven items, whether those items be digits, numbers, or words. The magic number, Miller argued, was more than just an experimental coincidence, but pointed to a fundamental limit in the number of things we can keep in mind at the same time. Thinking had a bottleneck and Miller had provided evidence for how wide it was.[*]

Observations such as Miller's led to a number of theories for how the mind processes information. This included a proposal by psychologists Richard Atkinson and Richard Shiffrin in 1968 that came to be known as the modal model of human memory. Their model suggested that we process sensory information—sights from our eyes, sounds from our ears, and sensations from our bodies—simultaneously, but that all this diversity of information must squeeze through a central bottleneck in order to become active in our thoughts. This short-term storage was also connected to our long-term memory, a repository of lifelong knowledge and experience that lay dormant, until we actively recalled its contents. Later, the psychologists Alan Baddeley and Graham Hitch proposed a theory of working memory, combining the short-term storage of the modal model with the ability to manipulate and transform its contents. All thinking occurred in this narrow window of awareness, filtering out most of the outside world of sensations, as well as the deep histories of our past experience.

If thinking is so constrained, how can we possibly function? In his original paper, Miller pointed to one possibility for loosening the constraint. His experiments observed that the bottleneck was limited

---

[*] Although Miller put the number at seven, he may have overstated the capacity. Careful measurements by contemporary psychologists suggest the number is closer to four. Cowan, "The Magical Number 4."

to the number of items, not the amount of information they contained. For instance, consider trying to keep track of the letters N U F H S B L A I. Most people would struggle to keep all of them in mind at once. But reorganize them to be FBI, USA, and NHL and most people would have little difficulty remembering the Federal Bureau of Investigation, United States of America, and National Hockey League. Both representations have the same letters, but the latter was reorganized into meaningful chunks. Those chunks, tied together through past experience, allowed you to easily keep track of nine letters, at the high upper bound of Miller's magic number. We overcome our limited working memories by assembling increasingly complex patterns of information. Because each pattern only requires one slot, the working memory demands for an expert are quite different than the strain on a novice, even for exactly the same problem and solution method.

In 1995, Anders Ericsson and Walter Kintsch proposed another way around the mind's bottleneck. Experience may allow us to make more efficient use of our long-term memory when dealing with short-term tasks. In Atkinson and Shiffrin's model, long-term memory is a near-infinite repository, storing every memory of our lives. Unlike the bottleneck of working memory, long-term memory is a vast reservoir. Yet most of our long-term memories lie inert. We may have the answer to a problem somewhere in memory, but if we can't recall it at the right time, it might as well not exist. With routine tasks, Kintsch and Ericsson argued, we learn to create retrieval cues that allow us to keep track of more information than the bottleneck normally allows. Kintsch offered evidence of this in story comprehension. Subjects read a story about the development of the steam engine, with distractor sentences inserted into every other line. In traditional memory experiments using meaningless words or digits, such distractions would quickly wipe out anything you were trying to keep in mind. This is why you need to constantly repeat a phone number to yourself to remember it before dialing—any interruption can easily erase patterns of information that aren't already chunked in memory. Yet subjects in the story condition were able to proceed with only minimal disruption, suggesting they had converted some of the story into more permanent memory and created retrieval cues to pick up where they left off.

Both Miller's chunking and Kintsch and Ericsson's theory have an important limitation: they're only possible after extensive practice. Chunks must first be assembled—we're not born knowing the acronyms FBI or USA, and many non-Americans might have failed to recognize NHL. Lacking efficient chunks, the beginner is effectively juggling more items in working memory than the expert. Similarly, fluent readers have mechanisms for keeping track of stories that aren't available to novices. Beginners, like those studied by Sweller, have tighter constraints in working memory than those who are already proficient.

Learning Within the Mind's Bottleneck

In the four decades since Sweller's initial experiments, numerous other impacts of working memory on learning have been studied by a diverse set of researchers. Collectively, these effects have coalesced into cognitive load theory, which argues that optimizing working memory space is a central issue for both educators and learners alike.

A central distinction in cognitive load theory is between intrinsic and extrinsic cognitive load. Intrinsic load refers to the necessary mental effort that accompanies learning. To benefit from a worked example, students need to study it, and this mental engagement requires an unavoidable amount of mental bandwidth. Extrinsic load, in contrast, is all the mental effort that is not directly associated with learning. Means-ends analysis, which requires juggling goals and methods to reach them, is a useful heuristic for solving problems. Yet it may be less useful for learning, because the extra burden it imposes on working memory leaves less space for observing the basic patterns used in solving the problem.

Not all extrinsic load is associated with problem solving. The split-attention effect refers to the added burden imposed by learning materials that require learners to move information around in order to understand the problem. Consider the following two diagrams. The left diagram has information located separately from its associated place in the diagram, requiring a key to reference the correct anatomical part. This mental juggling, not being essential to learning what the diagram teaches, becomes an added source of extrinsic load. In contrast, the right image places labels directly where they are located on the diagram and would presumably not create the additional cognitive load associated with the split-attention effect.

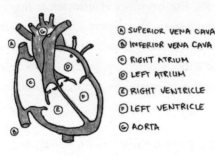
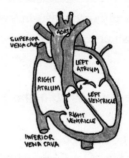

Figure 6

In the left diagram of the anatomy of a heart, labels are separate from their associated location on the diagram. This results in more cognitive work to interpret the diagram and would presumably make it harder to learn from, according to the split-attention effect.

The redundancy effect refers to the surprising interference from duplicated information. A diagram that presents the same information both visually and textually results in worse learning outcomes than one that only offers one. It appears that redundant information, such as saying aloud the exact same thing written on your slides, creates an additional working memory burden because the viewer gets distracted filtering out the irrelevant reproductions. "Most people assume providing learners with additional information is at worst harmless, and might be beneficial," Sweller argues. "Redundancy is anything but harmless. Providing unnecessary information may be a major reason for instructional failure."

While the origins of cognitive load theory come from domains such as algebra and geometry, research has recently expanded into less abstract domains. Studies with eye-tracking software show that students learn more when they can follow the eye movements of experts. It seems we are innately hardwired to follow people's gazes as a directive about where to pay attention, further reducing our cognitive load when we are presented with a complex scene and aren't sure what's important. This effect may also explain the success of Renaissance-era workshops in artistic production: being able to observe masters at work gives you not only their methods, but their eye for an artistic problem.

Does Discovering the Answer for Yourself Lead to Deeper Understanding?

Critics of worked examples often allege that it leads to shallower understanding. The Swiss psychologist Jean Piaget famously remarked, "Each time one prematurely teaches a child something he could have discovered for himself the child is kept from inventing it and consequently from understanding it completely." Being shown how to solve a problem, this line of reasoning goes, is inherently a shallower experience than solving the problem by yourself. One way we might test such a belief is by looking at how students apply a method they learned to more distant settings and problem types. If learning by example is just "teaching to the test," then we should be able to detect that: give students a different test, and those with a superficial grasp of the skill should fail.

Psychologists David Klahr and Milena Nigam examined this question in the context of learning to perform scientific experiments. The main reason for performing an experiment is to find out whether one thing affects another. For example, you might want to know whether the steepness of a ramp influences how fast a ball will roll down that ramp. The best way to do this would be to compare a pair of ramps that differ only in their steepness, while you make sure that the ramps have the same surface, same kind of ball, and so on. Klahr and Nigam wanted to know whether students who were given explicit instruction and examples of the strategy of varying only one thing at a time in an experiment would apply it to new situations less often than the students who managed to figure out the strategy through their own experimentation. They divided 112 third- and fourth-grade students into two groups. One was instructed in the strategy and shown examples of it working. The other was not told anything, but given a chance to discover the principle for themselves. The instructed group did much better on immediate performance—77 percent managed to conduct at least three out of four unconfounded experiments in the testing phase compared to 23 percent of those students in the discovery condition. This is not entirely surprising; it's obviously easier to learn something you've been taught than to figure it out on your own. More interestingly, Klahr and Nigam found that, regardless of how they learned it, those students who had done well in the original test also did better at applying the strategy to a later science fair contest. This suggests that not only was learning through example successful for more students, but it didn't seem to hamper their ability to apply the knowledge in diverse situations.

Examples alone are not always enough. Research finds that breaking apart worked examples into subgoals can help illustrate the reasoning behind a problem-solving procedure, and that encouraging students to engage in self-explanations of examples can enhance understanding. Worked examples are also more difficult to follow when steps are omitted. Few amateur artists could learn to paint like the Renaissance masters simply by looking at finished copies—it was also important to observe the painting process. And, as we shall see in chapter 4, experts often omit mental steps of a solution in their explanations. For abstract or intellectual subjects, we might need considerable training before we can hope to understand what an expert is doing just by watching their physical actions. However, Klahr and Nigam's experiment, along with the work of cognitive load theorists, challenge the assumption that knowledge acquired through seeing examples is inherently shallower than that acquired through direct experience.

When Is Copying More Effective than Creating?

The mind's bottleneck suggests a reason for learning failure: complex subjects and skills aren't broken down into simple enough parts. Faced with a confusing situation, novices must rely on means-end analysis and other effortful search processes to solve their problems. This problem-solving investment is often necessary for arriving at answers, but crowds out cognitive capacity that could be used for learning and generalizing patterns that could be applied to future challenges. Worked examples, goal-free exploration, and organizing materials to minimize split attention and redundancy can all make learning more effective.

This focus on complexity also means cognitive load theory is most relevant when solving a problem or understanding a concept requires integrating many different unfamiliar pieces of information simultaneously. This is certainly the case in producing art. Each brushstroke in a painting requires the simultaneous consideration of chromatic hue, color saturation, and tonal value. Each element of the painting must consider perspective, lighting, and size. Da Vinci's notebooks are filled with rule-of-thumb heuristics for the proportions of body parts and detailed anatomical studies of skeletal and muscular structures. A realistic depiction requires integrating far more information than a geometry puzzle, which is why few students can do so without considerable practice.

Not all problems of learning are an issue of complexity, however. Compare grammar and vocabulary when learning a second language. Grammar can be quite mentally demanding. An English speaker beginning to learn Japanese, for instance, must deal with the mental juggling of converting her thoughts from the familiar order of subject-verb-object ("Dog bites man") to the subject-object-verb order in that language ("Dog man bites"). For lengthy sentences such mental juggling can easily consume all of our cognitive capacity, which is why clear exemplification and practice on textbook exercises can be so helpful. Learning vocabulary, in contrast, is relatively low in cognitive load. Each word simply needs to be memorized. Thus it is much more feasible to acquire a wide vocabulary through immersion in conversations. In a similar way, chemistry involves concepts both complex (understanding quantum-mechanical electron orbitals) and simple (memorizing masses on the periodic table), and driving a car requires the complex process of simultaneously manipulating the steering wheel, gas pedal, and brakes, along with the simple process of recognizing what different traffic signs mean.

Because complex problems become simpler with experience, many of the effects of cognitive load theory disappear, or even reverse, as expertise develops. The expertise-reversal effect demonstrates that while problem solving is often ineffective for beginners compared to studying worked examples, this advice flips once students become more advanced. With the patterns of problem solving secured in memory, students benefit more from practice than simply watching. Just as nobody could become a skilled painter without actually painting, mastery requires doing, not just observation. The worked-example effect has its strongest influence when the patterns of problem solving are still unfamiliar. This is why, despite his advice to begin with copies, Da Vinci was a strong proponent of learning directly from nature as one's artistic abilities developed. Eventually, copying must be replaced with original observations for creativity to flourish.

This tension between the strategies of learning that work best when beginning in a field and those that work better as experience develops may also explain part of the tension in art education. Experienced artists, who benefit more from problem solving than from additional instruction, may incorrectly extrapolate the mental processes they use when creating new art with the methods that work best for teaching someone who lacks their extensive experience. Psychologist Paul Kirschner calls this the fallacy of confusing epistemology, or how experts invent new ideas and knowledge, and pedagogy, or how we ought to teach people to master the techniques already known. Because the mind's bottleneck is more constrained when learning new information than applying old information, problems can look trivial or excruciating depending on your past experience. Learning is the process of acquiring patterns in memory that help us cross that chasm.

Applications of Cognitive Load Theory

Cognitive load theory suggests a few steps we can take in order to learn new skills and subjects more efficiently.

Application #1: Seek Out Worked Examples

Whenever you're facing a new subject of any complexity, look for resources that have a lot of problems with worked-out solutions. In the beginning, these can offer a way to rapidly assimilate the problem-solving patterns. As you progress, you can cover up the answers to use them as practice opportunities.

Application #2: Reorganize Confusing Materials

Avoid the split-attention effect by reorganizing materials so that minimal mental manipulation is required. If you encounter a diagram that requires looking back and forth, recopy it so that the labels are right next to their referents. Comprehend formulas better by rewriting them with the plain-English meaning of each variable placed in context.

Application #3: Use the Power of Pretraining

Before embarking on a complex skill, see if it has any component parts that you're likely to find difficult. If you can practice these components, committing them to memory, you'll free up capacity for performing the skill later. Memorizing words in a new language with flash cards won't solve the problems of speaking, but it will ease one thing you need to think about while doing so. Similarly, understanding how color mixes, light shifts to shadow, or the rules of perspective before you begin a new painting can help you focus on expressing a vision rather than getting tripped up by technical problems.

Application #4: Introduce Complexity Slowly

Since the working memory demands of a skill decrease with experience, this provides a rationale for starting on simple problems and proceeding to more complicated ones. Video game designers use this brilliantly when they design tutorial levels that have a few of the game's features, allowing players to use goal-free exploration to learn the mechanics without laborious instruction. As you progress, introduce new complexities in a steady fashion.

Application #5: Put Craft Before Creativity

Originality is simply an exploration of an undervisited region of the problem space. There's certainly a difference between technical virtuosity and visionary creativity. Yet too often we put the two in tension, when they really are complementary. It is easier to see further when you have first mastered the techniques. It is only possible to bend the rules when you know which ones can be broken.

From Beginnings to Mastery

Much has changed since Da Vinci's day. Photography and mechanical reproduction of artwork mean that the skill of meticulously representing reality is no longer so remarkable. The avant-garde of art has shifted toward concepts, further removed from the verisimilitude of the Renaissance. It would be silly to suggest that all new artists should be trained in a style that flourished centuries ago. Art changes, and with it the techniques of great artists.

Yet, just as training regimens cannot remain static, it is important not to throw out the principles that worked well. Whether the goal is to produce the moody, chiaroscuro portraits of the Renaissance, the airy alla prima landscapes of the Impressionists, or even the bold arrangements of abstract art, creating something beautiful requires not just originality, but the means and methods to transform vision into a concrete manifestation. Studying the methods of those who came before us is not an impediment to originality, but an inescapable ingredient. In the next chapter, we'll look at how building that foundation is essential, not just for temporarily reducing cognitive load, but for motivation and long-term mastery.

CHAPTER 3

Success Is the Best Teacher

It is the duty of a student to get everything out of a teacher, and the duty of a teacher to get everything out of a student.

—*Kevin Kelly, founding executive editor of* Wired

- Does early success fuel future motivation?
- Are there skills that can bootstrap intelligence?
- Does a failure to learn stem from a lack of talent, or missing fundamentals?

Throughout her life, Helen Keller would celebrate two birthdays: one for the day she was born, and the second, her "soul's birthday" for the day her beloved teacher, Anne Sullivan, arrived at her home in Tuscumbia, Alabama. At only nineteen months old, Keller fell ill with what doctors at the time deemed a "brain fever"—most likely scarlet fever or cerebral meningitis. She recovered, but completely lost both her hearing and sight. Deaf and blind, Keller's communication was limited to a few dozen improvised hand signs to express her desires. More often, however, she threw tantrums. "Sometimes I stood between two persons and touched their lips," she wrote in her autobiography years later. "I could not understand and was vexed. I moved my lips and gesticulated frantically without result. This made me so angry I kicked and screamed until I was exhausted." By age six, those outbursts were occurring almost hourly. Exasperated, Keller's mother stumbled upon a story about another deafblind woman, Laura Bridgman, who had been educated. Hopeful that something similar might be done for her daughter, she reached out to Michael Anagnos from the Perkins Institute for the Blind. Anagnos recommended Anne Sullivan.

"The most important day I remember in all my life is the one on which my teacher, Anne Mansfield Sullivan, came to me," Keller would later write. Sullivan began by giving Keller a doll to play with. After letting her hold the doll for a while, Sullivan took Keller's hand and spelled "d-o-l-l" into her palm. "I was at once interested in this finger play," Heller recalls, "and tried to imitate it. When I finally succeeded in making the letters correctly I was flushed with childish pleasure and pride. Running downstairs to my mother I held up my hand and made the letters for doll." Over the next several weeks, Sullivan showed Keller dozens of new objects and their spellings. For Keller, the activity was still just a game, as she had not yet realized that each gesture represented a word. After confusing the words *mug* and *water* Sullivan took Keller to the well house and allowed the water to flow over Keller's hand. The moment, immortalized by William Gibson's 1957 play *The Miracle Worker*, was a revelation to Keller. "I knew then that 'w-a-t-e-r' meant the wonderful cool something that was flowing over my hand. That living word awakened my soul," Keller wrote. "I left the well-house eager to learn. Everything had a name, and each name gave birth to a new thought."

Over the next eight decades of her life, Keller would graduate from Radcliffe College of Harvard University; write twelve books; master Latin, French, and German; and become an ardent political activist, campaigning for women's suffrage, pacifism, socialism, and the rights of the disabled. Following her transformative education, it was arguably social attitudes, not her absence of sight and hearing, that ultimately held Keller back. As a young woman, she briefly became engaged, before the affair was called off by those who considered it inappropriate that a deafblind woman be married. Similarly, her life-long regret was not the inability to see or hear, but that she could not speak clearly enough to be easily understood, making her perpetually reliant on those who knew the manual alphabet to interpret for her. In the years since Keller's time, other deafblind people have gone further than Keller was allowed to, including Leonard Dowdy, who not only married but was gainfully employed for thirty years before retiring, and Haben Girma, the first deafblind woman to graduate from Harvard Law School. Keller's final legacy may not be in how far she was able to go, but how much further others have gone because of her example.

Bootstrapping Learning: How the Right Foundation Enables Future Progress

Keller's story illustrates the dramatic potential of education. Being taught the manual alphabet enabled her to learn words and commu-nicate. From that foundation she learned to read, write, and have an active intellectual life. Without that early opportunity, Keller might have remained in perpetual isolation. While Keller's complete deafblindness from such an early age might be comparatively rare—one estimate suggests as few as fifty people in the twentieth century have had such dramatic hearing and vision loss from such a young age—the basic phenomenon of missing an important, foundational skill in acquiring further skills is commonplace.

Consider reading. Without the ability to read, the vast majority of the world's knowledge is off-limits. Because of this, researchers have found that prior reading ability is closely linked to further devel-opment of intelligence. Stuart Ritchie and colleagues measured the reading abilities and intelligence scores of identical twin children at ages seven, nine, ten, twelve, and sixteen years old. At an early age, reading ability and intelligence were not highly correlated. However, the researchers found that when one twin of a pair had a stronger reading ability in an earlier period of time, it was correlated with higher intelligence scores at a later period of time. A suggestive interpretation from this study is that stronger reading ability makes it easier to learn other knowledge and skills, bootstrapping intelligence. Even more interestingly, the researchers found that the benefits to intelligence were not limited to verbal intelligence scores, suggesting strong reading abilities may have broader benefits than simply increased book knowledge.

Despite its importance, many struggle to read well. Data from the Program for the International Assessment of Adult Competencies (PIAAC) finds that, as of 2013, roughly one in five American adults lacks the reading ability to "complete tasks that require comparing and contrasting information, paraphrasing, or making low-level inferences." Nearly 10 percent are "functionally illiterate" in English. Nor is the issue limited to poor reading at the lowest levels. According to the same survey, less than 15 percent scored in the highest two levels of literacy, which includes test items such as pointing out a sentence in both an email and newspaper article that make the same criticism of a product, and reviewing a table of exercise equipment to identify the muscle group best exercised by a particular piece of equipment. With low levels of advanced literacy, even among adults, it is no wonder that many adults read few books. According to a Gallup poll, the average American in 2021 reported that they read almost a third fewer books than they did in 1999. While social media and internet articles might compensate for this decline somewhat, there's something special about the deep sustained engagement in an idea or story that only comes from a book. These statistics show that we should never take reading ability for granted.

Why is learning to read so difficult? One reason is that the alphabetic principle that underlies most writing systems is powerful, but unintuitive. Learning it requires memorizing an expansive set of arbitrary symbols—fifty-two, if we count only uppercase and lowercase letters; a few hundred if symbols, numerals, and alternative fonts are taken into account. Next, the sounds of a language must be consciously pulled apart into individual units that can be manipulated. Phonological awareness—which underlies the ability to say what the word *stink* would be without the *t*, or be able to point out which word of *tub*, *rug*, *mud* and *bean* doesn't belong—is one of the strongest predictors of early reading ability. Unfortunately, it does not come easily. Children are not spontaneously able to demarcate individual words in the sentences they can speak and comprehend, never mind individual sounds.* Then, those arbitrary symbols must be systematically associated with the freshly discovered building blocks of sound. This is a major task even in languages with highly regular spelling, such as Spanish or Italian. In English, it is an excruciating chore, with children forced to manage our highly irregular orthography, resulting in thousands of sound-spelling patterns, few of which apply entirely consistently. Finally, all of this mental work must be overlearned to the point where it can be done completely automatically. Only when the cognitive load for recognizing words is at a minimum can extra capacity be freed up for dealing with difficulties of interpretation, problem solving, and learning new concepts.

Given the importance of learning to read, and our difficulties in acquiring literacy, what is the best way to teach it? "By an overwhelming margin, the programs that included systematic phonics resulted in significantly better word recognition, better spelling, better vocabulary, and better reading comprehension," writes psychologist and reading expert Marilyn Adams in her comprehensive review of the published literature. In systematic phonics programs the basic letter-sound correspondences are explicitly taught and practiced. In comparison, reading methods that encourage students to guess at the identity of unfamiliar words by their overall shape, accompanying illustrations,

---

* If this sounds implausible, it is only because you've learned to "hear" silences between spoken words of sentences as a result of a lifetime of exposure to text. Analyze the audio waveforms in speech and you'll see that word boundaries are psychological, not acoustic. This is even more true for phonemic boundaries, as children have particular difficulty splitting apart consonant clusters like the *s-t-r* in *strong*. The alphabetic principle seems obvious only because we are so used to it. Adams, *Beginning to Read*, 486.

or the context implied by the story have more difficulties learning to read. An obvious advantage to systematic phonics is that memorizing the basic sound-spelling patterns is a fantastically helpful, if imperfect, tool for sounding out unfamiliar words. By giving new readers a tool for making sense of words they haven't already memorized, they gain the ability to learn more from their independent reading than they would if they were restricted to words they knew by sight. Sounding out words, however, may not be the most important reason phonics works. Instead, encouraging new readers to systematically pay attention to the letter combinations that make up words facilitates an automatic and effortless processing that frees up resources for other parts of the reading experience. Research shows that strong readers are particularly good at pronouncing pseudowords—nonwords that conform to the rules of English spelling like *bluck* or *squimper*—compared to weaker readers. This facility comes not from laboriously spelling them out, but from the fluent spelling-to-sound associations stored in memory.

Successful early experiences can create a virtuous cycle. The early reader who has a strong grasp of the sound-spelling patterns in English will read with less effort than her peers. That reduced effort will also make her more likely to read. Reading more, she will further master the sound-spelling patterns, including those that were not explicitly taught. In a study, Connie Juel and Diane Roper-Schneider compared the word recognition abilities of students who were given phonics instruction and one of two different series of books to practice with. One group was given a reading series that stressed words that were decodable by the phonics rules the children were being taught. The other focused on frequently used words instead. At the end of the year, those in the phonics-oriented program were more successful at recognizing new words than those in the frequency-oriented readers. What's more, on separate tests, the phonics-oriented students did better at sounding out pseudowords that had spelling-sound correspondences that had not been explicitly taught. This suggests that they were extending their early phonics lessons to new patterns. This virtuous cycle may help to explain how those taught in some phonics programs see sustained advantages: their students experience success, see themselves as readers, and continue to practice, further entrenching their proficiency.

Just as learning to read is a foundation for other knowledge, mastering the sound-spelling patterns present in English is a foundation for reading. Some precocious students will figure this out on their own, but many will not. For those who don't, their early reading experiences will be frustrating ones, perhaps turning them off reading forever.

The Two-Sigma Problem: How Can We Make Classrooms as Effective as One-on-One Tutoring?

The research on reading illustrates an important principle: early experiences with a subject are important, not only to build the cognitive foundations for executing the skill, but for sustaining interest that will lead to long-term engagement. Unfortunately, in many classrooms students who struggle in the beginning simply get left behind. Failure to master prerequisite material means they find it harder to follow subsequent lectures, homework becomes frustratingly difficult, and opportunities for applying the skill in real life become increasingly unlikely. Continued far enough and it's not hard to see how those early experiences can calcify into a negative self-concept: "I'm not a math person," "I'm not artistic," or "I'm not good with languages." Instead, we would like to create a positive feedback loop, where early mastery experiences encourage further investment of effort in learning and practice.

One way to achieve this virtuous cycle of early success generating greater learning outcomes is through one-on-one tutoring. Helen Keller's deep relationship with her teacher was a striking example. Not only did Anne Sullivan teach Keller the manual alphabet, and how to read and write, but she even accompanied her to college, dutifully transcribing the content of spoken lectures so her pupil could follow them. A direct tutoring relationship is powerful because the tutor can quickly adjust the material to suit the pupil's needs, jumping in with explanations when they're needed, holding back when the student needs practice applying the knowledge herself. In a famous paper, psychologist Benjamin Bloom discussed the strong benefit that one-on-one tutoring appears to impart onto students, arguing that tutoring can raise student achievement by two standard deviations above the average without it. This "two-sigma problem," following the statistical convention to represent standard deviations with the Greek letter σ (sigma), he presented as a challenge to educators. Bloom argued that because we know such increases of achievement occur with tutoring, it cannot be said that such gains in learning are simply not possible, owing to deficits in the students' ability to learn or the intrinsic nature of the subject. But tutoring is also expensive. Schools can scarcely afford to hire one teacher for every student. Hence the two-sigma problem was a call to find methods of teaching that could approach the benefits of one-on-one support, but which were feasible to implement in a classroom with dozens of children. Bloom believed he had found such a technique with mastery learning.

Mastery learning breaks the curriculum down into cycles of teaching, practice, and feedback. Units are first taught, and then students are given a test. Unlike the typical tests given in classrooms, however, these ones are not for grades. Students are not penalized for failing to do well on these tests. Instead, the tests are used purely for assessing which students have mastered the material and which have not. Those students who have not mastered the material are then given new explanations and practice to ensure that they can pass the test before moving on. Those who pass the first time are given enrichment activities instead. While mastery learning can take more time initially, proponents argue that the total time spread over the entire semester is usually only slightly more than a typical classroom. That is because, having their difficulties corrected early, many more students are able to follow the classroom lectures and assignments in later units without difficulty.

Mastery learning upends many of the conventions we take for granted about classroom learning. A central assumption of mastery learning is that 95 percent of the students in a class have the ability to master the material. Contrast that with the practice of grading on a curve—the assumption that for any material, some students will get it, some won't, and a passing grade merely means being better than one's peers. Such a practice may be fine if the skills and knowledge taught are only useful as a sorting mechanism, to separate students by their natural aptitude, with no intrinsic value. But it's a terrible mechanism if the aim is to teach all students useful skills. Grading on a curve encourages students to be competitive, where one's gains equal another's losses. Why would students in such a classroom feel inclined to help a struggling peer? Proponents of mastery learning argue that classes should never be graded on a curve. Instead, teachers should get a clear idea of what skills and knowledge students ought to be able to perform, and then create an environment where every student is expected to succeed.

Or consider another assumption of most classrooms: that early test scores should contribute to the final grade. Such an assumption isn't unreasonable. After all, many teachers would argue that without offering class credit for completing homework or interim exams many students might not put in any effort to study. But offering grades for early quizzes has a pernicious effect on students who struggle initially. By failing at the beginning, those students see their chances of succeeding in the class steadily diminish. A student who failed early homework and tests might see the only way to pass with a C+ is if they get a perfect score on the final exam. But this is ridiculous! Unless the final exam is not truly comprehensive, a perfect score should mean the student has mastered the material. Yet this is the inevitable logic of a system that punishes early learning stumbles rather than quickly correcting them. In mastery learning, in contrast, tests aren't used to punish students who don't understand the material, but to identify and support them. By quickly intervening when some students are struggling, some of the magic of one-on-one tutoring can be replicated in a classroom environment.

Another major tenet of mastery learning is that the material shouldn't be taught the same way twice. If a student struggled with some of the initial lessons, the same explanations shouldn't simply be provided again. Instead, students who are working through a unit they struggled on should be provided with new material to try to present the information in a different way. Different examples, explanations, or practice activities ensure that if the previous route to learning was a dead end, those students will have an alternative path.

This sounds nice in theory, but does mastery learning work? Systematic meta-analyses find that mastery learning is one of the more effective educational interventions. Effect sizes find mastery learning tends to improve student achievement between one-half and one standard deviation. These analyses show that mastery learning appears to work in elementary, high school, and college classrooms, with particularly large effects among lower-ability students. This is still shy of Bloom's original goal, to raise student achievement by as much as one-on-one tutoring does. But given the constraints of delivering material to a large student body, mastery learning provides one of the more promising educational interventions that has been studied to date.

A related approach, Direct Instruction, may have even stronger effects than mastery learning. While mastery learning is focused on ensuring early success, it is agnostic to the specific teaching strategy used. Direct Instruction curricula, in contrast, work by systematically breaking down complex skills into their component parts, and rigorously testing the sequence of instruction to be delivered. The end product is a highly scripted set of lessons, which quickly alternate between examples, teacher-led practice, and feedback. DISTAR, the Direct Instruction system for learning to read, which applies systematic phonics, was found to be the most successful program studied for reading achievement in a large-scale experiment. Despite some technical differences, mastery learning and Direct Instruction have considerable overlap in their aims and philosophy. Both are committed to the principle that all students can learn, regardless of talent, and that the way to ensure this occurs through closely monitored cycles of examples, practice, and corrective feedback.

Why Success, Not Failure, Is the Best Motivator

Motivation plays an outsize role in learning. Some students show up to class eager to learn. Others arrive with barely concealed contempt for the subject. We've all personally experienced moments where we became engrossed in a subject that captivated us, and we've all experienced torturous moments in the classroom, watching as the second hand on the clock slowly swept out the remaining minutes of the lecture. As important as motivation is, it often feels mysterious, perhaps something that's impossible to understand in a fully rational way.

In this history of psychological theories of motivation, one strand of thought firmly rejected the supposed irrationality of our motivations. Independently, psychologists Kurt Lewin and Edward Tolman each proposed that motivation was a calculation of expected benefits. We were motivated, they argued, when we anticipated the likely outcomes of our efforts were valuable. Yet this explanation seems to falter when we consider our actual behavior. Why do we fail to feel motivated to study for an important exam, even though we know the consequences if we don't pass? If our motivation were purely rational, we'd experience fewer inner conflicts over the seemingly right thing to do and our own inability to push ourselves to do it. A purely rational calculus also seems at odds with explaining the diversity of motivation we see. Why do some students study hard while others slack off? Explaining the desire of some to work hard and think deeply in terms of "achievement motivation" or a "need for cognition" borders on circular reasoning. The question isn't whether some people have greater motivations to learn, but why?

The psychologist Albert Bandura helped to clarify the issue by arguing that it wasn't only our expectations of the possible outcomes of our actions that led to motivation, but also our beliefs about how capable we were at taking those actions. Self-efficacy formed an intervening link, and could explain why two people, in similar life circumstances and with similar options, might nonetheless feel radically different motivations about what course of action to pursue. The person who chooses not to study for an exam may not do so because she believes passing is unimportant. Rather, she might fail to be motivated to study if she doesn't believe she's capable of learning the material.

Formulated this way, self-efficacy is distinct from related ideas like self-concept or self-esteem. Self-concept is a global property, how you think about yourself as a whole. Similarly, self-esteem is a valuation of your self-worth. Someone can have high self-esteem or a favorable self-concept and still have low self-efficacy for a particular task. I might be confident in myself as a person, perhaps valuing my athletic skills, but still believe I'm unlikely to succeed on a math test. Similarly, I might feel like I'm a whiz at programming but wilt at the

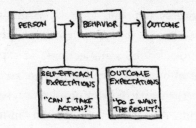

Figure 7
Bandura's concept of self-efficacy links motivation to two types of expectancies: the chance that I'll be able to perform the necessary action (self-efficacy expectations) and the chance that action will achieve a desired result (outcome expectations).

thought of giving a presentation onstage. Self-efficacy is much more granular than your personal identity and can vary between different situations and tasks. Yet, as Bandura argued, our self-efficacy for a particular course of action goes a long way in explaining our motivation to pursue it.

If self-efficacy is so important, how does it come about? Bandura argued there were four major influences, with two being particularly important. The two minor influences were bodily state and persuasion. Someone who is highly agitated may feel like they're unable to take an exam, simply because their hands are shaking and their heart is racing. Verbal persuasion refers to encouragement, like the cheering crowd that gives you energy to cross the finish line. In contrast to these two minor moderators of self-efficacy, Bandura argued there were two more important factors: vicarious experience and personal mastery. Vicarious experience refers to seeing someone else succeed or cope with the situation faced. As we've already seen, learning from others forms an important cognitive component in learning skills—by eliminating the trial-and-error experimenting needed to figure out the best way to perform a skill, we are able to learn much more quickly through instructions and examples than individual invention. Bandura argued that such experiences have a motivational role to play as well. When we can witness someone succeed, particularly when we have reason to believe we could imitate their success, then we're more likely to be motivated to take the same actions. This is why role models, particularly those who we can see ourselves in, are so important. They not only illustrate the way to solve a problem or the correct technique, but they can build our self-efficacy, and thus motivation, to achieve the same outcomes. Personal mastery refers to directly experiencing success ourselves. This is particularly powerful, since while vicarious success experiences can be discounted based on perceived differences between ourselves and our role models, nothing gives a greater boost to our confidence than seeing ourselves succeed.

Bandura summarizes the essential role of direct experiences of success in setting up conditions favorable to future learning:

> Performance accomplishments provide the most dependable source of efficacy expectations because they are based on one's own personal experiences. Successes raise mastery expectations; repeated failures lower them, especially if mishaps occur early in the course of events. After strong efficacy expectations are developed through repeated success, the negative impact of occasional failures is likely to be reduced. Indeed occasional failures that are later overcome by determined effort can strengthen self-motivated persistence through experience that even the most difficult of obstacles can be mastered by sustained effort. The

effects of failure on personal efficacy therefore partly depend on the timing and the total pattern of experiences in which they occur. Once established, efficacy expectancies tend to generalize to related situations.

Success, not failure, is the best teacher. The outcome of repeated early failure experiences is more likely learned helplessness or avoidance, not grit. Failure, when it is helpful, tends to be built on top of a history of previous successes. It's only when we believe we can eventually succeed within a pursuit that persisting through failure even makes sense. While it may be beneficial to have some humbling moments in a long process of mastery, both as a corrective to overconfidence and to make our motivation robust in the face of difficulties, repeated, sustained failures are hardly motivating.

As we've seen, the benefits of early mastery experiences to later learning are multiple. Mastering the basic building blocks of complex skills gives the cognitive foundation for further learning. Repeated practice reduces the total effort needed to use the skill, which further expands the range of situations that passes our internal cost-benefit test, making using the skill outside the classroom more likely. Finally, a history of success within a domain tends to bolster self-efficacy, making it more likely we'll be motivated to continue learning as well. Let's examine some ways we can apply these lessons, both to our own learning and to the skills we'd like to cultivate in those around us.

Lesson #1: Begin with the Basics

A lesson from reading instruction is that many of the skills we struggle with are those for which we lack the basic building blocks. Unfortunately, omissions of needed knowledge are the rule, not the exception, in most classrooms. As we'll discuss in the next chapter, as we gain expertise, we often lose the ability to articulate the building blocks of our own skills. Since most teachers generally know their topic already, this can make them ill-equipped to notice their own assumptions of what students should already know upon entering a classroom. Yet it's not simply having knowledge that makes the difference, but fluent, overlearned skills. Solving algebra problems is really hard if you haven't adequately memorized your multiplication tables. Similarly, literary analysis is impossible if it takes all of your mental bandwidth just to decode the letters. By getting the right foundation, and following it up with extensive practice, we can free up mental resources for handling more complex tasks. Therefore, before declaring that you're unfit to learn a particular subject, you should always ask yourself if you've actually mastered the prerequisite material that's assumed before you start.

Lesson #2: Hire Help

Bloom's challenge was to find teaching methods that worked as well in a classroom as we know is possible from one-on-one tutoring. But that's a strong argument in favor of individualized tutoring! While we may not be able to afford private tutors for every subject, all of the time, hiring help can be well worth the cost, especially if it is applied at the right moments. Hiring a tutor or coach or finding a personal mentor can be helpful if you have them view some of your practice efforts. Since even a small amount of instruction usually requires a large dose of practice to make the skills automatic, the ratio of coaching to practice can still be beneficial, even if it is small.

Unfortunately, tutoring often comes with a stigma that it is only for struggling students. As a result, stronger students often scoff at the idea of using a tutor. But this is not a useful attitude. Many of the intellectual greats had strong tutor-like relationships that enabled them to master their material. Robert Boyle, one of the first scientific chemists, was extensively tutored by George Starkey in the chemical arts. Terence Tao, one of the greatest living mathematicians, received tutelage from Paul Erdős. In many fields, one can even trace out an intellectual lineage of teacher-student relationships extending back to the founders of the discipline. While tutoring may not be affordable in all situations, that doesn't mean we shouldn't take advantage of it when it is feasible.

Lesson #3: Confidence Comes from Competence

The lesson of self-efficacy is not that we should try to psych ourselves up to be more confident (for example, "fake it until you make it") nor that we should try to shower ourselves with phony praise. In Bandura's research, both arousal and persuasion were relatively weak moderators of our self-efficacy. Instead, we become confident through seeing other people succeed and experiencing success ourselves. This suggests that when we lack confidence, the key is to build a positive track record, starting with easier, simpler tasks, and getting plenty of help from other people who can do what we want to do. Kindling a fire is a good metaphor: igniting a spark requires careful sheltering from the wind and an abundance of material that will easily catch flame. Once motivation is higher, we can increase the challenge level. A heavy log that might have smothered a spark is robust fuel for a roaring fire.

For complex skills the best way to achieve these conditions is to get thorough instructions on the basics of the skill you're trying to perform, plenty of practice on examples that aren't too far outside your ability, and support and guidance for whenever you get stuck. Focusing on a sequence of tasks, building from simple to more complex, and ensuring that you're hitting high levels of success on the simpler ones before moving on can also be a good tool for ensuring fluency. For language learning that might mean working through a series of graded readers that use mostly vocabulary you've already learned. For math that might mean mastering the equations before moving on to the word problems. Building a foundation of success makes tackling thorny challenges later much more likely.

From Early Success to Eventual Expertise

As we've seen with reading, well-practiced skills can become so automatic that we lose awareness of the underlying process we use to execute them. For a fluent reader, the idea that we recognize every word by its letter-by-letter combination strains credulity. We read too fast to do that! And yet that's exactly what psychologists find. Eye-tracking studies show that expert readers fixate on nearly every word on the page, and that we resolve the identity of words by recognizing their letter patterns. It's simply that, with years of experience reading, this cognitive work happens at an unconscious level so that, most of the time, we're only aware of the meaning of the text, not how we're actually reading it.

In the next chapter, I'll delve deeper into the research on expertise, showing that deep mastery of skills often comes with a subsequent fading of awareness of the basis for how we execute them. For the experts themselves, this can be a great boon. Not needing to pay attention to the individual letters is how we're able to analyze the meaning of texts. Yet for learners, this can create a disadvantage in learning from others, as the experts that we want to model are often only unconsciously aware of how it is that they're able to perform complex skills.

CHAPTER 4

Knowledge Becomes Invisible with Experience

We know more than we can tell.

—*Michael Polanyi, philosopher and chemist*

- Why are experts not always the best teachers?
- How does expertise transform explicit thinking into tacit knowledge?
- Can we make experts' intuitions clearer, so we can learn from them?

Few molecules are more recognizable in the public imagination than the structure of DNA. The twisted ladder signifies the triumph of our scientific understanding of life itself, appearing everywhere from company logos to movie posters. Given its prominence, it's hard to appreciate that as recently as 1950, nobody knew what it looked like. That image of a spiral staircase, and the consequences it has had on our understanding of ourselves, owe much to the work of the intrepid X-ray crystallographer Rosalind Franklin. Although her contribution was initially overlooked, it was her photographs that made it possible to unravel the mystery of the world's most iconic molecule.

X-ray crystallography makes a peculiar kind of picture. The images taken are not light reflected off an object, as the light bouncing off a bowl of fruit illuminates a still life. Nor are they silhouettes, like the shadows cast by an X-ray when imaging a broken bone. Instead they're created by the quantum-mechanical principle of diffraction. X-rays, like all light, are made up of waves. When the waves hit something, like atoms in a crystal, they scatter in all directions. Like stones cast into calm water, ripples from different sources travel outward and eventually overlap. In some places, where a crest of one wave meets the crest of another, those waves amplify. In other places, where a crest meets a trough, they cancel out. When shone on a crystal, most waves cancel out, except for those that exactly correspond to the regular spacings of the atoms inside. Put a light-sensitive film in the way and you can deduce the structure of the molecule that generated it. Decoding the image requires not only a detailed understanding of the theory of diffraction, but the practical experience needed to make clear pictures out of unruly materials.

Rosalind Franklin was such an expert. Trained as a physical chemist at the University of Cambridge, she had mastered the technique of X-ray crystallography by conducting cutting-edge studies on the crystal structure of coals. Her work helped determine why some pieces of coal reduced to graphite when heated while others did not. Although far removed from biology, the subject had important industrial applications and provided excellent practice in crystallographic techniques. Coal is not a perfect crystal, with impurities and irregularities making interpreting images more difficult. After being recruited to King's College London, she was asked to study biology's most enigmatic molecule: DNA.

Imaging a biological molecule like DNA isn't easy. For one thing, living molecules are wet. There are two different crystal forms of DNA—the compact "A" form and the slightly stretched "B" form. Which form predominates depends on the humidity of the sample. Earlier photographs were smudged because the sample changed from one form to the other in the middle of a long imaging process. Another complication was that getting a good picture of DNA required finding a tractable sample to work with. This meant grinding up animal organs and purifying extracts. But despite the precision to which science aspires, the processes for generating usable samples weren't well understood. Rudolf Signer, a Swiss chemist, had found a technique for generating samples where the molecule hadn't broken down much—what chemists refer to as high molecular weight. "It's just like snot!" commented Maurice Wilkins, another researcher working on DNA, about the high quality of the Signer samples. Despite the fact that the molecule is in every living cell on the planet, the Signer DNA formed a near monopoly for usable samples. Getting good pictures meant carefully pulling the threads of DNA, using a series of salt solutions to keep them ideally wet, and beaming X-rays for exposure times of a hundred hours or more.

The images Franklin created were exquisite. The British crystallographer J. D. Bernal remarked that they were "among the most beautiful x-ray photographs of any substance ever taken." Her experimental dexterity was matched with theoretical insights into attacking the problem. When James Watson and Francis Crick showed her their first model, with three phosphate backbones on the inside and the bases sticking out, she immediately saw what was wrong. The model they had suggested had far too little water and the sodium ions they had placed on the outside would be wrapped in water molecules, unable to bind as their model predicted. Later, when the world-renowned chemist Linus Pauling entered the race with a similar three-chain model, she had no compunctions against writing directly to the celebrated genius to point out his mistake. Her photographs helped her see that the phosphates had to be on the outside, with the bases in the middle. For months she went back and forth with her assistant, Raymond

Gosling, producing images of the A and B forms, carefully narrowing down the exact atomical structure.

In the end, it was James Watson and Francis Crick who first cracked the puzzle of DNA. In an infamous moment from scientific history, they relied on X-ray photographs taken by Franklin used without her knowledge or consent. Without those photographs the duo might not have moved past their mistaken three-chain models. Similarly, had Franklin been given a few more months to analyze her own data, the correct structure might have been hers to discover. By 1962, when Watson and Crick received the Nobel Prize for the discovery, Franklin had died four years earlier from cancer. Despite not receiving science's highest honor—the Nobel is not given posthumously—Franklin's work has since been appreciated as pivotal in unraveling one of life's greatest secrets.

The Elusive Nature of Expertise

How did Franklin know at a glance that Watson and Crick's first model of DNA couldn't possibly be right? How did she immediately infer the right way to prepare the delicate fibers, despite never having handled the molecule before? Furthermore, how did Watson and Crick, being shown only a momentary glimpse of Franklin's X-ray diffraction picture, manage not only to recognize the overall shape of the molecule, but eliminate enough possibilities to reach the necessary answer? Science is often seen as the pinnacle of rationality—a priesthood using pure reason to deduce the nature of the world, divorced from sentiment or intuition. Yet the examples from working scientists betray this philosophy. Intuition seems to play as large a role as deliberate method in the annals of great discoveries.

Hungarian philosopher and chemist Michael Polanyi defined the term "tacit knowledge" to describe the things we know, but cannot say how we know them. Science, he argued, depended as much on inexpressible know-how as it did on explicit reasoning. Contrary to the vision of the impartial researcher, Polanyi saw science as being inextricably tied up in the personal convictions of the individual scientist. Tacit knowledge could not be eliminated from science, and attempts to rid science of its intuitive foundations would destroy the very thing philosophers had hoped to protect.*

The mathematician and physicist Henri Poincaré similarly argued for the importance of intuition in making great discoveries. In his 1908 book, *Science et méthode*, he wrote:

> The sterile combinations do not even present themselves to the mind of the inventor. Never in the field of his consciousness do combinations appear that are not really useful, except some that he rejects but which have to some extent the characteristics of useful combinations. All goes on as if the inventor were an examiner for the second degree who would only have to question the candidates who had passed a previous examination.

If we can anachronistically interpret this in the language of Herbert Simon and Allen Newell, Poincaré was arguing that the expert's thinking does not seem to search through large, random swaths of the problem space. Good ideas occur automatically, allowing one's initial guesses to be more accurate than pure chance would predict.

Since Polanyi and Poincaré's speculations, psychologists have gathered a wealth of evidence on the nature of expertise. Different theories support the idea that expertise involves considerable tacit knowledge, although the exact role of intuition differs in each. What is recognized, however, is that the process of becoming an expert often involves knowledge receding from conscious awareness. The right move appears obvious, often without much reflection, even if experts themselves cannot always explain how they reached their conclusion.

---

* Coincidentally, Polanyi also pioneered fiber diffraction analysis, a central technique used in unraveling the structure of DNA.

Grandmasters, Firefighters, and the Power of Recognition

The origin of the scientific study of expertise is often dated to the work of Dutch psychologist and chess master Adriaan de Groot. His 1946 thesis, *Het denken van den schaker* (Thought and Choice in Chess), compared the performance of elite chess masters to weekend club players. By asking players to think aloud as they planned chess moves, de Groot could compare the thinking styles of the stronger and weaker players. An initial hypothesis might be that good chess players are able to think more moves ahead. The rational mind hypercharged, perhaps they dive deep into the problem space to see moves the lesser player cannot imagine. Yet, in the range of experts de Groot studied, players did not differ much in terms of depth of search. Another hypothesis might be that chess masters simply have higher-powered intellects, able to solve all sorts of problems much better. Yet studies have found that experts of all stripes, including grandmasters, typically show little enhanced ability to perform in problems outside their experience. Whatever separates the grandmasters, it seems to be neither deeper analysis, nor generic smarts.

William Chase and Herbert Simon replicated and extended de Groot's work on chess in the early 1970s. They confirmed de Groot's finding that stronger chess players do not seem to rely more heavily on deeper search. Instead, chess masters seem to intuit better moves. The initial moves they choose to explore are better than the weaker players, explaining their superior performance. Chase and Simon explained this intuitive ability in terms of better memory. Experienced chess players, when shown a naturally occurring board configuration for a brief period, are able to quickly re-create the complex patterns of the board. Novices, in contrast, can usually only recall a few pieces, poorly. But when the board positions were scrambled, experts performed no better than novices. This enhanced recall ability was first documented in chess, but has since been shown to be a nearly universal feature of expertise. Experts in medicine, programming, electronics, athletics, and music all show enhanced recall of naturally occurring patterns, but their advantage sharply declines when the same information is presented in formats atypical for the discipline.

Another feature of Chase and Simon's grandmasters was the order in which they placed their chess pieces. Experts tended to set down meaningful configurations of pieces in chunks, with pauses between. An expert might first recognize a forking position with a knight and two rooks, or that the king was castled queenside. They suggested that the expert is able to better recall the game positions because they perceive chessboards in terms of a collection of meaningful arrangements. Novices, who lack these patterns, cannot help but see each piece in an arbitrary position, and thus must juggle the remaining pieces in their working memory. Intuition, according to Simon, "is nothing more and nothing less than recognition." The expert, having saved countless patterns in memory, perceives that a position is like one she has seen before and merits the same response. This enables her to avoid extensive search through the possibilities.

Psychologist Gary Klein, conducting field research with experienced firefighters, found that they also seemed to diagnose the right course of action from an intuitive process. Under the danger and time pressure of needing to react in a burning building, few firefighters acted the way formal models of decision making said they ought to: generating multiple options, weighing the pros and cons of each, and taking action. Instead, Klein argued, experts in real situations used a process he described as recognition-primed decisions. Looking at a situation, if it conforms to a typical one from memory, experts go forward automatically with their initial option. Only when factors intrude suggesting the current situation is strange in some way do they engage in more extensive problem solving. Continuing the tradition of research in expertise, Klein also conducted a study of chess players, finding that the first move generated was much better than would be predicted by chance, and was frequently the best move considered, even when given longer periods to think it over. Five-time World Chess Champion Magnus Carlsen seems to agree, explaining in an interview that "I usually know what I am going to do after 10 seconds;

the rest is double checking," adding, "Often I cannot explain a certain move, only know that it feels right, and it seems that my intuition is right more often than not." Just as Poincaré observed, our intuitive hunches seem much more accurate than random guessing would allow.

Does this mean intuition is simply memory, in disguise? This would suggest that experts are only skilled when working from cases they have seen before—either the same situation or a similar situation which calls for the same response. This explanation of intuition isn't entirely satisfying. Chess has an enormously large problem space. While many situations in the opening and the endgame may be nearly identical to ones from memory, the middle game often puts experienced chess players in positions no one has ever encountered. Adaptive expertise requires finding a good move in the presence of a novel combination of constraints. Evidence that experts can do this comes from studies showing that, while recall ability doesn't seem to be better than novices for atypical board positions, the masters do seem to be able to pick better moves.

An alternative to the simple recognition account of intuition argues that experts comprehend the meaning of situations by first unconsciously creating multiple, conflicting representations of the situation, which stabilize into a single, most-likely interpretation. Walter Kintsch's Construction-Integration model of reading performance provides an example. The sentence "He met the man at the bank" would simultaneously activate an understanding of a meeting at a financial institution and at the side of a river. As we read further, inappropriate meanings are suppressed. The subsequent sentence, "They withdrew two hundred dollars," would support the notion that the duo met at a financial bank and not a riverbank. Studies that measure how quickly people process words like *river* or *money* suggest that both meanings are temporarily activated, but that the inconsistent understanding is suppressed before it rises to the level of conscious awareness. Intuition, in this account, works because the expert comprehends the meanings of patterns. Initially, those patterns produce conflicting ways of understanding the situation, which, as more data comes in, suppresses less likely explanations. When a novel combination shows up, the comprehension process suggests a coherent answer.*

Both the recognition account of expertise, and the more complex process of comprehension through conflicting representations that compete for consciousness, suggest a role for tacit knowledge. Expertise may begin with application of formal rules and procedures. However, over time, this may come to be replaced by recognition of specific situations. In this case, the expert's knowledge is tacit because there is no reasoning at all—the process of getting the correct answer is simply remembering it. Similarly, in the intuition-as-comprehension account, knowledge is hidden because the web of associations that make sense of a situation is not open to conscious introspection.

Why Experts Don't Always Make the Best Teachers

Tacit knowledge provides one barrier to learning from experts. Relying on recognition and intuition, experts generate good answers but aren't always able to explain how they spot them. Another obstacle is knowledge that could be stated but is often omitted because the expert believes it is obvious. Rosalind Franklin's objection to Watson and Crick's three-chain model was of this type. She had no difficulty explaining why their model didn't work—the phosphate backbones had to be on the outside of the model to account for the water content. This was clear to Franklin, but apparently not to Crick or Watson, neither of whom was an expert in chemistry. Communication naturally omits information that interlocutors believe is redundant. Anyone who has dealt with the incessant "why" questions of a toddler knows how painstaking it can be to explain every detail of what you're doing. Yet when two groups of people have vastly different levels of skill, what is obvious to one person can be inscrutable to another. This has been

---

* Coherent doesn't always mean correct. As we'll see in chapter 9, expert intuition often does poorly compared to simple statistical approaches in uncertain environments with poor feedback.

called the "curse of knowledge" whereby expertise causes you to take knowledge for granted, thus overestimating the knowledge possessed by those you are talking to. It's the reason why many world-class experts make lousy teachers for introductory subjects, and it's also the reason many popular scientific books alternatively swing between aggressive dumbing down of the topic and confusing sections—the author, usually an expert in the field, struggles to calibrate just what will be obvious and what will be confusing to her audience.

Another obstacle to learning from experts is the presence of lore, or knowledge that is known within a particular community but is not written down. An instructive case occurred during Watson and Crick's model-building efforts. They had initially explored the possibility that DNA's bases might fit on the inside. But the possibility seemed remote because they had learned from textbooks that the shape of the nucleic acids was unstable. Two similar structures, an enol form and a keto form, with hydrogen atoms in slightly different positions, were thought to occur in about equal ratios. This meant trying to squeeze them in the middle would make joining their structure difficult. Imagine fitting Lego pieces together when the shape of the bricks keep oscillating back and forth. Jerry Donohue, a crystallographer, claimed that the textbook they were using was simply wrong. He argued, on the basis of only a few published studies, that the actual shape was the keto form. Sure enough, using this form, the bases clicked together nicely.

Lore forms a greater role in the frontier of many fields, because many of the findings scientists must build upon to reach new heights haven't yet solidified into established fact. When Franklin, Watson, and Crick began their investigations, it wasn't even clear that genes were made of DNA. Many researchers still believed that proteins were the best candidate. A few years earlier, Oswald Avery had shown a compelling demonstration in favor of DNA being the molecule of heredity. He injected harmless bacteria with purified DNA from a pathogenic strain and watched the safe microbes become toxic—a trait that endured as they replicated. Watson's dogged insistence to study DNA was based on his hunch, still not the scientific consensus, that Avery's experiment was sound. Similarly, Erwin Chargaff had noted an unusual correlation between the ratios of the nucleic acids. The amount of adenine (A) always seemed eerily close to the amount of thymine (T), as were the guanine (G) and cytosine (C) similarly matched. Some DNA samples had more A-T, and others had more G-C, but the two ratios were fixed. In retrospect, this was a powerful clue to the structure of DNA—A's match with T's while G's match with C's inside the molecule's structure. Yet this hard, scientific fact was much squishier when Watson and Crick were forming their models. Watson reports that his colleague Roy Markham was equally insistent that Chargaff's results were incorrect. This might have been on the basis of studies where cytosine was absent, owing to some viruses using an alternative chemical instead.

Tacit knowledge, "obvious" facts, and unwritten lore all form barriers to learning advanced skills. Some have argued that the presence of such barriers is so extensive that a process of apprenticeship is needed to learn elite-level scientific work. Harriet Zuckerman, in her survey of American Nobel laureates, found that more than half had worked in an apprentice-like relationship with another laureate. In 69 percent of those cases, the master laureate had yet to win the prize when the mentorship began, suggesting the influence had more to do with the master's acumen than institutional prestige. Being able to witness how skills are performed, access to the lore which has yet to be written in the textbooks, and hands-on practice may be prerequisites for the highest levels of scientific achievement. Of course, few of us will have the opportunity to study under Nobel-winning scientists, or the extreme elite of our chosen profession. Nonetheless, the ability to see what experts know is essential to accelerating our own improvement process.

Cognitive Task Analysis: Extracting Expert Knowledge

Cognitive task analysis is a family of techniques designed to extract knowledge from experts. The practice grew out of a frustration with earlier behavioral task analyses. These older methods were developed to investigate the exact movements and actions people took when performing skills, such as a riveter fastening bolts on an assembly line. Cognitive task analysis attempts the more difficult job of trying to figure out what knowledge and skills are being used as the basis for a decision. As the authors of one handbook on cognitive task analysis explain, the technique "becomes more valuable as the nature of the work becomes more conceptual than physical, when the tasks can't be boiled down to procedures, and when experts clearly outperform novices." The tools of cognitive task analysis have been used to understand the buying behavior of shoppers, develop curricula that reduce training time, engineer tools to help professionals in their work, and as basic research to understand psychological processes.

The discipline of cognitive task analysis is itself quite large. One review lists over sixty different techniques that have been developed. This includes low-tech methods like structured interviews and concept-mapping, all the way to detailed computer simulations of expert performance. Conducting a cognitive task analysis is itself a skill that takes considerable training and practice to develop. A thorough analysis may involve hundreds of hours of work interviewing experts, organizing the data, and confirming conjectures about the nature of expert thinking. Even if applying the full power of a cognitive task analysis is impractical for most of our individual efforts at improvement, we can leverage informal methods to gather similar information, albeit imperfectly. By understanding the major lessons of cognitive task analysis, we can avoid some of the pitfalls typically encountered when trying to learn from experts.

Insight #1: Ask for Stories, Not Advice

Talking to experts is one of the best ways to figure out what they know. But there are many pitfalls to avoid. One is to assume that the expert can easily act as a teacher and directly provide the advice you need to move forward. As the authors of one guide argue, "self-report methods assume respondents are capable of 'self [cognitive-task analysis]' and of reporting tacitly held knowledge. . . . That assumption is not backed up by research—in fact the evidence suggests quite the opposite: people have considerable difficulty reporting on their own cognitive processes." Ask for advice and you might get a sermon, when what you want to hear is the knowledge they think is too obvious to be worth mentioning.

One way around this is to focus on stories. The Critical Decision Method focuses on asking experts to recount a particularly challenging incident. Telling stories focuses on the concrete details of when decisions occurred, how they were made, and what their consequences were, in ways that asking for generic advice or routines often omits. This can also be beneficial when the situations you need to understand occur too infrequently to be easily observed. A difficult surgery, fire-fighting rescue, or tricky business decision occurs rarely enough that recalling stories may be the only way to gather information about the events.

A good protocol is to act like a journalist preparing for a story—focus on gathering facts, establishing a timeline, and walking through the decisions step-by-step. This provides the raw material for asking follow-up questions to investigate why the expert made certain choices. A focus on the facts tends to highlight details of a story that may be obscured when simply asking for the broader lessons from the experience.

Insight #2: Talk Through Tough Problems

Another strategy in cognitive task analysis is to watch experts as they solve problems. The PARI method (Precursor, Action, Result, Interpretation) focuses on having experts generate typical problems they face, and then swapping those problems with other experts. By thinking aloud as they work on the peer problems, researchers can investigate the basic flow of the problem-solving process. After solving the problem, experts can rehash what they did so further details can be illuminated.

Being able to watch an expert perform a task, along with the ability to ask why they made the choices they did, can often reveal much about the thinking behind it. The focus on solving an actual problem, rather than simply recollecting a story or giving advice, has two distinct advantages. First, the problem situation is likely to act as a reminder of knowledge that might be harder to retrieve outside of its natural context. Second, observing the problem-solving process itself can be one of the best ways to learn how it is done. Research often vindicates the power of learning from examples over explicit instructions. This may be an evolutionary adaptation from an era before instruction manuals, when watching other people was the only way to learn how to solve problems.

Insight #3: See Where They Seek Answers

Sociogrammetry is another method in the cognitive task analysis arsenal. This is a method for mapping out knowledge as a social network and starts by asking experts who they go to for advice on particular topics. Since knowledge needed to perform in tough problems is often held diffusely, it's rarely possible to find a singular expert who knows all the answers. Instead, mapping out a list of useful contacts is often the first step to understanding a problem yourself. Herbert Simon noted this method as one of the most efficient processes he has found for answering questions:

> On the receipt of an inquiry, I pick up the phone and call the person, among my acquaintances, whose field of expertness is as close as possible to the target (it need not be very close at all). I ask my respondent, not for the answer to the question, but for the name of the person in his or her circle of acquaintance who is closest to being an expert on the topic. I repeat the process until I have the information I want. It will be a rare occasion when more than three or four calls are required.

Despite Google searches, Amazon books, and free public libraries, often the best method to answer a question is simply to pick up the phone and ask around for who knows the answer.

From Seeing to Doing

Over the last four chapters, we've discussed how people solve problems by exploring a problem space, the importance of managing cognitive load when learning new skills, the self-reinforcing cycle of early mastery experiences, and the tacit nature of expertise. But skill doesn't come from observation alone—considerable practice is required to get good at anything. In the next four chapters, I'll discuss the role doing plays in learning, from finding the difficulty sweet spot to the importance of creating a practice loop; the research that shows our mental abilities are more specific than we realize; and why variability beats repetition for acquiring flexible skills. Finally, I'll talk about the importance of increasing our productive output if we wish to move beyond imitation and find truly creative solutions.

PART II

DO

LEARNING FROM PRACTICE

CHAPTER 5

The Difficulty Sweet Spot

This is a fundamental truth about any sort of practice: If you never push yourself beyond your comfort zone, you will never improve.

—Psychologist Anders Ericsson and Robert Pool

- When is difficulty helpful for learning?
- Should you solve problems first or study an example?
- How can you integrate examples, action, and feedback into a practice loop?

Octavia Butler was one of the most celebrated science fiction writers of all time. Recipient of multiple Hugo and Nebula awards, she was the first science fiction author to receive a MacArthur "genius" grant. Her novels have reached bestseller lists and are taught in college English classrooms throughout the country. Her success is all the more remarkable for the fact that, for a time, she was the only Black woman writing science fiction professionally in America.

Butler's literary triumphs had an unlikely start. Her father died when she was seven. Her mother, possessing only a third-grade education, worked as a domestic servant to put food on the table. Shy and awkward, she was bullied until, reaching six feet tall, she literally outgrew her attackers. For years Butler had no contact with any successful writers. Even the idea that she could become one was in doubt. "Honey, negros can't be writers," an aunt told her when she confessed her aspirations.

Butler began writing at age ten. At thirteen, she found a discarded copy of an industry magazine, *The Writer*, while riding the bus. The periodical explained how to submit short stories for publication. Soon after, Butler had mailed off her first story—and promptly received her first rejection. After she sought help, a fraudulent literary agent bilked her out of sixty-one dollars—more than a month's rent for her and her mother. "I didn't know what I was doing and I didn't really have anyone to help me," Butler later said of her early years of frustration, later adding, "I had no examples, I had no idea what I was doing wrong in my work. This is true of a lot of people who are beginning to be writers. They don't know what's wrong. They don't know why it keeps getting rejected."

Still, Butler wrote. Obsession, she stated, "is about not being able to stop just because you're afraid and full of doubts. . . . It's about not being able to stop at all." A typical routine was to wake up at 3 a.m. and write all morning before leaving to work odd jobs. "I preferred blue-collar work," she admitted, "because with white-collar work you have to pretend you were enjoying it, and I wasn't." Avoiding stable employment allowed Butler mental freedom, but it came with financial costs. "I was lucky," she explained, "I had an extra typewriter. And anytime I got really low on food, I would go and pawn that." Butler was rarely happier than when she was laid off from one of her dead-end jobs—for that gave her more time to pour into her writing.

A turning point came during a free class put on by the Screen Writers' Guild. One of the instructors was Harlan Ellison, himself a successful science fiction author. Ellison encouraged Butler to attend the six-week Clarion Workshop for science fiction. Butler was terrified at first. She had hardly ever left Pasadena, California, where she grew up. Despite her trepidation, she managed to scrape together the funds to take the Greyhound bus to Pennsylvania.

At Clarion, most of the instructors were established authors. They understood the industry and what kind of writing was needed to get published. Butler discovered that "the things I had been learning in English class weren't that useful because it's a different kind of writing. I mean, academic writing is just plain different from fiction." Students at the workshop were pushed to write a new short story every night, so it could be dissected in class the following day. At first Butler struggled to deal with the aggressive pace. However, by the end of the workshop, she had sold her first story.

After Clarion, Butler decided to switch from writing short stories to novels. The pay for short stories was meager. Writing novels, with larger publisher advances, was the best route to make writing full-time a reality. Yet the length of a novel intimidated her. "I had been able to finish some short stories, which were about twenty pages long, and I finally decided to try writing twenty-page chapters until I finished each novel," Butler said of her strategy. These efforts allowed Butler to sell her first novel, *Patternmaster*, to Doubleday.

Following *Patternmaster*, Butler began the most prolific period of her writing career, producing five novels over the span of five years. By her third, she had earned enough money to write full-time. For her fourth novel, she wanted to try something more ambitious. As a child, she had been embarrassed by her mother's work as a servant. Employers frequently spoke in degrading terms about her mother while she was within earshot. Yet, as she grew older, she saw the dignity in those who, like her mother, manage to endure. She imagined the story of a Black woman thrown back in time in the antebellum South, contrasting modern attitudes with the reality of slavery, as the perfect setting for exploring this theme. Requiring far more research and attention to historical accuracy than Butler was accustomed to, she used some of her advance money to plan a trip to Maryland, visiting plantations where she intended to set scenes for the novel.

Her additional efforts paid off. *Kindred* became Butler's most commercially successful work and secured Butler's literary legacy.

The Writer's Paradox

According to the view of expertise discussed in the previous chapter, experience transforms problems into routines. Beginners struggle with searching through the problem space. Experts recognize the situation and proceed directly to the answer. If so, studying expert writers complicates this picture. Transcripts of expert writers thinking aloud as they work on a writing task make them appear like novices—effortful problem solving, frequent impasses, and means-ends analysis. In contrast, young children often write with expert-like fluency. There is little planning, organization, or thought about what might be interesting or persuasive for a potential reader. During one investigation, researchers Marlene Scardamalia and Carl Bereiter remarked that children were bewildered when it was explained to them that adults sometimes spend as much as fifteen minutes thinking about what they want to say before starting to write.

Writing seemingly violates the standard findings on expertise because a writing task isn't a single problem. Solving a Rubik's Cube, answering an algebra question, or even finding the proof to Fermat's Last Theorem is the same puzzle, regardless of how you approach it. The starting point, maneuvers, and what counts as an acceptable solution are the same for everyone. In contrast, two different writers given the same writing prompt may conceive of the problem in completely different terms. Even a simple task like composing an email can be conceived as a perfunctory assignment or an opportunity for expressive prose. In short, children behave like experts while skilled writers behave like novices because the two groups of people are actually solving different problems. Children produce text fluently because their self-set aim is to write things as they come to mind on a particular topic, what Scardamalia and Bereiter call a knowledge-telling strategy. This strategy can even persist into adulthood, as anyone who has been forced to read a disorganized, stream-of-consciousness email from a colleague can readily attest. In contrast, experts usually choose for themselves more difficult problems to solve: crafting an original story, persuading an audience, or expressing something interesting.

Butler's literary growth was a steady progression of increasingly difficult problems. Her early writing was highly imitative. "The short stories I submitted for publication when I was thirteen had nothing to do with anything I cared about. I wrote the kind of thing I saw being published—stories about thirty-year-old white men who drank and smoked too much." As she wrote more, she developed original themes with personal significance. The first story she sold, "Childfinder," dealt with a struggle between covert groups recruiting children with peculiar mental abilities. These early works would mature into lifelong interests in themes of hierarchy and dominance within society. After Clarion, she progressed from short stories to novels. With three novels under her belt, she deepened her ability to do research—from the historical setting of *Kindred* to later novels that drew upon indigenous languages and inspiration from scientific texts.

Owing to her progressive problem solving, writing never got easier for Butler. She dealt with creative blocks her entire life. A compulsive rewriter, she sometimes threw out large sections of books when they failed to meet her standards. At one point, she offered to give back the advance for a novel she had sold after it wasn't turning out to her satisfaction. Asked in an interview during the peak of her success whether her writing was "organic," Butler replied, "No, it's work," adding, "It's certainly not a matter of sitting there and having things fall from the sky." Butler's occasional frustration at her own writing is evidenced in her personal journals, yet I would argue that it was her very tendency to seek out increasingly challenging problems that allowed her to develop her literary talents. Ernest Hemingway stated it best when he supposedly uttered that writers "are all apprentices at a craft where no one ever becomes a master."

In this regard, writing is far from atypical. Physicists may breeze through textbook problems that stump an undergraduate. But in their jobs, they aren't simply solving textbook problems more quickly.

Instead they're tackling the most challenging problems at the frontier of science. Similarly, chess grandmasters aren't practicing how to checkmate novices, but engaging in deeper analysis to battle wits against tougher opponents. Indeed, the mindlessness of expertise seems mostly at play when we are dealing with skills we aren't trying to improve. Driving, for most of us, becomes a thoroughly automated task, not because there aren't deeper problems of driving-related skill for us to solve, but because we don't care to solve them. Progressive problem solving is essential for mastery, even if it occasionally frustrates our performance.

When Is Difficulty Desirable?

As we've seen from previous chapters, added difficulties aren't always helpful. Problems can be impossible to solve if they're too far out in the problem space, given your current supply of strong methods to search for them. Even if you can reach the solution, the extra cognitive load of means-ends analysis can distract from recognizing reusable patterns. Finally, the tacit knowledge possessed by experts can make extraction tricky without direct access and observation. Butler certainly faced all of these difficulties in her early writing. "Frustrating. Frustrating," she said of her beginnings. "During those years I collected lots of frustrations and rejection slips." It is a testament to her character that she persisted while wholly lacking guidance for so many years. It is also unsurprising that her biggest breakthroughs came after she finally had insider access to the world of science fiction writing.

Yet researchers have discovered that not all difficulties are unhelpful. Psychologists Robert Bjork and Elizabeth Bjork have studied the conditions under which more difficult practice leads to greater improvement than easier efforts. One of these desirable difficulties is the added effort of retrieving information from memory, compared to seeing it again. Successfully recalling a fact, procedure, or idea strengthens memory more than repeat viewing. This is why flash cards are such an excellent tool when studying for a test. Simply looking over your notes is far less efficient for improving your ability to recall it in the future.

Another desirable difficulty is spaced practice. Practicing the same thing, multiple times in a row, rapidly improves performance. But it also results in equally fast forgetting. This explains why cramming is popular among students, but a bad way to study. Cramming does fill your head up before an test—temporarily—but you'll quickly forget most of it before you get a chance to use it outside the examination hall. A better strategy is to space your reviews out, a little bit each day, so that the same amount of time has a greater impact.

Why do some difficulties help? One reason is that the brain is a fantastic effort-saving machine. If you can access the solution pattern to a problem just by looking at it, there's no need to store the answer in memory. Similarly, if you expose yourself to a problem multiple times in a burst, this suggests that the answer may only be needed temporarily—and can also be forgotten quickly. When helpful hints about what knowledge is needed are present, the brain can save effort retrieving it when those hints are absent. Psychologist John Anderson has proposed that these rules guiding memory can be understood as a rational adaptation to deal with the need for knowledge in the real world.

Creating a Practice Loop

Desirable difficulties suggest a tension between seeing and doing in our practice. Without the opportunity to see a pattern for solving a problem, we have to invent it for ourselves. In the best case, this can involve added cognitive load. In the worst case, we may never learn the helpful strategy. Conversely, if we always have easy access to helpful hints, we may not internalize the lessons. One way to resolve this tension is to combine the three components of seeing an example, solving a problem, and getting feedback into a practice loop. By repeatedly cycling through the loop, we ensure that all three ingredients of successful learning are available to us.

Butler applied a similar process when advising new writers. "For instance, if they have difficulty with beginnings—they have wonderful stories to tell but don't know where to begin or how to begin—I have them look at work they enjoy reading. . . . I then ask them to copy half a dozen beginnings; I ask them to copy directly, word for word." Butler explains her strategy, "This is not about imitating someone else's beginnings; that's why I want at least a half a dozen. It's about learning what is possible. One of the problems we have as writers is that we either know too much or not enough. . . . We know that there is an ocean of possibilities out there, and we're overwhelmed. We don't know how to take from the ocean just what we need." By studying how other authors have solved similar problems, you can sample from a range of options when dealing with your own stories. Seeing examples is the first step in building new skills.

Next, you need to actually perform the skill you're trying to practice. Seeing can assist with doing, but it can never replace it. To learn a skill, we need to overcome the brain's effort-saving tendencies that avoid internalizing knowledge we aren't actively using. Action guides attention. Researchers have found that students tend not to study worked examples until they encounter a problem that requires using them. By cycling back and forth between examples and practice questions, you ensure you're attending to the lessons and not just skimming them over.

Finally, we need to get accurate feedback on the quality of our attempt. This is a clear stumbling block for skills like writing. Butler struggled for years owing to a lack of high-quality feedback telling her what mistakes she was making in her work. When given the opportunity, Butler aggressively sought feedback on her work. During her classes at the Screen Writers' Guild, she sought out feedback from one of the teachers, Sid Steeple. "Whatever you wrote he would go over it and talk to you about it and you might go home feeling like you didn't much like him but it was the kind of criticism I needed," Butler explained.

As you progress in a skill, the practice loop can be made more challenging. Seeing examples can fade away as you increasingly tackle problems using your internal reservoir of knowledge. The problems you choose can increase in complexity, as you can manage extra cognitive load from bigger projects. Finally, self-assessment can play an increasing role over external feedback as you develop refined intuitions as to what counts as excellent work. The practice loop creates an opportunity to optimize the level of difficulty.

Should You See Examples First or Try for Yourself?

Seeing, doing, and feedback are all required for improvement. Pure discovery learning, where the aim is to omit instruction or examples and have the student find the best method, routinely underperforms guided forms of learning. Psychologist Richard Mayer suggests there ought to be a "three strikes rule" against pure discovery learning, owing to a number of prominent failures. Psychologists John Sweller, Paul Kirschner, and Richard Clark go further, arguing against all "minimally guided" forms of learning that ask students to solve problems prior to being taught required knowledge and methods. "After a half century of advocacy associated with instruction using minimal guidance, it appears that there is no body of research supporting the technique. In so far as there is any evidence from controlled studies, it almost uniformly supports direct, strong instructional guidance," the authors write.

On the opposite end, few can doubt the importance of practice. John Anderson, Herbert Simon, and Lynne Reder counter the claim that excessive practice leads to shallower understanding. "Nothing flies more in the face of the last 20 years of research than the assertion that practice is bad. All evidence, from the laboratory and from extensive case studies of professionals, indicates that real competence only comes with extensive practice." Omitting either seeing or doing from the learning experience is ineffective.

Yet between the extremes of completely omitting examples or practice, there is a question of sequencing. Do we learn better when we encounter problem situations first? Or should we start by seeing examples? In other words, is the ideal practice loop "see, do, feedback" or "do, feedback, see"? As of the writing of this book, this question is hotly debated. In favor of the problem-solving first approach, psychologist Manu Kapur has argued that the "productive failure" paradigm shows that some students can benefit when problem solving precedes instruction. In his experiments, groups of students are presented with difficult, but still comprehensible, problems to work on. Lacking instruction, they typically fail to solve the problem the way an expert would. After, they're shown the canonical solution procedure and their early attempts are contrasted with the superior method. For instance, students might be given a problem of a baseball manager trying to draft the player with a more consistent batting average. After students experiment with various ways to calculate this, the concept of variance would be taught and compared with the methods they had initially tried. A 2021 meta-analysis conducted by Kapur reviewed over 160 experimental effects and found a benefit to students who were instructed under the productive failure paradigm. In a related experimental paradigm, Daniel Schwartz and Taylor Martin argue for allowing students to invent their own methods before explaining the correct one. Students are thought to benefit by observing gaps in their own knowledge and then recognizing problem situations where knowledge might apply.

Other studies have found the opposite pattern, with examples preceding problem solving to be more effective. Greg Ashman, Slava Kalyuga, and John Sweller compared the two sequences of instruction for a science lesson on the efficiency of lightbulbs and found students performed better in the example-first condition. A study led by Inga Glogger-Frey similarly found an advantage for seeing examples before attempting problems. The study's authors argue that the results are in line with arguments that "a worked example is more effective than working on an open (inventing) problem when providing equal time on task during such a preparatory activity." In a study looking at teaching the strategy of controlling variables in experiments, Bryan Matlen and David Klahr found the group with the greatest guidance performed best, but found no difference for timing. They argue that students "learned and transferred relatively well as long as they received high guidance at some point during instruction."

Researchers are still probing the boundary conditions for when problem-first or example-first approaches are more successful. Yet, in some ways, this contrast is less significant than it seems. Provided you're engaging in a practice loop, you should be able to cycle back and forth between encountering a problem situation, attempting to solve it for yourself, and seeing examples of how it is done. The effect of sequencing may be of theoretical interest, but it has fewer practical consequences than the harms of omitting one of the ingredients altogether.

Strategies for Fine-Tuning Difficulty

The idea that we need an optimal level of difficulty to make progress in skills is central to many theories of learning. The influential Russian psychologist Lev Vygotsky proposed that we learn through a zone of proximal development—the gap between what we can do with the assistance of others and what we can do on our own. Psychologist Walter Kintsch argued for a zone of learnability drawing from studies of text comprehension. His research found that students with low prior knowledge learned best from well-organized texts. Somewhat surprisingly, he found that texts with poorer organization led to better learning for high-knowledge students. In a similar light, the expertise reversal effect proposed by cognitive load theorists finds that changes that make learning easier for beginners become less helpful as they progress. Eventually, those same interventions can actually be negative, as students benefit more from retrieving knowledge in uncertain contexts than seeing further examples. Progressive problem solving is needed for mastery.

While it's easy to agree on the benefits of the optimal challenge level, it can be tricky to achieve it. Butler's early days were beset with frustration. In contrast, her switch to novel writing, a move that eventually secured her professional status, was likely delayed by at least a few years owing to her apprehensions about tackling more complex works. Getting the difficulty right isn't easy, but there are a few strategies we can pursue that can help.

Strategy #1: The Workshop Method

Butler credited the workshop environments she participated in Clarion and elsewhere as having a major influence on the development of her craft. "A workshop is a way of renting an audience, and making sure you're communicating what you think you're communicating. It's so easy as a young writer to think you've been very clear when in fact you haven't." A workshop environment, especially if it is led by an experienced teacher, also affords an excellent opportunity for a practice loop. By forcing her to write new stories daily, see the stories of her peers, and have them all compared and dissected in class, Butler's experience at Clarion allowed her to more rapidly assimilate the patterns of good science fiction writing. Far from inhibiting creativity, this library of patterns gave her more space to pursue a unique vision rather than the superficial imitation she engaged in with her early stories.

Workshop environments also act as a forcing mechanism. While Butler never struggled to submit her work for publication, many writers hold off on getting feedback for fear of scrutiny. Butler remarks that "getting a rejection slip was like being told your child was ugly. You got mad and didn't believe a word of it." It's easy to slip into desk-drawer syndrome, where work gets submitted to a dusty file folder, never to be seen by anyone. While such ego-saving maneuvers can reduce the sting of rejection, they also guarantee stagnation.

Strategy #2: Copy-Complete-Create

Copying from an example is an underrated strategy for learning. Yet critics of mindless imitation have a point—it's easy to cut-and-paste a solution without really understanding why it works. One workaround is to use completion problems. Instead of studying a fully worked-out example, you try to fill in the blank with one or more parts of the example omitted. Jeroen van Merriënboer has found completion problems help in speeding up the acquisition of programming skills by novices, since deleting a key step forces students to mentally engage with understanding the solution, but avoids overloading working memory by trying to generate a full answer. Cloze deletion is a similar strategy advocated by language learning enthusiasts—in this case, you create flash cards that ask you to fill in the blanks in a sentence. This avoids the problem of studying isolated words (which often omits the context needed to truly understand them) without creating the problem of needing to recall entire sentences.

Ultimately, of course, the goal is not to copy or complete, but to generate a solution using the knowledge you have saved in your head. This is why completion problems should be viewed on a continuum, starting with simply studying the example, then filling in the blanks, and finally, producing it for yourself in varying contexts.

Strategy #3: Scaffolding

In architecture, a scaffold is a temporary structure that assists in constructing a building before it is completed. Following this analogy, instructional scaffolding is a technique for indirectly modifying the problem situation so as to reduce degrees of freedom. Training wheels are a kind of instructional scaffold, preventing novice cyclists from falling over when they're still getting used to steering the handles. Motherese, the habit of talking to babies with exaggerated cooing sounds, may also be an instinctual kind of scaffolding that parents use to assist their infants in acquiring language. Marlene Scardamalia and Carl Bereiter, in their work on writing instruction, found that they could activate a more expert-like writing process from children by providing prompts the students could select to evaluate the sentences they just produced. By encouraging students to choose from statements like "People may not believe this" or "I think this could be said more clearly" after each sentence, investigators were able to force a reflective process of writing that isn't generally exhibited until later grades.

Scaffolding can work by simplifying some of the difficulties encountered in realistic situations. But scaffolding can also be additive, as the intervention by Scardamalia and Bereiter demonstrates. Practicing a conversation in another language with the explicit aim of using a certain phrase or grammatical pattern may be contrived, but it also reduces the working memory burdens compared to trying to use the knowledge when you have genuine communication goals.

What's Your Practice Loop?

Our ability to improve as writers, programmers, athletes, and parents depends on the quality of our practice. Only by integrating seeing examples, solving problems, and getting feedback are we likely to improve at the skills that matter most. Fine-tuning the difficulty is an essential part of that process. In the next chapter, we'll look at what actually develops as we practice skills. Contrary to popular belief, our minds are not like muscles that strengthen broadly through training—the skills we learn are surprisingly specific.

CHAPTER 6

The Mind Is Not a Muscle

Strengthening muscle in one task improves its performance in another task. It is now abundantly clear that the mind is not a muscle in this sense.

—*Psychologists John Anderson and Mark Singley in* The Transfer of Cognitive Skill

- Does brain training work?
- Does learning chess, music, or programming make you smarter?
- What are the building blocks of complex skills?

I n January 2016, Lumos Labs agreed to pay two million dollars to settle charges from the Federal Trade Commission that they deceived customers with their brain-training program Lumosity. According to the FTC complaint, the company claimed that users who participated in their specially designed games for "10 to 15 minutes three or four times per week" would "perform better at work and in school and reduce or delay cognitive impairment associated with age and other serious health conditions." The company was also barred from suggesting that their product "improves performance in school, at work, or in athletics," or that it "delays or protects against age-related decline in memory or other cognitive function," unless it could back those claims with reputable scientific evidence.

It's easy to understand the appeal of brain-training programs like Lumosity. Intellectual ability is correlated with nearly every important life outcome psychologists have chosen to measure. Even a small boost to mental functioning could easily make the time investment worthwhile. Unfortunately, there's scant evidence that brain training works. In a six-week cognitive-training experiment with a staggering 11,430 participants, Adrian Owen and colleagues found that while participants improved on the games they practiced, "no evidence was found for transfer effects to untrained tasks, even when those tasks were cognitively closely related." Another study looked at ninth graders as they went through working memory training. Even after two years of continued practice, improvements in the tasks trained didn't extend to similar tests for measuring fluid intelligence. Nor does brain training appear to protect against age-related cognitive decline. One review of the literature finds that "most of [the studies] have failed to observe generalizable performance improvements." Aggregating the results of eighty-seven studies in a meta-analysis, Monica Melby-Lervag and colleagues write, "working memory training programs appear to produce short-term, specific training effects that do not generalize to measures of 'real-world' cognitive skills." Brain training makes you better at the games you play, but little else.

The failure of brain training may not be surprising. Countless products promising to improve our bodies and minds fail to withstand scientific scrutiny. Yet unlike the case of fad diets or multivitamins, the failure of brain training gets to the heart of one of the oldest debates in psychology.

The Enduring Allure of Formal Discipline

Brain training owes its justification to a tempting analogy: the mind is like a muscle. Just as lifting weights can later make your arms stronger for carrying groceries or hauling luggage, the analogy goes, so too can strenuous mental activity make the mind sharper for all sorts of unrelated tasks. But while playing digital games to strengthen thinking is a novelty, the mind-muscle analogy is ancient. Plato suggested in *The Republic* that training in arithmetic, even if it were not used, would nonetheless quicken the mind for other kinds of knowledge. The analogy became the basis for the doctrine of formal discipline, often credited to the English philosopher John Locke, which argued that the value of education came not only from the skills directly taught, but for the general improvement of mental faculties. Learning Latin improved memory, not just for the words studied, but for all sorts of knowledge. Similarly, geometry enhanced the powers of reasoning, poetry cultivated sensitivity, and drawing promoted accuracy.

Beginning in 1901, the psychologists Edward Thorndike and Robert Woodworth conducted a series of experiments to investigate the extent that improvements caused by practice of one skill transferred to other abilities. Thorndike found that geometry and Latin didn't assist other school subjects more than mundane topics. In laboratory experiments, subjects who learned to estimate the size of small rectangles only improved by a third as much in estimating the size of larger rectangles. Children who practiced discriminating hues made no improvements in their accuracy for guessing lengths or weights. Subjects who greatly improved their ability to detect English verbs showed almost no improvement in recognizing other parts of speech. In contrast with the expansive view of formal discipline, Thorndike argued for a theory of transfer based on identical elements. Improvement in abilities transfer to the extent that those skills share overlapping components. Thorndike concluded that "the mind is so specialized into a multitude of independent capacities that we alter human nature only in small spots."

Learning Latin to strengthen memory sounds antiquated today, but the doctrine of formal discipline is hardly a relic of the past. It is implicitly invoked whenever advocates argue that we ought to teach chess for its ability to impart strategic reasoning, music in order to enhance creativity, or that programming teaches problem-solving independently of the ability to write actual code. Just as in Thorndike's day, careful research casts doubt on the wide-ranging benefits often ascribed to these specific subjects. Giovanni Sala and Fernand Gobet conducted meta-analyses of the general cognitive benefits of chess and music instruction. Only small effect sizes were found on enhanced measures of mathematical reasoning or academic ability. "Overall these results may be considered 'cautiously promising,'" the duo explain. "In fact they are not. The size of the effects was inversely related to the quality of the experimental design." Considering only studies where the experiments were rigorously performed, "the overall effect sizes were minimal or null." Similarly, programming does not appear to make you a better problem solver. As the authors of one study explain, "The rationale for teaching computer programming is that it aids in the development of critical thinking, problem solving and decision-making skills. This contention is not supported by empirical data." Whether the activity is brain training, chess, or programming, the results appear to be the same: training improves the tasks directly practiced, but there's little evidence of substantial improvement to other topics.

How Much Does Learning One Skill Generalize to Another?

Practice in one skill is unlikely to produce wide-ranging benefits. But Thorndike's experiments didn't settle the debate. Many critics were quick to latch on to the word *identical*, in his theory of identical elements, pointing out the absurdity of believing learning was limited to exact copies of the original training. "Think of learning to drive a nail with a yellow hammer, and then realize your helplessness if, in time of need, you should borrow your neighbors' and finding it painted red," mocked the educator Alexander Meiklejohn. Thorndike's own experiments, while hardly providing support for the mind-muscle analogy, nonetheless showed more transfer than his own theory predicted. Training experimental subjects on a task to strike out words from a passage containing both the letters *e* and *s*, subjects performed better when only one of those letters was substituted (for example, crossing out words with *e* and *r*) than when it involved two new letters. However, subjects who practiced the first task still did better than untrained controls. Similarly, in experiments with mathematical equations, subjects did better when formulas were presented in the form typically taught in school, but their ability didn't drop to zero when new forms were presented. Whatever the identical elements among skills were, they seemed to be somewhat more general than straightforward pairings of stimulus with response.

Others pointed out that the transfer of improvements made from one skill to another depended on how it was taught. In one experiment, Charles Judd had boys practice throwing darts at an underwater target. One group was taught the principle of light refraction; the other was not. While both groups performed about the same while attempting to hit the first target, when the depth of the target was changed, those who knew how the direction of light bends as it exits the water's surface adapted better to the new task. In a similar vein, the Gestalt psychologist Max Wertheimer showed that the extent of skill transfer depended on how the problem was perceived. He gave the example of finding the area of a parallelogram. It's possible to memorize that the answer is base times height. However, if the student understands the logic behind the method, it's possible to apply it to a wider range of shapes. Understanding leads to more flexible skills than memorizing by rote.

The mind may not be a muscle, but the components that transfer between skills can't be reduced to simple patterns of stimulus and response either. Memorizing an answer and understanding a method may both solve a problem, but the latter is considerably more flexible. Wertheimer and Judd demonstrated that predicting transfer unavoidably depends on how skills are represented in the mind of the student.

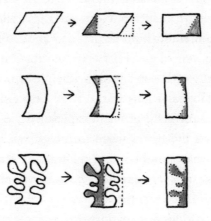

Figure 8

The area for a parallelogram can be solved by cutting it vertically and moving the left side to the right, so it is transformed into the more familiar rectangle whose area equals length times width. Properly understood, this trick applies to many shapes that have the same abstract property, including the highly irregular shape at the bottom.

What Are the Building Blocks of Skills?

Early psychologists were handicapped in discussions of transfer because they lacked a precise language for discussing mental representations. Notions of "identical elements" or "good gestalts" were too vague to make predictions about the degree of transfer expected between two tasks. This changed with the cognitive revolution in psychology. Researchers began couching their theories in a language of information processing, producing models that could be simulated on a computer and directly compared to subjects' performance. From these theories,

one of the most serious attempts to model the process of skill acquisition has been John Anderson's career-spanning work on ACT-R
theory.

Skills, according to ACT-R, are built out of atomic units called
production rules. A production rule is an if-then pattern that combines a condition with an action. Wertheimer's parallelogram trick, for
instance, could be described as the production rule, "IF the left side is
congruent to the right side, THEN cut the shape and shift the right
side to form a rectangle." Production rules inherit the simplicity of
stimulus-response associations, but with two key differences. The first
is that production rules can be abstract. The reference to the "left side"
of the shape in our hypothetical production rule doesn't need to refer
to any particular shape. In the same way, once you learn the algorithm
for long division, you can perform it on any numbers—you don't need
separate practice on every possible combination of digits. The second
difference is that production rules involve not just overt behavior, but
mental actions as well. Complex skills can break down into multiple mental steps, such as setting subgoals or manipulating imagined
contents. As a result, even if two problems are superficially different,
there can be transfer if there are common psychological steps in their
solution.

Abstraction and mental actions help explain how a programmer
who learns one programming language can acquire a second one much
faster. While the exact format of the commands in each language is
different, a complex skill like coding also involves more abstract production rules like deciding to make a variable or a function. Similarly,
artists and musicians can often pick up new media and instruments
faster than untrained beginners because a lot of their knowledge may
be abstract. The finger movements for playing the piano are completely
different than for the violin, but timing, melody, and the ability to read
sheet music are the same. Production rules offer a middle ground between Thorndike's extremely narrow views on transfer, and the overly
optimistic account suggested by the mind-muscle analogy.

One prediction the theory suggests is that with continued practice,
skills will become asymmetric. Production rules flow from condition

to action but not in the reverse direction. In support of this prediction, Anderson gave students the rule for integration and differentiation in calculus. Like addition and subtraction, these operators are opposites of each other, so the output for differentiation is the same as the input for integration for pairs of formulas. Those who repeatedly practiced applying the rule for making a derivative got better at this rule, but not with forming integrals and vice versa. Similar results have been found with second language learning. Robert DeKeyser showed that students who practice generating a particular sentence pattern made little improvement at understanding it, while those who practiced understanding improved little at generating the pattern. The asymmetry of skills has real-life consequences. Research has shown that French-immersion students in Canada, where schooling is conducted in French from kindergarten to grade 12, typically acquire fluent comprehension, but lag in productive abilities as they have fewer opportunities to practice speaking.

Beyond the asymmetry of skills, how well do production rules predict transfer? Anderson tested his theory by having students acquire different skills that were each modeled as sets of production rules. The theory predicts that the speed of learning a new skill will depend on the number of production rules shared between skills (and the degree of learning for each individual production). Overall, the relationship between observed and predicted transfer is an almost perfectly straight line. Despite the near-uniform linear relationship, transfer observed is still somewhat higher than predicted by the model. Anderson argues that this might be because the model omits some of the more general production rules that would be shared between the skills trained.

Production rules are one component of the more elaborate ACT-R cognitive architecture. According to this theory, knowledge of facts, concepts, and examples relies on a separate memory system. Overlapping production rules are thus best equipped to explain the amount of transfer we can predict after repeated practice. Nor are all theories of skill are built on production rules. Connectionist systems model skills out of the interactions of countless, simple information-processing units, schema theories represent knowledge in terms of abstract templates, and exemplar-based accounts ground skilled performance on the accumulation of countless remembered instances. Given the amount we still don't know about the human mind, it's possible that future researchers will find even more elaborate explanations that fit the data better. What we can say is that production rules, and the ACT-R theory that uses them, is a strong candidate theory and that alternatives, even if they end up describing skills with completely different mechanisms, will have to fit to the same mountain of psychological data that has been amassed to provide support for the theory.

The Power and Limits of Abstraction

Production rules provide one account for how much we can expect practice in one skill to transfer to another. But even if two problems have overlapping solutions, we don't always avail ourselves of this similarity. A representative example comes from an experiment conducted by Mary Gick and Keith Holyoak. They presented subjects with a story about a general attacking a fortress. The roads leading to the fortress were booby-trapped with pressure sensitive mines. If the general attacked with his full force along any road, the mines would detonate. A smaller force, while escaping the mines, would be easily rebuffed by the defenders. After presenting this story, they gave subjects a problem of treating a stomach tumor with a beam of radiation. A high-intensity beam would destroy the tumor, but also kill any surrounding healthy tissue. A low-intensity beam, in contrast, would spare the healthy tissue but not be enough to eradicate the tumor. The solution to both was structurally the same: split your attack up along multiple trajectories and converge on a central target. Yet few subjects spontaneously made use of the analogy. Despite them being presented side by side, only 20 percent of subjects made the connection, and of those, two-thirds reached only a partial solution. In contrast, when the researchers gave a hint to subjects to use the story when solving the problem, the solution rate jumped to 92 percent.

Another example of failing to use analogous knowledge and skills is the difficulty people have with the Wason four-card task. In this puzzle, subjects are given the rule that "if a card has a vowel on one side, it must have an even number on the opposite side." Shown the cards K, E, 4, and 7, the task is to pick which cards have to be flipped over to verify if the rule is correct. Which cards would you choose?

Figure 9

Wason Card Task: Which cards must you flip to verify that the rule "cards with vowels on one side must have even numbers on the opposite side" holds?

In the original study, nearly half of subjects incorrectly choose E and 4. The correct answer is E and 7. While the rule would be violated if an odd number were on the reverse side of an E, there was no rule saying that consonants could not be behind even numbers. Instead, we need to check the 7 because a vowel on the opposite side would violate the rule. Only 7 percent of subjects made the right choice. Fascinatingly, subjects do not seem to perform better at this task even if they have formal training in logic.

Now consider a different puzzle: You're an inspector investigating underaged drinking at a bar. You see an old man, a teenager, a person drinking milk, and a person drinking beer. Whose ID or drink do you need to examine in order to see if the rule "nobody under the age of twenty-one is allowed to drink alcohol" is being violated? Obviously, you need to check the beer drinker and the teenager. Yet these two puzzles have the same structure and solution.* Why do so few people

---

* To see the connection, we replace "vowel" with "teenager" and "even number" with "non-alcoholic drink" in the wording of the rule, and swap the examples "K" -> "old man," "E" -> "teenager," "4" -> "milk," and "7" -> "beer."

get the first question right, while the latter seems fairly straightforward? One explanation is that due to our experience dealing with norms in social situations, we have an ability to detect rule violations. This allows us to correctly spot the solution when framed in terms of enforcing a law, but it doesn't get activated when solving the structurally identical card-sorting task.

The difficulty of transfer between analogous tasks isn't limited to problems concocted in a laboratory. Psychologist Stephen Reed studied how students who had taken an algebra class but had yet to practice word problems would fare when given an example solution and a new problem to solve. When the example and problem shared both the same story and solution structure, students performed well. Yet when the story content differed between them, success rates dropped. If the problem required modifying the solution given in the example, few students could cross the gap. Word problems are challenging for most students, and a dominant strategy for dealing with them appears to be memorizing different problem subtypes and their appropriate responses. This is a far cry from the goal of most algebra teachers, who would hope that their students could readily apply their skills to real-life problems requiring algebra, not just the stereotyped problems used in textbooks. Worse, applying algebra skills spontaneously in real life is usually harder than word problems, as being in an algebra class is an enormously powerful hint as to what kind of knowledge is required. Problems outside the classroom requiring algebra rarely announce this fact when you encounter them. The mathematician and philosopher Alfred North Whitehead lamented the problem of "inert knowledge" in education, of those ideas and methods that could potentially apply broadly, but which lie dormant instead. Even if knowledge is potentially available to solve a problem, we often don't use it.

Not all findings on the transfer of analogous skills are entirely pessimistic. Geoffrey Fong, David Krantz, and Richard Nisbett found that students taught statistical heuristics like the law of large numbers were successfully able to apply that knowledge when given a quiz disguised as a phone survey. Subjects who practiced solving superficial variations of the Tower of Hanoi puzzle struggled at first to transfer knowledge between structurally identical puzzles. However, these problems lessened as they were given more opportunities to practice. Research on physics experts finds they tend to categorize problems in terms of deeper principles, rather than superficial features. A reasonable interpretation of this research seems to be that while knowledge has a potentially abstract character, it often takes considerable examples and experience to take advantage of even this constrained degree of generality.

Practical Consequences of Precise Skills

The research on transfer should temper our expectations about broad benefits derived from learning specific skills. The most sensible prediction about learning chess is that it will make you better at chess. There might be some benefit to learning to play similar games, such as from learning to manage your time or from sizing up an opponent. But most of what is learned will likely be specific to chess. Subjects like mathematics, whose abstract structure has broad potential uses in many other concrete tasks, may be more generally useful. Yet, here too the full generality of mathematics isn't always achieved, as many students fail to spontaneously apply the math they've acquired in everyday life.

What about learning how to learn? After all, for a book such as this one to have any practical importance, presumably a reader like you would need to extract general ideas about learning and apply it to your specific pursuits. Here I'm cautiously optimistic. I think improving learning is possible, if only because few of the insights gained from research are widely known. The value of retrieval practice over passive review, or spacing over cramming, is not widely appreciated by students and many appear not to choose them when given the option. Yet controlled experiments repeatedly demonstrate they're more effective generic strategies for learning. Similarly, I believe there are probably shared production rules involved in the planning that goes into a self-directed learning project, conducting research, or studying for classes that extends beyond the concrete material taught. We live in a world quite different from our ancestors, with incredible demands for the acquisition of knowledge and skills, so it wouldn't be surprising if our instincts regarding learning in our modern environment were occasionally misleading.

That exception notwithstanding, the research on transfer makes it clear that the broad-based abilities we see in others are built out of myriad smaller parts. Just as fluency in a language is inherently built upon knowing lots of words and phrases, so too is smart thinking built upon having large quantities of specific facts, methods, and relevant experiences. Below, I want to outline three practical consequences of the research just discussed.

Takeaway #1: Focus on the Tasks You Intend to Improve

Broad abilities, like fluency in Spanish or proficiency in Python programming, are really collections of much smaller units of knowledge and skill. While transfer within subjects is certainly greater than zero, it's also usually less than 100 percent. As we've seen, proficiency generating a sentence pattern does not necessarily lead to proficiency understanding it. It makes sense, therefore, to break down large goals into more specific sets of tasks you want to improve at. Knowing how to ask directions to the supermarket in Spanish is a much more modest goal than conversational fluency, but there's every reason to believe the latter is simply the aggregation of success at the more specific tasks.

Selecting and sequencing the order of tasks to learn is an important part of any practical curriculum, but it can also apply to intellectual skills. After all, the value of subjects like economics and physics lies not in their generic mind-strengthening powers, but for giving you intellectual tools for dealing with concrete problems involving money or motion. Here too we should keep an eye on the tasks we want to be able to perform and ensure that they receive ample opportunity for practice.

Takeaway #2: Abstract Skills Require Concrete Examples

The research on transfer suggests a tension exists in how skills should be taught. On the one hand, we want to teach skills in their most generic form possible, to ensure the maximum breadth of application. Students taught the same equations in the context of an algebra class, for instance, later applied this better to a physics class than vice versa. One explanation is that the algebra class is deliberately abstract, and so students take that as a cue to apply it more broadly. On the other hand, abstract skills may remain inert unless we can recognize that they apply in new situations. Avoiding particulars may end up omitting many needed specifics, which is one reason new college graduates often need more specific training before they can do anything useful on the job.

One fix seems to be that providing lots of examples is more likely to ensure students generalize a principle, rather than get stuck on concrete particulars. Instead of a single demonstration, most students probably need to see multiple examples in order to appreciate the full range of a method or idea. Similarly, abstract skills may require further training before they can be practically useful. A person who learns concepts in a computer science class may need additional knowledge and skills to bring that to bear in the particular software projects she encounters at work. Difficulties of application may be compensated for by faster learning when the connection between past skills and new knowledge is pointed out.

Takeaway #3: Learn Things for Their Own Sake

Skills genuinely worth learning shouldn't need the false promise of generic mental enhancement. Chess is a fine game with a rich history. Mastering its intricacies doesn't require the justification that it also assist with formulating business strategies. Appreciation of music doesn't need the additional promise of enhancing one's ability to brainstorm marketing campaigns, nor does the utility of being able to write computer code hinge on whether it enhances intelligence. Instead of doing the activities with questionable intrinsic merits, we can devote ourselves more fully to the skills and topics we care about for their own sake.

Replacing the Mind-Muscle Metaphor

The history of thinking about the mind is a history of metaphors. Plato likened the soul to a chariot driver, pulled by the horses of righteous virtue and irrational passions. René Descartes saw the nerves as a system of hydraulics. Associationists argued habits organized the mind and Gestaltists viewed thinking through the lens of perception. More recently, the computer metaphor has become dominant, both in the serial machine formulation of classical cognitive science and the web of interconnected information-processing units of neuroscience. All metaphors reveal in some ways as they mislead in others. The metaphor that the mind is like a muscle is no different. Skills certainly strengthen with practice, so in this sense, the metaphor is correct. Where it misleads is the suggestion that strengthening on one task will lead to general mental fitness in many unrelated tasks. Perhaps a better metaphor is that the mind is a collection of tools, built out of knowledge. Each tool may be specific, but in total they can add up to sophisticated abilities.

"It may dishearten the teacher to be compelled to think that the gain in power in arithmetic, grammar or translation does not pass over to all other capacities and powers," wrote Edward Thorndike over a century ago. "There is however, no real cause for discouragement in finding out these facts. There will be as much disciplinary value to studies as there ever was; indeed more, for having found out how little there is and how that little is obtained, teaching is more likely to have general value than it was so long as we trusted that the subjects themselves would in some mysterious way improve the mind as a whole. The real discouraging thing would be for teachers to delude themselves into wrong choices of subject matter and unwise methods on the basis of false notions about the improvement of one mental function upon another." The value of learning is not diminished if we set aside the notion that the mind is like a muscle. Instead it provides clarity about the nature of the task ahead. Problem solving develops when you have learned how to solve many types of problems. Critical thinking comes from a broad base of knowledge to question dubious assumptions. Accuracy develops from meticulousness in all of your tasks. As Thorndike concludes, "The mind does not give something for nothing, but it never cheats."

The mind may not be a muscle, but we still want to ensure the greatest generality possible for the skills we learn. In the next chapter, we'll look at how variable practice is one of the most promising approaches for achieving flexible skills.

CHAPTER 7

Variability Over Repetition

I used to think, "How could jazz musicians pick notes out of thin air?" I had no idea of the knowledge it took. It was like magic to me at the time.

—*Calvin Hill, jazz bassist*

- How can we learn to improvise?
- How does varied practice lead to flexible thinking?
- When is varied practice more helpful than repetition?

n the early 1940s, on the second floor of Minton's Playhouse in Harlem, a new kind of music was born. There, musicians such as Thelonious Monk, Charlie Christian, Dizzy Gillespie, and Charlie "Bird" Parker played for each other during the customary Monday night off for performers. Bebop, as the new style came to be known, was a reaction to the swing music dominating dance halls across the country. Swing jazz was played by big bands, in prearranged melodies you could easily move your feet to. In contrast, bebop was limited to just a few instruments, with the emphasis on improvisational solos performed with complex chord changes and rhythms. Free from the demands of a paid performance, the players could challenge each other in increasingly virtuosic displays of technique and creativity. Recalling his time at Minton's, a young Miles Davis remarked, "You brought your horn and hoped that Bird or Dizzy would invite you to play with them up on stage. And when this happened, you'd better not blow it." He recalls, "People would watch for clues from Bird and Dizzy, and if they smiled when you finished playing, then that meant your playing was good." Just as often, however, the new demands for spontaneous performance could lead to failure. In one episode, stand-up bassist and Minton's veteran Charles Mingus reduced a saxophonist to tears after talking over his solo with "Play something different, man; play something different. This is jazz, man. You played that last night and the night before." It is difficult to overstate the influence bebop has had on jazz, with the ability to improvise on complex material now considered an essential part of the craft.

Improvisational ability has long been cherished in the African American musical culture where jazz originated. Music ethnologist Paul Berliner, in his fantastic survey of jazz improvisation, *Thinking in Jazz*, recounts an anecdote from a gospel singer, when a classically trained pianist filled in for her church's choir:

> After an introduction to the choir, the pianist asked the director for her "music." The director explained that they did not use "sheet music" and that the pianist should take the liberty to improvise her part in relation to the choir's. Taken aback, she replied apologetically that, "[without] music," she was unable to accompany them. She had never before faced such artistic demands. The choir members were equally astonished by the pianist's remark, never having met a musician who was dependent upon written music.

This cultural emphasis on improvisational skills found its way directly into the new jazz. As early as 1944, Charlie Parker improvised

multiple unique solos for different takes of the same song while recording for Tiny Grimes's quintet. Miles Davis showed the extent of
his improvisational prowess when he had a trumpet valve get stuck
during a solo. Unperturbed, he simply carried on playing, treating
the now-inaccessible notes as a new musical constraint. "Energized
by its vitality," writes Berliner, "listeners might well imagine that jazz
was thoroughly composed and rehearsed before its presentation. Yet
artists commonly perform without musical scores and without a specialized conductor to coordinate their performances."

Spontaneity should not be confused for a lack of discipline. "Jazz
is not just, 'Well, man, this is what I feel like playing,'" remarks trumpeter Wynton Marsalis. "It's a very structured thing that comes down
from a tradition and requires a lot of thought and study." Experienced players liken jazz to a language, with both infinite expressive
capabilities, but also strict rules of vocabulary and syntax that prevents those expressions from devolving into gibberish. Saxophonist
James Moody likens notes played in the wrong context to "a scream
in the middle of a peaceful street scene." Similarly, Miles Davis once
chewed out a young Lonnie Hillyer for not knowing his chords
after he clashed with the band during an improvised solo. The
anything-goes impression of improvisational jazz is best refuted
by the fantastic precision experienced players possess when playing
spontaneously. "My teacher would have you improvise over a song,"
one student recalls, "and when you tried, he'd sit at another piano and
play your improvised lines a fraction of a second behind you. It could
drive you nuts."

Learning to improvise presents a serious challenge to the would-be
jazz musician. How do you develop proficiency to flawlessly execute the
complex chord changes and rhythms on your instrument, while maintaining the flexibility to avoid constantly repeating yourself? Decades
after Minton's Playhouse, aspiring players have used an assortment of
techniques to master the ability to improvise. A key feature of many
of these techniques is exploiting variability to deepen the effects of
practice. Performing the same skills in varied orders, seeing the same
concept in varied examples, and thinking about the music through

varied representations are central not only to fluent performance, but to creative expression.

Contextual Interference: Making Practice Less Predictable

A first source of variability is simply mixing up what you practice within a session. While improvisational jam sessions clearly embody this kind of variability, many jazz musicians have applied systematic variability within their more structured practice efforts. A simple exercise like practicing the scales, for instance, can explode into endless variations by drilling not just their inversions, but also exploring all the possible intervals and chord combinations. A student of pianist Barry Harris remarked that he used to hate playing the scales as teachers would push students to play it "straight up and down the octave." Working with Harris, however, he learned how to improvise with scales, remarking, "I never get tired of playing with them." Another student in one of trombonist Jimmy Cheatham's workshops described his advice to "exhaust all the possibilities" by working through each available permutation. Another example comes from trumpeter Henry "Red" Allen reportedly learning to play in all keys by playing along to records set to different speeds. Each speed would correspond to a different pitch, giving him greater variety with the same fundamental source material. Practicing multiple skills within the same session helps performers stay flexible.

Psychologist William Battig was one of the first to study the connection between practice variability and learning. In his contribution to a conference on the acquisition of skill in 1965, he observed the "somewhat paradoxical principle" that training conditions which produced greater interference between items studied, and thus worse performance, nonetheless often accelerated learning for new tasks. For psychologists studying memory, interference was viewed as a major obstacle to learning. The observation that increasing interference on one task might improve performance on a different task surprised many. John Shea and Robyn Morgan extended Battig's early observations to motor skills. In an experiment, they had subjects quickly knock down a sequence of wooden barriers using a tennis ball, in response to one of three different colored indicator lights: red, blue, or white. While the movement skill is purposefully unusual (otherwise some students might have had prior experience with it), it's not entirely dissimilar to the difficulty faced by musicians, who produce notes and chords through correctly pressing a sequence of keys or valves. They split training into two groups. The first group had a blocked practice schedule, with training on one sequence at a time. The second group trained on all three sequences, in a random order. Consistent with Battig's theory, the group that practiced in a blocked fashion was faster than the group that practiced under conditions of greater contextual interference. Yet when the groups later practiced two novel sequences—black and green—the group who trained in the varied order performed the new skill faster. This effect remained consistent even after a ten-day delayed test, suggesting the benefits of variable practice were relatively durable.

One explanation for the benefit of contextual interference is that it helps the performer develop control processes for deciding which action to take. Practicing in a blocked fashion makes it easier to acquire the individual pattern being learned. However, because the practice is highly predictable, the process of deciding which action to take isn't developed. Evidence for this view comes from studies that show that the benefits of a randomized practice schedule are higher when the practice involves choosing between different movements (for example, playing one note instead of another) rather than executing the same movement with varying intensities (for example, playing the same notes at different volumes). These results support the view that what variable practice assists with is the process of choosing which action to take, not the fine-tuning of those movements. Such control processes clearly play an outsize role in improvising jazz, where a considerable part of the difficulty is simply deciding which note to play next.

The value of varied practice isn't limited to motor skills. Jeroen van Merriënboer, Marcel de Croock, and Otto Jelsma found a similar effect in training engineering students to troubleshoot a simulated chemical plant. In their experiment, one-half of the students worked on four different types of malfunctions, with twelve problems presented from each type as a block before moving onto the next. For the other half, the same forty-eight problems were presented in a random order. Once again, the random group did more poorly at solving the problems during practice, and no difference was observed on a later test that quizzed malfunctions previously studied. However, when a new malfunction was tested, the group that practiced under varied conditions performed better. Similar effects have been found in second language learning, where practicing multiple conjugations in Spanish led to better retention when practiced over multiple sessions (although not when the conjugations were first introduced). Another study reports that Japanese learners of English grammar did better on follow-up tests when they engaged in varied, rather than consistent, practice sequences.

Despite its potential benefit, variable practice remains underused. Most classroom homework assignments minimize contextual interference by carefully segregating questions taught in each unit. Some exams even feature an order of questions that mirrors their order taught within the curriculum, furthering the distortion. Variable practice may be less common because it falls into the unintuitive category of desirable difficulties discussed in chapter 5. Recall that these were situations where an intervention, say spacing the presentation of material out over time or requiring students to practice recall instead of repeated review, resulted in worse immediate performance but greater long-term learning. Practicing multiple skills in the same session may be overlooked because it appears to result in slower progress.

Generating Abstraction: Hearing Sameness and Difference

Jazz improvisation requires performers to generate something new, but which still sits comfortably within the language established by convention. Direct copying, while an important stepping-stone, cannot be the final interpretation or the performer will be seen as a mere plagiarist. Conversely, a performer who defies all convention wouldn't be playing jazz at all. Meeting these contradictory constraints requires performers to develop an abstract representation of the music itself, both its restrictions and its possibilities.

Concept formation is the process of figuring out what different examples have in common, as well as what separates them from similar instances that nonetheless don't count as an example. A child learning the concept "red" might initially include things that adult English speakers would call "brown" or "orange." If the concept of "red" was only shown in the context of, say, a fire engine, it would be impossible for the child to properly evaluate whether the red of a tomato or a rose merits the same label. Being exposed to a wider range of stimuli that all fall under the same classification helps to generalize an abstraction. Trumpeter Tommy Turrentine recalls that during his early musical education, one teacher would sustain a B on the piano and ask him to remember it. As they walked home the teacher would hit iron poles along the way to set them ringing and quiz Turrentine on the note it created in comparison to the remembered piano key. Such sensory discrimination plays an important role in learning to recognize notes and chords after hearing them played. Musician Howard Levy argues that one of the best ways to learn is to transcribe music heard from recordings. It's inevitable that you'll make mistakes in the beginning, he argues, but the act of doing the work yourself to listen builds up perceptual discrimination skills. "In the beginning I couldn't hear the chords," a novice student explained. "I couldn't feel where the chords changed in a piece. Today, I might not be able to identify all the chords in the tunes I hear, but I can hear it when they do change, and that's a big step from where I started."

Learning sameness and difference in sensory qualities is only the beginning of the skills needed to improvise fluently. Composer Chuck Israels remarks that an "essential ingredient in learning to be a musician is the ability to recognize a parallel case when you're confronted with one." In high school, Israels played games with his peers to learn to recognize a song solely from its chord progression. Transposition exercises, where the student shifts a familiar phrase into a new key, can be useful not just for increasing the variety of practice, but also for learning to recognize the hidden link between seemingly different pieces of music. "Discovering that certain, apparently different phrases gleaned from disparate solos share a similar basis is a familiar revelation for students," writes Paul Berliner. Making finer distinctions, not just revealing hidden commonalities, is an equal component of developing one's knowledge base. Singer Carmen Lundy remarked that at first she could only recognize "jazz licks" but as her experience progressed, she could distinguish "bebop licks" and eventually "Charlie Parker licks and Sonny Rollins licks."

Research on interleaving has confirmed the value of presenting different, but easily confused, concepts together, rather than the more typical approach of separately teaching examples of each concept in isolation. Rose Hatala and coauthors found that medical students studying electrocardiogram readings did better when patterns for different diseases were mixed together during presentation, compared to presenting patterns for one disease at a time. Similar results have been found in learning to recognize categories of molecules in organic chemistry, painting styles by different artists, and different species of birds and butterflies. Showing examples of different concepts in succession appears to assist with noticing the features that help to separate them, while showing seemingly different examples of the same phenomenon helps students to recognize what they have in common. Direct Instruction, the successful teaching methodology developed by Siegfried Engelmann and Wesley Becker we encountered in chapter 3, exploits this effect by carefully sequencing examples and similar-seeming nonexamples to illustrate concepts. For instance, in trying to teach children to recognize the letter **d**, the instructor wouldn't just show the letter in a single typeface, but varied fonts to show the full range of visual displays that literate adults correctly categorize: d, d, d, d, **d**, etc. Then, mixed in with these presentations, the instructor would show similar, but distinct, letters. For instance, **a** has a similar visual shape to **d**, but a different sound and name; **t** has a similar sounding name, but different shape; and **p** has both a similar sounding name and shape, but all refer to different letters. Letter recognition tasks may seem trivial, but that's largely because of our extensive experience with reading. If you're not able to read Chinese characters, consider trying to discriminate 已 (for example, 巳, 巳, 己, 巳) from the highly similar 己 (for example, 己, 己, 己, 己) in various fonts, and it's easy to see why letter recognition takes considerable practice! By juxtaposing maximally different examples of the same concept, with minimally different examples of different concepts, the student can more quickly home in on the exact boundaries of the ideas.

Multiple Representations: Having More Ways to Play

A final source of useful variability that jazz improvisors exploit is possessing multiple systems for thinking about music. "The more ways you have of thinking about music, the more things you have to play in your solos," remarks Barry Harris. One source of representational variety is training both the ear and the eye to understand music. Many great jazz improvisors, lacking formal music education, had extensive aural practice, being able to pick out what sounds good simply by listening to it. Trombonist Melba Liston remarks she "knew what notes didn't fit the chords and didn't sound good," and so she "tiptoed around" the notes that didn't work. This knowledge, however, often runs into limitations as songs become more complex. Saxophonist Gary Bartz struggled during jam sessions to improvise on tunes like "You Stepped on a Dream," relying on aural skills alone. It wasn't until trombonist Grachan Moncur taught him the theoretical principles of harmony in jazz that he was able to understand how the music worked. Conversely, artists with more extensive formal education often find their overreliance on a visual understanding of the music to be a handicap. Paul Berliner documents one student, who was originally trained as a classical musician:

> It was not until he was immersed in his jazz training that he discovered that his exclusive dependence on written music had, in fact, undermined the development of his aural skills. As a result,

his retention of material learned from recordings greatly lagged behind that of musicians who had grown up in the jazz tradition. It required years of experience with the jazz community's methods for him to close the gap.

Just as being able to understand a song from a recording or sheet music gives performers more flexibility, so does having multiple mnemonic systems to recognize it. Chords, scales, and intervals all provide ways of representing pitch relationships within music. However, each divides up the musical possibilities in different ways. "For learners, the discovery of scales and their theoretical relationship to chords constitutes a major conceptual breakthrough with immediate application," writes Berliner. Musician Greg Langdon reportedly had a "revelation" when he discovered that "G harmonic minor scale up from the fifth degree" had the same pattern as "E-flat major arpeggio with half steps" added below each degree. Being able to see the same music in different ways gives improvisors more possibilities.

The value of varied representations isn't limited to jazz. Physicist and Nobel laureate Richard Feynman remarked on the exceptional usefulness of having multiple ways of thinking about the same phenomena:

> Suppose you have two theories A and B, which look completely different psychologically, different ideas in them and so on, but all the consequences that are computed from them are exactly the same. . . .

> [In this case] people usually say in science that one doesn't know how to distinguish them. However, for psychological reasons . . . these two things are very far from equivalent, because one gives a man very different ideas from another. . . .

> Therefore, psychologically, we must keep all the theories in our head and any theoretical physicist that's any good knows six or seven different theoretical representations for exactly the same physics.

Multiple representations are equivalent to having the ability to formulate the same problem in different problem spaces. Herbert Simon and Allen Newell provide a helpful demonstration with the game of number scrabble. This is a two-player game where tiles having the digits one through nine are placed face up between them. Players then take turns choosing a tile, with the first player to possess three tiles that sum to fifteen winning the game. For instance, if the first player draws 2, 7, and 6 (2 + 7 + 6 = 15), they win the game. Interestingly, it can be shown that number scrabble is actually structurally identical to tic-tac-toe. A correspondence can be found simply by labeling the squares with the numbers 1–9 according to the diagram below. Drawing a tile is equivalent to putting an X or O on the square, and you'll have a set of three that combine to fifteen if and only if you have made a corresponding row, column, or diagonal on the labeled tic-tac-toe board. Just because two representations are formally equivalent does not mean they are psychologically equivalent, and what might be obvious in one format may require intensive thinking to deduce in another.

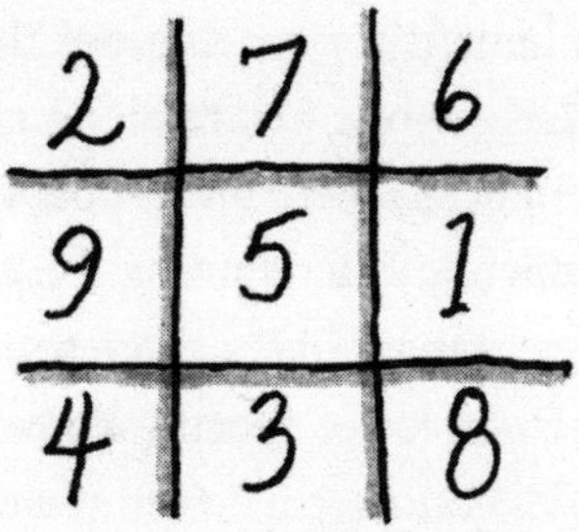

Figure 10

By assigning each grid square the numbers above, the game of number scrabble transforms into the more familiar tic-tac-toe.

The psychologist Kurt Lewin famously opined, "There is nothing so practical as a good theory." In our current culture, theoretical and practical knowledge are often contrasted as belonging to different domains, or worse, being in active opposition. While it's true that theoreticians and practitioners often belong to different groups, with differing goals and needs, theories themselves are simply tools. With more tools, better adapted to the reality we work on, we can solve a greater variety of problems.

When Is Variability Helpful?

Practicing multiple skills in the same session, seeing a full range of examples with interleaving contrasting cases, and learning to represent the same ideas in multiple ways can all be beneficial. But obviously, there are limits to how much variability can help. As we saw in the last chapter, training that results in improvement to skills that don't share overlapping knowledge or procedures has often been difficult to demonstrate. Most of the benefits of variable practice center around practicing patterns within the same overall skill. Juxtaposing different examples or exercises is beneficial to the extent that we're likely to confuse the problems. We wouldn't expect interleaving math questions with history homework to yield the same benefit (although there might be a separate benefit for spacing out the material, as discussed in chapter 5). Similarly, while abstractions generated from multiple examples may be beneficial, there are probably limits to how abstract concepts can become while still retaining their usefulness. While chess strategy and business strategy likely share some concepts in common, success at each requires a lot of specific knowledge that doesn't really have an analogue in its counterpart, even if we can use the same word, *strategy*, to describe them.

Another factor that determines the usefulness of variability is how much variation the final skill requires. A classical pianist, who doesn't need to improvise new tunes, may benefit from a more repetitive practice schedule, since she can safely assume the notes from Beethoven's Ninth Symphony will always be played in the same order. Learning is slower under a variable practice schedule, so benefits only emerge when a variety of skills are actually needed. A linguist studying Romance languages might develop a more abstract and flexible understanding of Latin if she practiced French, Spanish, and Portuguese in sessions close together. However, if a person only needs to live in France, then learning three languages is certainly slower than simply learning one. What variable practice shows is that if she needed to speak all three languages, she might benefit from practice sessions that alternated between the languages. How much variability is helpful depends critically on the skills that eventually need to be performed.

A final moderation on practice variability is under what conditions variability is helpful. Gabriele Wulf and Charles Shea note that complex motor skills and performers with low prior experience to a domain often benefit from blocked practice rather than varied practice schedules. An easy way to understand the apparent contradiction is in terms of cognitive load theory. Variable practice creates greater cognitive load, and so if the task is too difficult to perform correctly in optimal conditions, adding extra load will tend to make it even harder to grasp. However, as performers gain familiarity with the underlying movements, the skill becomes more automatic and so practice schedules that cultivate the ability to discriminate between patterns become more useful. Evidence for this perspective comes from research that finds English learners with more experience benefited more from practice listening to multiple speakers, while lower-experience learners benefited more from listening to a single speaker. Similar results were found with practice variability in mathematics—students with less prior knowledge benefited from practice on questions that were minimally different, while students with greater prior knowledge learned more from practice questions that varied more substantially.

This perspective suggests variability is something to ramp up over the course of learning, rather than simply start out at a maximal level. For skills that are extremely difficult to perform correctly even once, consistent repetition, rather than variation, is probably called for. This is also clear from Berliner's study of jazz improvisors. Faithful imitation, produced through hours of attempting to play along to recordings—rather than improvisation—was the typical starting point for musicians. "Woodshedding," where artists retreat into the figurative woodshed to repetitively practice in isolation, was a common habit among skilled performers. The strident efforts to replicate the published solos of master jazz players can themselves produce ingenious results. Bassist George Duvivier developed an unusual fingering technique to master a complex solo he heard recorded, repeating it endlessly until he had mastered it. It wasn't until he heard the band play live that he discovered what he originally thought of as a solo was actually two musicians playing on the same instrument! Even Charlie Parker, one of the originators of bebop, reportedly retreated into lengthy practice sessions after finding himself outmatched at an early showing at Minton's Playhouse. As we've seen in the previous chapters, repetition and imitation are not antithetical to spontaneous creativity, but essential precursors to it.

Part of the motivation for wording this maxim as "Variability Over Repetition" and not "Variability Instead of Repetition" was to acknowledge this tension between imitation and improvisation that exists in a complex skill like playing jazz. Variability is essential to flexibly execute skills in new ways. However, that variability grows on top of, and not opposed to, the continual repetition of component skills that ensures fluency.

Strategies to Make Use of Variable Practice

Variable practice is one of the best strategies researchers have uncovered to promote transfer of skills to new contexts. Unfortunately, it's also a method that has remained underused. Classroom curricula often minimize variability, limiting questions to those from the most recent chapter or presenting a sequence of practice problems of exactly the same type. Below are four different strategies that you can use to make use of variable practice in your own efforts.

Strategy #1: Shuffle Your Studying

The easiest way to apply variable practice is simply to randomize what you practice within a studying session. Since most learning materials are carefully organized into different topics, this can take a little bit of extra work. If you're studying flash cards, for instance, you might want to test yourself in a random order, rather than going through one topic at a time. If you're working through practice problems for a test, you might want to shuffle the problems together so you can't tell which ones come from which unit. If you're practicing tennis shots on the court, you might want to mix up backhand and forehand shots, rather than work on them individually.

One way to benefit from a randomized schedule is to start with a list of different problems you want to practice from a particular skill, and assign each a card from a deck of cards. A Spanish student could list out different conjugation exercises and assign each exercise a playing card. A similar approach can be applied to learning programming functions, guitar chords, badminton serves, or physics problems. The only thing that matters is that their performance is short enough that you would be able to work on more than one in a single practice session. Then shuffle a deck of cards with the ones you've assigned and draw them out, practicing one at a time.

Strategy #2: Play with More Performers

Randomizing your practice schedule is a highly structured way of approaching variability, but a more organic method is simply to increase the number of people you learn from and practice with. Jazz players frequently worked with a range of other players, often improvising onstage with band members they had only met that same evening. Since all players have their own idiosyncrasies, such frequent rotation exposes a performer to more potential music than playing for the same gig in a fixed band.

For professional skills, look for job opportunities that put you in contact with a wider variety of cases typical of the discipline. Following his in-depth study of firefighters as discussed in chapter 4, psychologist Gary Klein remarks, "In research on firefighters, we observed that ten years with a rural volunteer fire department were not as valuable for skill development as a year or two in a decaying inner city. Urban firefighters are exposed to a wider variety of fires and a vastly higher incidence rate than rural firefighters are." Similarly, the path to becoming elite in many professions often involves beginning work in stressful, highly variable environments before settling down to positions with a more routine set of duties. Accountants and lawyers often cut their teeth in big professional firms with a wide diversity of clients, before choosing a focus area. Doctors rotate through multiple emergency rooms before beginning a family practice. In situations where such professional opportunities are not the default, it may be beneficial to seek out high-variability workplaces when you're still establishing yourself in your career.

Strategy #3: Learn the Theories

Theoretical knowledge, as we've seen, helps foster multiple representations for dealing with a problem. This is also the kind of knowledge that's difficult to develop through experimentation alone. Good theories are rare, and so you're far more likely to find them by reading books. Deeper theoretical understandings are often an investment, however, as they usually assist largely with making other knowledge easier to acquire, not with getting results themselves. A musician who spends hours in the library isn't immediately going to play any better. However, a deeper understanding of harmonies will make it easier to assimilate new patterns of music. Miles Davis, an alumnus of the Juilliard School, often rebuked the tendency he saw in fellow musicians to avoid studying music theory:

> I would go to the library and borrow scores by all those great composers, like Stravinsky, Alban Berg, Prokofiev. I wanted to see what was going on in all of music. Knowledge is freedom and ignorance is slavery, and I just couldn't believe someone could be that close to freedom and not take advantage of it.

Of course, not all theories are academic. Practical theories, professional rules of thumb, and industry standards are just as valid ways of thinking, even if they aren't derived from a scholastic source. Talking to people in the field, and finding out what tools they're using and theories they're working with, gives a road map for acquiring more tools to work with.

Strategy #4: Get It Right, Then Vary Your Practice

Variability, as we've seen, is something best viewed as building on top of, rather than opposed to, repetition. However, finding the exact dividing line for where greater variability is helpful can be difficult. Most of the studies reviewed here have focused on a snapshot of learning, thus making the dividing line between when repetitive practice or variable practice is more helpful difficult to discern. Worse, variable practice falls into the unintuitive category of desirable difficulties, so people may not accurately gauge when it will be most useful. Nate Kornell and Robert Bjork found that, as with similar studies on retrieval practice and spacing, participants generally believed they learned better with a blocked presentation than a variable presentation, even though later tests indicated otherwise. This was true even after participants had completed a final task in which they performed better after the interleaved schedule—students still believed blocking worked better.

As the research on variable practice is still evolving, I'm not aware of any scientific guidance for deciding the dividing line. However, it seems fair to say that if you're unable to perform a skill correctly in isolation, greater variability is probably not going to be helpful. Similarly, if you're able to perform a skill correctly most of the time, while variability will probably make learning slower, it will also likely be beneficial in developing those control processes. Jazz soloists frequently begin by repeating a solo multiple times, checking their performance against the recording they are trying to emulate. Only once they can do this without mistakes do they start adding embellishments, interpretations, or entirely new sections. Variation, built over repetition.

From Improvisation to Invention

Variable practice is an important contributor to flexible skills. Fluent improvisation, however impressive, is still firmly within the bounds of an existing tradition. Invention, the process of generating something that breaks with tradition, such as the development of bebop itself, seems further still. In the next chapter, we'll move beyond the development of flexible skills to the roots of inventive creativity.

CHAPTER 8

Quality Comes from Quantity

Well, you just have lots of ideas and throw away
the bad ones!

—*Linus Pauling, on the secret to his scientific
insights*

- Are geniuses typically prolific?
- How large a role does chance play in
  invention?
- How can you improve your creative output
  without sacrificing quality?

F ew in history can compete with the inventive productivity of
Thomas Edison. His creative accomplishments include multiplex
telegraphy, the first practical system for sending multiple signals
down a single telegraph wire; the fluoroscope, the first device for taking
clear X-ray pictures; the kinetograph, one of the earliest motion picture

cameras; the tasimeter, for measuring infrared light; the carbon micro-phone, a practical necessity for telephones; rechargeable batteries; and—most incredibly for someone who was almost completely deaf—the phonograph, the first audio recording device. His laboratory in Menlo Park, New Jersey, became a model for corporate innovation, later inspiring the industrial research facilities of Bell Labs, General Electric, and DuPont. Superstitious locals attributed his inventive genius to sorcery. For the "Wizard of Menlo Park" there seemed to be no device he couldn't develop, at a cost that was affordable for everyday people.

The most famous invention associated with Edison, the electric lightbulb, wasn't, strictly speaking, his own. Electric arc lighting, whose blinding illumination came from the continuous spark created in the gap of a high-current circuit, was already available by the time Edison made his lighting experiments. Early incandescent bulbs also existed, although they burned out quickly and consumed too much power to be commercially viable. Yet, in some ways, crediting Edison with the light-bulb actually undersells his accomplishment. For it wasn't just his insight to seek a high-resistance filament to make incandescent lighting practical, but his simultaneous invention of the surrounding infrastructure—including parallel circuit connections, high-efficiency electric dynamos, and the concept of a central power station—that enabled not just lighting, but the entire electric industry we know today. Edison produced an astonishing 1,093 patents in his lifetime, making a strong claim to having been the most inventive person in all of human history.

When Edison died in 1931, it was briefly considered that all electricity should be shut off for two minutes to pay respect for the deceased inventor. However, it was quickly realized that such an outage would cause widespread chaos. Edison's legacy was so pervasive that the world couldn't contemplate turning it back, even for a moment.

Da Vinci or Picasso: Is Genius Typically Prolific?

Edison embodies the prolific creative. His inventions were as influential as they were numerous. But Edison's example raises a question about creative productivity more generally: Do the creators who make the best works tend to make more or fewer works than their less eminent colleagues? Compare Leonardo da Vinci and Pablo Picasso. Both are regarded as eminent artists, albeit of vastly different time periods and styles. However, the two left markedly different bodies of work. Da Vinci completed fewer than two dozen works in his lifetime, and left many others unfinished. Picasso finished over thirteen thousand original paintings, bringing his total artistic output to over one hundred thousand works when including engravings and prints. Both figures spring to mind plausible, competing models of creativity: the dedicated artist who imbues a handful of works with the entirety of their vision, and the copious creator who spews forth ideas without pause. Yet the data suggest that Edison and Picasso are more typical of creative success than Da Vinci. The world's most successful scientists, artists, and innovators are also the most prolific.

One of the earliest investigators to consider this question was Belgian sociologist Adolphe Quetelet. In his 1835 treatise, he counted the number of works produced by French and English playwrights. He discovered that creative output was strongly correlated with literary impact. Nearly two centuries later, psychologist Dean Simonton has gathered research supporting Quetelet's early observations: the most accomplished scientists, artists, and scholars are also those who produce the most. Simonton explains that across many domains, personal productivity and social creativity are highly correlated. If we look at the pattern of creativity across an individual's career, Simonton argues, the periods when a person produces their best work also tend to be the periods when they produce the most work. Measuring the number of highly acclaimed works and dividing them by the total can produce a kind of quality ratio. "This ratio of hits to total shots does not change in a regular pattern with age," Simonton explains. "The ratio neither increases nor decreases, nor exhibits any other form. This remarkable result suggests that quality is a function of quantity." Simonton proposes an "equal-odds baseline," which suggests that, once a person begins contributing original work to their field, every attempt has roughly equal potential for world-changing impact. While we can look back in awe at Edison's achievements in creating an electric lighting system, and be baffled at his failed venture applying electromagnets to iron mining, which squandered his previous fortune, Edison himself couldn't foresee which of his innovations would have built his legacy.

The equal-odds baseline suggests that creative potential doesn't vary throughout an individual's career. But what about between individuals? Is there evidence to support the idea that some people regularly churn out mediocre works while geniuses relentlessly perfect a few precious ideas? While perfectionists producing only a handful of high-quality works and mass-producers churning out mediocre products do exist, historical data supports the idea that prolific creators tend to be the most influential. Price's law, named after British physicist and historian of science Derek John de Solla Price, finds that half of the scholarly output of a given field will be produced by a number of researchers that is approximately the square root of the total. A subdiscipline with one hundred authors producing papers will have approximately half of the total output produced by only ten researchers. Harriet Zuckerman's work studying American Nobel laureates finds that the most highly cited scientists wrote almost twice as many papers as similar but less influential colleagues. Richard Davis similarly observes that the neurosurgeons with the most citations were those who wrote the most papers. Consistent with the equal-odds baseline, however, citations per paper did not depend on how prolific the author was. However, since more productive authors wrote more papers, they were also more likely to have generated highly cited works.

Despite the haphazard character of creative success, it isn't as if all creators are made equal. Edison, as we have seen, was singularly productive—inventing far more than most inventors of his era, not to mention the millions who never invented anything. To make sense of this pattern of productivity, and what it means for how we should cultivate our own creative success, we need to consider three different explanations of creative accomplishment: expertise, environment, and randomness.

Explanation #1: Creativity as Expertise

"Creativity," wrote cognitive scientist Herbert Simon, "is 'thinking writ large.'" In this view, creative success depends on the same mechanisms of thinking as ordinary problem solving. What distinguishes a world-changing invention from ordinary troubleshooting isn't the kind of thinking, but the degree of difficulty and social significance. Creativity depends on the same search through a problem space that character-izes more trivial puzzle-solving efforts. Echoing this "nothing special" view of creativity, Albert Einstein once remarked that "science was nothing more than the refinement of everyday thinking."

Examining Edison's track record of inventing lends support to the creativity-as-expertise theory. The theory predicts that creative success will be concentrated in a particular field. Despite his aura of poly-mathic brilliance, Edison hews close to this prediction. Although his inventions impacted many disparate industries, Edison's innovative progress was largely concentrated in novel applications of electrical circuitry. His decision to focus on the electric lightbulb came from his understanding of Ohm's law, which showed that a high-resistance filament would draw less current than a low-resistance one. While many of his competitors were focusing on robust materials that could withstand intense heat and currents, Edison pursued increasingly deli-cate filaments for his lightbulb. By reducing their thickness, resistance would increase, using less current and making the product economi-cally viable. Building on more than a decade of hands-on experience with electrical circuitry, Edison could narrow the search space to an area more likely to contain the desired result.

Edison's failures, as much as his successes, provide evidence for the expertise view of creativity. In his experiments with lightbulbs, Edison noticed that the interior of the bulb became blackened from the inside with continued use, except for a "shadow" left by the pos-itive end of the filament. He reasoned, correctly, that particles of carbon must be shooting off the negative end. Connecting a second wire within the glass bulb, he found he could even get a current to pass through the vacuum. This "Edison effect" lamp, seen by the inventor as a mere curiosity, was actually the first step toward building vacuum tube electronics, the central building block of early computers. With more theoretical knowledge, it's possible Edison might have pursued this development further, discovering the electron and ushering in the electronic age. As it stands, however, he left the path untrodden to focus on more commercial applications for his lightbulb.

Other evidence for creativity as an extension of expertise comes from the dependence on long periods of training. Psychologist John Hayes reviewed 76 famous composers and found that of the 500 notable works they produced, only three occurred before the tenth year of their musical instruction (and those occurred in years eight and nine). He conducted a similar analysis of 131 painters, finding at least six years was needed before a masterwork was recognized, with the quantity of masterworks steadily increasing for the subsequent six years. A similar analysis of poets revealed no notable poems before five years in a career and of the 66 poets studied, 55 did not have a notable poem until after their tenth year. Although Edison was largely unschooled, he was a voracious reader and extensive experimenter. Edison recounts, "My refuge was the Detroit Public Library. I started with the first book on the bottom shelf and went through the lot, one by one. I didn't read a few books. I read the library." Still, it was not until he was twenty-two that he received his first patent, for an electronic voting machine, and not until he was twenty-seven that he produced his first widely celebrated invention for multiplex telegraphy.

The importance of accumulated knowledge to creative success may also explain the overall changes in scientific innovation since Edison's day. Edison lived through the transition from the "heroic" age of American innovation, characterized by the lone inventor attempting to profit from a novel gadget, to the institutional model, where innovation grows out of industrial laboratories and university research departments. If invention is a process of searching a problem space, then we might expect innovations to require more training and specialization as search delves deeper. Edison's ability to make useful inventions with limited schooling may have been a side effect of the relatively impoverished state of electrical understanding at the time. Innovations in electrical engineering today involve refinements of integrated chips with billions of transistors per square inch, or finding superconducting materials at ultracold temperatures. These esoteric advances require far more abstract knowledge, explaining the trend toward large teams of doctorate-holding specialists in producing cutting-edge work.

Yet the creativity-as-expertise view is not a full explanation. While it can explain why some creators are more successful than others, it doesn't explain the equal-odds baseline. If steadily increasing expertise explained success, we should expect the quality of creative contributions to go up over a creator's career, rather than remain flat beyond an initial training period. Similarly, equating creativity with expertise also leaves open the question of why some experts are exceptionally creative and others are entirely routine. Expertise may be a prerequisite to creative accomplishment, but it isn't sufficient.

Explanation #2: Creativity as Environment

Francis Bacon, whose writing helped spur the Scientific Revolution, once wrote that his contribution was, "a birth of time rather than of wit." In this way, he was heralding another of the great explanations of scientific creativity: the theory that ideas are a product of their cultural moment, not merely individual genius. The zeitgeist, or "spirit of the times," argues that cultural context provides the soil in which ideas germinate. That context not only defines where innovators tend to look for new ideas, but also which of those ideas, once found, receive broad acceptance. Even the most brilliant ideas will fade into obscurity if the environment is not receptive.

Evidence for the environmental view of creativity comes from the long and surprising list of multiple discoveries. The theory of evolution was simultaneously and independently worked on by Charles Darwin and Alfred Russel Wallace. Both Isaac Newton and Gottfried Wilhelm Leibniz invented calculus. Alexander Bell and Elisha Gray famously submitted patents for the telephone within hours of each other. Four different scientists discovered sunspots, all in 1611. And no fewer than nine different inventors claim credit for the optical telescope. Even the concept of multiple discovery, often credited to sociologists William Ogburn and Dorothy Thomas, who published an extensive list of examples, has been rediscovered countless times. The sociologist Robert Merton counts eighteen instances where the concept of multiple discoveries was suggested independently, drawing from the nineteenth and twentieth centuries alone. The inevitability of certain discoveries is seared into the mentality of working scientists. Fierce debates over priority, with sealed and postdated manuscripts providing evidence about the timing of key discoveries, would not be necessary unless scientific innovations were already "in the air" before their exact formulation.

Social psychologist Mihaly Csikszentmihalyi argues that creativity cannot be judged in a vacuum. While many psychologists have endeavored to study creativity as a purely mental function, Csikszentmihalyi argues that such studies neglect the field of experts who collectively decide what counts as creative. He argues that perhaps ten thousand people constitute the modern art field, whose acceptance any new artist must receive if their work is to be considered innovative. Computer analyses of musical compositions lend support to this view, with those compositions of moderate "melodic originality" having the greatest popularity. Being original is important for artistic creativity, but being too original may make your work incomprehensible. Similar social gatekeeping occurs in science, where small communities of experts set the standards of peer review before findings can be published. Intellectual fashions can dictate the palatability of certain kinds of ideas: talk about mental states in psychology went from the wild conjecture of introspectionists to taboo under the influence of behaviorism, only to be resuscitated by cognitive psychologists. That scientific ideas are occasionally rehabilitated depending on the intellectual fashion suggests that many potential fruits of discovery wither on the vine. Nor is popular reception limited to cloistered groups of judgmental experts. Commercial products and mass media must face the gauntlet of public opinion that decides whether they're popular or a flop.

Thomas Edison was acutely aware of the importance of the receptive environment, not mere technological possibility, in his inventive work. "Anything that won't sell, I don't want to invent. Its sale is proof of utility and utility is success." Yet this sentiment was hardly motivated by greed. "My main purpose in life is to make enough money to make ever more inventions," he remarked. Edison could have retired multiple times over on the profits generated from his early creations. Instead he invariably plowed all his earnings back into risky new ventures, often bringing him and his family to the brink of bankruptcy before he hit upon a new success. Edison seemed to have a keen understanding of the distinction between invention and innovation. An invention is a creative work, judged on its technical merits. An innovation, in contrast, is measured by its social impact. Ever the pragmatist, Edison wanted to create useful devices, not mere technical curiosities. His focus on a high-resistance filament for his lightbulb came not from technical considerations, but from a careful analysis of the cost of lighting. A bulb that used a lot of current wouldn't be economical, even if it might be technologically feasible.

A receptive environment for invention also explains many curious examples of world-changing inventions going unused. The wheel was invented in Mesoamerica centuries before the arrival of Europeans, yet it seemed to be used only in children's toys rather than agriculture. An explanation for this missed opportunity comes from the lack of native beasts of burden that could have made wheel-driven carts practical. Similarly, movable type was created in Korea hundreds of years before Gutenberg's world-changing printing press. Yet the literary language was written in Chinese characters. This meant printing books required representing thousands of unique symbols, greatly increasing the material cost. "The common belief is that if creativity is rare," Csikszentmihalyi argues, "it is because of supply-side limitations; in other words, because there are few geniuses. The truth seems to be that the limits to creativity lie on the demand side. If there is too little creativity, it is because both individually and collectively we cannot change our cognitive structures rapidly enough to recognize and adopt new ideas."

Explanation #3: Creativity as Randomness

Both expertise and environment suggest creativity is a deterministic process. A more humbling explanation may be that chance plays a far greater role than either cognitive or sociological theories give credit. Paralleling the process underlying Darwin's theory of natural selection, psychologist Donald Campbell proposed in 1960 that creative thinking can be understood as a similar process of blind variation with selective retention. Biological evolution is enormously creative, as witnessed by the incredible diversity of life. Yet Darwin famously showed that all that was required was chance mutation, along with heritable accumulation of useful adaptations. In a similar light, perhaps theories of creativity that seek complicated mechanisms are overwrought. Creativity, Campbell argued, might be better understood as simply a process of generating a lot of potential ideas and retaining those that work. As quoted in the epigraph to this chapter, Linus Pauling attributed his Nobel Prize–winning chemical insights to a similar process of generating copious ideas, retaining only the best.

Evidence for the role of chance comes from the long history of accidental inventions. Penicillin was invented accidentally after the Scottish physician Alexander Fleming noticed mold growing that seemed to suppress the surrounding bacterial samples. The artificial sweetener saccharin was stumbled upon by Russian chemist Constantin Fahlberg after he accidentally ingested the products of one of his reactions. The recipe for superglue arrived unexpectedly after Harry Coover was looking for a way to create cheap, plastic gun sights for the military. Serendipity also explains the invention of Teflon, dynamite, vulcanized rubber, safety glass, and Viagra. "Le principle de l'invention est le hasard," wrote French philosopher Paul Souriau. Chance, not necessity, is the mother of invention.

Edison was intimately familiar with the role of accident in discovery. "In experimenting, I find a good many things I never looked for." He tested countless materials for his incandescent lightbulb before finding a workable material with carbonized paper strips. With this observation made, he then proceeded to test thousands of other carbonized plant fibers, finally settling on bamboo as the ideal source. Later in his life, when looking for a substitute source for rubber, he examined fourteen thousand different plants, looking for one with sufficiently high latex content that could be cultivated in a temperate climate. His efforts to find a high-capacity, rechargeable battery were similarly cut-and-try. His friend Walter Mallory went to offer his sympathies after hearing that he had failed to gain any results despite months of work. Edison replied, "Why, man, I've got a lot of results. I know several thousand things that won't work!" Edison's embrace of chance, and his willingness to test thousands of combinations in pursuit of an answer, were derided by his onetime employee and later rival Nikola Tesla. Of his working habits, Tesla remarked, "If Edison had a needle to find in a haystack, he would proceed at once with the diligence of the bee to examine straw after straw until he found the object of his search." Yet this embrace of trial and error may not have been as foolish as it sounds. The state of chemical research was still nascent, and few reliable predictions could be gleaned about which materials would work except from trying them out. Even today, innovations owe a great deal to chance. Despite the impressive advances in biological and chemical theory, pharmaceutical discovery still depends a great deal on serendipity, as the effects of drugs are often stumbled into rather than theoretically predicted. The weight-loss drug semaglutide, sold under the name Ozempic, was originally developed for diabetes, and sildenafil, sold as Viagra, was originally developed to treat hypertension. Chance, not design, led to their discovery.

Combining the Three Explanations

The three explanations of creativity—expertise, environment, and randomness—are not mutually exclusive. A fairly simple model of creativity incorporates all three. In this model, the existing stock of knowledge defines the possible innovations that can be made. Expertise is required because, unless you are at the frontier, your insights may be individually creative, but not socially creative. An illustration of the difference comes from a story about a six-year-old Carl Gauss. Asked to find the sum of 1 + 2 + 3 . . . all the way to 10, he quickly responded "55!" How did he answer so quickly, the teacher asked? He responded that he observed that the numbers can be paired off into five sets that each sum to eleven (1 + 10, 2 + 9, 3 + 8 . . .), so the answer must be 55. Although we can marvel at his cleverness, such a trick was not unknown to mathematicians, so the ingenious solution had no social influence, even if it heralded a particularly creative mathematical mind.

Beyond the frontier of knowledge, chance plays two important roles in creative success. The first is within the problem-solving process itself. As we saw in chapter 1, people use both general-purpose strategies like means-ends analysis and generate-and-test, as well as domain-specific heuristics to guide problem-solving search. But even if problem solving is far from an unthinking activity, there remain plenty of possibilities left over in the problem space. This is true by definition, since if the problem space collapsed to a single, obvious answer we wouldn't consider it beyond the current frontier of knowledge. Thus random processes of exploration are needed, even for the most intelligent and knowledgeable experts, to venture beyond what has already been mastered. The second role of chance occurs with the receptive environment. Even the most astute technologists, investors, or scientific forecasters can only modestly predict which works will be supremely important and which will fizzle out. Creators themselves have only a limited ability to foresee the long-term impact of their works. This lack of predictability means that each invention, essay, product, or scientific paper is always partly a gamble.

The difference between routine and creative experts can be seen in the decision to work on risky problems. Important work can be done entirely within the current frontier of knowledge. Even if creativity itself depends on chance, some experts will choose to stick to tried-and-true methods, while others will take risks to explore new areas of the problem space. This notion of the creative as a gambler is clearest in Robert Sternberg and Todd Lubart's investment theory of creativity. In their model, creators are like stock pickers, making bets on which ideas, methods, or areas of investigation will rise in value. Like stock market speculation, this process depends a great deal on chance—some creators will gain fame, while others fade into obscurity. The difference between routine and creative experts is largely due to their appetite for risk. Edison was no stranger to economic tumult resulting from his risky inventive pursuits. "At least I did not have ennui," he later reflected on the wild swings of fortune and failure of his inventing career. An investment theory also helps to reconcile why some individuals are unusually inventive, compared to their equally knowledgeable peers. Historian Anton Howes finds that inventors are much more likely to have had contact with another inventor prior to inventing something on their own, suggesting that the desire to engage in a risky line of business may be something culturally transmitted, beyond simply the expertise needed to be successful at it.

This model of creativity helps to explain the seeming contradiction between Simonton's equal-odds baseline of creative accomplishment and the rarity of world-class innovators. Getting to the frontier is difficult and takes years of study and practice. However, once the frontier has been reached, since further developments depend a great deal on randomness, creative accomplishment comes from being willing to take a lot of chances.

Does Increasing Creative Output Increase Creative Quality?

Simonton's research and the equal-odds baseline do not imply any effort to increase output will automatically increase the likelihood of creative success. After all, I could write more books if I simply banged on the keyboard and published whatever nonsense text emerged, but few would argue that was a reliable strategy to authorial eminence. The tight coupling between quality and quantity might emerge, for instance, if creators develop internal standards that they rarely violate when publishing work. A writer going through a creative drought may not find it impossible to write anything, but simply find it difficult to write anything that she judges publishable. Such a dearth of ideas would then show up as a productive slump, even if it might be equally described as a problem of creative quality. Similarly, if creators tend to adopt a dominant style or method, that may artificially mask any quantity-quality trade-off. Picasso's oeuvre is much broader than Da Vinci's, in part, because the Cubist style he cultivated lent itself to more prolific production. We don't have access to data from a counterfactual scenario where the Spaniard labored for years to produce hyperrealistic work, or the Renaissance man switched to churning out paintings like a factory. But within the normal bounds of creative acceptability, and holding the usual variations in method and style, quantity and quality are closely correlated in creative careers.

A straightforward, if unappealing, implication of the equal-odds rule is that successful creatives will tend to be workaholics. Edison offers a striking example. One story puts the inventor, lost in thought, late at night in his laboratory. After being asked why he was working so late, he asked what time it was. "Midnight," came the reply, to which Edison responded, "Midnight! Is that so. I must get home then, I was married today." Although certainly hyperbole, it appears more credible in light of the inventor's habit of staying at the laboratory for weeks on end, returning home only to pass out in his soiled clothes. One of the most famous photos of the man has him slumped and disheveled, listening to his phonograph after a seventy-two-hour binge of nonstop tinkering to improve the quality of the sound.

An extreme dedication to work can be found in countless other eminent creatives. Herbert Simon, whose work won a Nobel Prize in economics, reportedly worked one hundred hours per week during his most productive periods. Albert Einstein focused so intensively during his work on general relativity that he developed stomach problems. Honoré de Balzac wrote his eighty-five novels by working fifteen hours a day for twenty years. Research suggests this work ethic pays off, with distinguished researchers in physical and social sciences working sixty to seventy hours per week with few vacations. Other research finds that psychologists who fit the hard-charging "Type A" profile are more likely to be highly cited than their relaxed "Type B" counterparts.

Given this pattern, it's not surprising that Edison claimed "genius is one percent inspiration and ninety-nine percent perspiration." Yet these intense work schedules often impose considerable costs. Edison was an absent father and husband, as his quest for inventing left little time for anything else.

Strategies for Creating More (Without Reducing Quality or Working Overtime)

The key to creative success is phenomenal productivity. Assuming, for a moment, that you're already working as many hours as you can (or would like to), this raises a question if there are any other ways to increase one's creative output without making obvious sacrifices to the quality of one's work or personal life. Here are four strategies to consider for making a bigger impact.

Strategy #1: The Assembly-Line Method

Few images are as antithetical to the popular image of creativity as the assembly line. Mechanically reproduced sameness, at the surface, appears to be the opposite of ingenuity. However, if we take the idea of creativity-as-productivity seriously, then we might have more to learn from the assembly line than we think. Routinizing the non-creative aspects of creative work can streamline their production. The comedian Jerry Seinfeld, on his hit television show *Seinfeld*, chose to organize the writing of new episodes by separating different phases of the creative process to different writer's rooms: one for pitching ideas, one for outlining, and another for edits. In keeping with the role of chance in creativity, ideas and story lines were drawn out of the real-life experiences of comedy writers. However, the workflow ensured that polished episodes, not just half-baked ideas, made it on-air.

Routines, checklists, and systematic phases for different aspects of your creative work are a few ways you can automate the regular part of making new work. While you may not have control over the content of the ideas and insights, if you can systematize some of the other aspects, you can ensure that you're able to consistently take chances. For instance, a scientist may not always know which research avenues are most promising, but she can streamline her process for writing grants and submitting papers to devote more time to her lab work. Adopting an assembly-line mindset can also help shake you of creative resistance, where anxiety or perfectionism hold you back from publishing regularly. When the working up and releasing of new creative works is on autopilot, there's little time for paralytic self-censoring.

Strategy #2: Allow Ideas to Ripen

The problem-solving aspect of creativity suggests some ideas may be "ripe" for implementation, while others are missing key components. An inventor may be stuck on a particular technical hurdle that she can't seem to overcome. A novelist may have a great idea for a character, but no plot. Pursuing unripe ideas takes more time because the combinatorial process of trying alternatives has to be brought to bear to break through the impasses. While the celebrated image of creative genius often focuses on a persistence through difficult projects, it's equally the case that successful creatives manage to avoid problems that are not ripe for discovery. Robert Kanigel, in his extensive review of the illustrious Johns Hopkins research dynasty, remarks that Lasker Award–winning neuroscientist Solomon Snyder "had almost a sixth sense for scientific questions apt to leave him batting his head against the wall—and he avoided them."

Edison dealt with this problem by pursuing many different inventive projects simultaneously. Having multiple irons in the fire at once, he could switch between efforts when he was stuck. He also was able to take advantage of chance discoveries, if a new possibility turned up that cleared a path that was previously obscure. Many authors maintain extensive notes on potential stories, waiting until a sufficient number of pieces have assembled in the background before doggedly pursuing the work. While it may be impossible to anticipate creative solutions, it is often possible to see how large the gaps are that separate the current reservoir of knowledge and what would be needed for a solution.

Strategy #3: Moderate the Risks

The role of chance in creativity suggests another reason people fail to produce inspired work: they're not able to take the risks required. Those who produce the most creative successes also have quite a few creative failures. While sufficient expertise and productivity can increase the average quality of the results, the volatility involved in creative work can prevent many people from embarking on innovative careers. Edison was able to stomach the risks of inventing by rationalizing to himself that he could always start over as a telegraph operator if things didn't turn out well. It's also possible that an early life of frugal living convinced him that falling back down in financial fortunes was not such a disastrous setback as it might have been for someone who had only known a comfortable existence.

For those of us without Edison's stoicism, we can increase our creative risk taking by ensure we have more reliable sources of work and income we can fall back on in the case of failure. Following the investment theory of creativity, we can think of our work as a kind of creative portfolio. Creative projects are like owning high-risk stocks—they may pay off spectacularly, or we may lose all our money. To make these investments palatable, we want to combine them with the intellectual equivalent of treasury bonds—low-risk investments we can fall back on in a crisis.

Strategy #4: Spend Less Time in Noncreative Work

Not every working hour is used for new work. Much of our potential creative output is eaten up by meetings, email, administrative overhead, and other minutiae. In Harriet Zuckerman's study of Nobel laureates, many scientists remarked that their research careers slowed considerably after having won the prize. While some of this might come from reduced motivation, many remarked that they felt overwhelmed by all the extra public attention. When they had labored in obscurity, they could put many hours solely toward their work. As they became famous, they were increasingly asked for interviews, invited to attend public functions, and offered to chair prestigious committees. Edison's productivity also dipped as he aged, as his business interests grew more expansive and he managed ever-larger teams of engineers.

Creativity requires nimbleness and the ability to put in hours on uncertain projects, both of which may get harder as the obligations of success set in. Being more creative, then, requires a pushback against the encroachment of noncreative work. Nobel-winning physicist Richard Feynman used the strategy of feigning irresponsibility to avoid being roped into time-wasting assignments in his university department. Author and computer science professor Cal Newport advocates setting up strict boundaries to surround one's "deep work" to ensure a sufficient supply of uninterrupted thinking time in order to make progress on difficult problems. Whatever strategy is used, only by maintaining a high ratio of hours worked on creative projects to hours worked in total can we possibly have a productive career without completely sacrificing our personal lives.

From Practice to Feedback

Over the last four chapters, we've discussed finding the difficulty sweet spot, why the mind is not like a muscle, the power of variability to ensure flexible skills, and the surprisingly tight connection between quantity and quality in creative achievements. Over the next four chapters, we'll look at the role feedback plays in learning. We'll start with learning in environments with uncertainty, and see the importance of enhancing feedback to ensure accurate judgments. Next we'll look at the problem of interaction in learning, where contact with reality is both necessary and fraught for mastering real-life skills.

Then we'll examine the role of unlearning, and how correcting our mistakes and misconceptions becomes increasingly important as our skills develop. Finally we'll look at anxiety in learning, and how direct feedback from the situations that scare us is one of the most effective ways to overcome our fears.

PART III

FEEDBACK

LEARNING FROM EXPERIENCE

CHAPTER 9

Experience Doesn't Reliably Ensure Expertise

True intuitive expertise is learned from prolonged experience with good feedback on mistakes.

—*Daniel Kahneman, psychologist*

- What are the prerequisites for intuitive expertise?
- How can we improve in uncertain environments with noisy feedback?
- When should you trust your gut, and when should you stick to the numbers?

On September 17, 2007, a day before her nineteenth birthday, Annette Obrestad made history by becoming the youngest-ever winner of a World Series of Poker tournament. Competing in Europe—she'd have two wait another two years before she was old enough to play in Las Vegas—the young Norwegian took home the one-million-pound prize. She had beaten out 362 other entrants, each having paid ten thousand pounds in order to participate. Although poker may be a game of chance, Obrestad's win was hardly a fluke. She had already become a dominant player online. While still in high school, she was winning more money from poker than her mother was earning from her full-time job. Just a couple of months before the World Series of Poker event she entered an online tournament with 179 other players. For fun, she decided to see how far she could get while having a piece of tape on her computer screen, preventing her from seeing her own cards. She won.

Obrestad got her start after seeing an ad for an online poker site while watching bowling on television. She had enjoyed playing card games with her father as a young girl, and thought it might be fun. Only fifteen, she was too young to gamble with real money, so she joined the play-money games online. To her surprise, she found out she had a knack for it. "I just kind of had a thing for the game," she later reflected. "You know when you start something and all of a sudden you realize you're really good at it and everyone else sucks? That was my experience with poker." A play-money tournament online led to her winning nine dollars. From that minuscule start, she steadily grew her bankroll. Despite never having invested any of her own cash, Obrestad was now playing—and winning—games involving real money against other players. Over the next four years, she won hundreds of thousands of dollars online. Once she was old enough to gamble legally in a casino, she started playing live games as well. By the end of her poker career, Obrestad had won over $3.9 million from live games alone.

Obrestad represents a new breed of poker player. Far from the stereotype of swaggering gamblers playing for high stakes in smoke-filled casinos, this new generation mastered the game at home, on their computers. To understand how Obrestad, and players like her, have gotten so good in such a short time, we have to see how the game of poker has evolved over time.

A Brief History of Poker

In the earliest days, being good at poker meant being a good cheat. Gambling riverboats took players—and their money—along the Mississippi River, spreading the game throughout the American South. From this era, we have accounts of people like George Devol, who bragged about his swindling exploits in his autobiography, *Forty Years a Gambler on the Mississippi*. A common trick was to use a marked deck—cards with subtle smudges on the back side—that could inform an unscrupulous player who held the better hand. Devol bragged about catching another player using a marked deck against him and turning the tables, cheating the cheater. In another episode, Devol's reputation as a shrewd poker player attracted an investor who wanted to front four thousand dollars to Devol for a share of his winnings. He promptly lost it all to a conspirator, allowing him to walk away with most of the investment without needing to repay his backer. "The common belief was that if you sat down to play a poker game on a Mississippi steamboat, you were basically asking to be cheated," writes poker player and author Màrton Magyar.

Despite these unseemly beginnings, poker also acquired a reputation as a game of skill, not just deviousness. Mark Twain was an avid fan of the game. "There are few things as unpardonably neglected in our country as poker," he wrote. That neglect would not last for long. Franklin Delano Roosevelt regularly played stud games during his four-term stint in the White House, and Dwight Eisenhower counted himself a poker player. Richard Nixon even managed to fund part of an early congressional campaign with poker winnings. The game allowed players to size up not only the odds, but also their opponents. "Poker is a game of people," wrote professional gambler and author of one of the first popular books on poker strategy Doyle Brunson. "A man's true feelings come out in a poker game." In his book, Brunson mixed careful strategic reasoning based on probability with more fanciful additions, such as his belief in extrasensory perception and the importance of trusting gut feelings over a more rational analysis. Brunson's book captured a popular perception of poker that remains to this day—that savvy poker playing is largely a matter of psychology, not probability.

Poker's next revolution came in 2003, when Chris Moneymaker (that is his real name) won a seat at the World Series of Poker tournament after winning a $39 online tournament. The full-time accountant and amateur player bested 839 other entrants—each paying $10,000 to participate—for a grand prize of $2.5 million. Moneymaker's surprise win over seasoned pros led to an explosion in the interest in online poker. Dubbed the "Moneymaker effect," online poker websites ballooned in size, attracting tens of thousands of new players.

Playing poker on a computer differs from a casino. Most obviously, there isn't a lot of room for psychoanalysis. All you can see of your opponent is a screen name. This means carefully observing an opposing player for signs of a bluff takes a back seat to more fundamental analyses of the way the cards are dealt. Less obviously, online poker dramatically accelerates the pace at which someone could acquire experience in the game. "It used to be if you didn't see a guy in Las Vegas playing in the high-stakes, then he probably wasn't very good," explains professional poker player Daniel Negreanu. He notes that the new breed of online player "is gaining experience so quickly because online you can play multiple tables. So, some of these guys are playing twelve games at once." He adds, "A guy like Doyle Brunson, who's eighty-four years old right now, he's been playing every day pretty much for fifty, sixty years. He still hasn't played as many hands as some of these twenty-three-year-old kids." Perhaps even more important than extensive experience is the enhanced feedback that can be gained by playing online. Old-school players largely had to rely on their memory for how key hands played. Online play allows players to replace frail human recollection with a hard drive, keeping track of their hand history and those they regularly play against. Obrestad, who began her poker journey at the beginning of the Moneymaker era, would be able to take advantage of that early opportunity to gain experience and feedback in a way no casual player, and few casino-bound professionals, could have imagined.

Poker and the Art of Learning Under Uncertainty

To understand the difficulty of mastering a game like poker, it helps to compare it to another famously cerebral game: chess. In chess, play is completely deterministic. Make the same moves and the outcome will be the same every time. In contrast, poker is a game of chance. Even being dealt two aces—the best starting cards in Texas Hold'em—your chances of losing against a random hand are still one in six. This randomness makes it much harder to learn from your mistakes. Did you lose because you were unlucky, or just unskilled? One remedy for randomness is simply more experience. Play enough and eventually luck averages out. Many of the earliest players, unschooled in probability, likely acquired their intuition simply through repetition. See the same hand dozens of times and your average sense of its potency will gradually approach the true value. But, given the vast quantity of possible poker hands, it becomes clear that this approach to gaining poker skill has serious shortcomings.

Fortunately, there's an alternative: use probability theory to calculate the correct move and ignore the actual outcomes. Today, all aspiring poker players quickly become well versed in the basic math. Players count the number of "outs" or cards they need to complete their hand, and count the number of hands that could beat theirs. Calculating the odds, and comparing that to bet sizes, can make it clear whether a bet is for "value" (meaning it is made because the player thinks the odds of winning are worth the price) or a bluff. Poker may be random, but since the cards obey the laws of probability, calculation is a superior strategy to basing decisions on gut feelings alone.

But luck isn't the only thing that makes poker difficult. Comparing it again to chess, poker is a game of hidden information. A chess player never needs to worry about an opponent hiding a queen up her sleeve for a surprise checkmate. In contrast, you can rarely be sure of your opponent's cards before you make a bet. This means the optimal strategy depends not just on the bare odds of your hand winning against a randomly selected hand, but on the odds of winning against the hands you think your opponent might have, and in turn, what your opponent thinks you have. This makes poker a game of calibration. If you only bet when you have good cards, your opponents will quickly realize your playing style and fold every time you make a big raise. In contrast, if you bluff frequently, opponents will realize that too and start calling you more often. Poker strategy requires a careful balancing to eliminate patterns in your playing style that could be exploited by your opponents.

Both the intrinsic randomness of poker outcomes, and the careful calibration needed to develop a good strategy, are made easier by playing online. While old-school casino players might have jotted down a handful of their key hands for later analysis, the new generation of players can download every hand they've ever played and run it through software analysis. This can not only help point out mistakes in the calculation of the probabilities, but also help you spot patterns in your own playing style that other players might exploit.

The rise of analytical tools has already begun fueling the next evolution in poker. Players are applying increasingly sophisticated calculations from game theory—a branch of mathematics that deals with strategic choices in hidden-information games. These "game-theory optimal" strategies seek to find the exact calibration of bluffing and betting for any hand combination so that there's no possibility of an opponent exploiting a pattern in your play. Many players today randomize their choices, say, by looking at the second hand on their watch and choosing one play if the number is even and another if it is odd, in order to escape the mind-reading abilities of veterans like Doyle Brunson. The Massachusetts Institute of Technology even offered a poker theory course at its Sloan School of Management, reflecting an appreciation for the mathematical sophistication of modern play. Regardless of the new directions poker takes, it's clear that it will not stop evolving as players develop more sophisticated theory and learn from ever-more-detailed feedback to enhance their game.

When Should You Trust Your Gut?

Poker illustrates some of the difficulties of learning under uncertainty. Players use probability theory and enhanced feedback to calibrate their decisions beyond what could be easily achieved from raw experience alone. But what about situations where strong theory or corrective feedback isn't easily available. How do experts acquire useful intuitions then? The surprising answer may be that in many cases they simply don't.

In 1954, the psychologist Paul Meehl wrote a slim volume titled *Clinical versus Statistical Prediction: A Theoretical Analysis and Review of the Evidence*. In it, he wanted to compare two modes of decision making. The first, which he called "clinical," referred to the subjective impression of the doctor, counselor, teacher, or parole board judge in reviewing cases and making a prediction about the future of an individual. The second he referred to as the "statistical" or "actuarial" method. This method worked by a simple formula, taking basic data about the patient and computing an answer. Despite the complaints from countless experts that their professional opinion could never be substituted by a mechanical formula, Meehl found that the statistical method tended to outperform clinical judgment. Nor did the formulas need to be particularly sophisticated to beat gut feelings. In one experiment, sociologist Ernest Burgess looked at three thousand parole decisions for criminal offenders to predict rates of recidivism. Burgess took a list of twenty-one basic factors about each offender (for example, age, previous offenses, nature of crime, etc.) and simply added the number of factors in the parolee's favor and subtracted those against. In comparison to this unweighted sum, Burgess compared the expert opinion of three psychiatrists. The result? Burgess's simple arithmetic slightly underperformed the psychiatrists in predicting success, but greatly surpassed them in predicting failure. This was even under the somewhat unfair comparison that the actuarial tally was used in every case, where the psychiatrists omitted an opinion on some of the more difficult cases. In short, in a heads-up comparison between the intuition of an expert and a simple calculator, the calculator won.

At the time of the publication of Meehl's book, fewer than two dozen studies existed directly probing the relative efficacy of intuitive judgment and statistical calculation. As a result, Meehl was unsure about which would win out in the long run. Perhaps there were some domains where subjectivity beat cold number-crunching? In his book, Meehl was sympathetic to the potential advantage of the clinician:

> For instance, suppose . . . we are trying to predict whether a given professor will attend the movies on a given night. On the basis of [a hypothetical calculation] we arrive at a probability of .90 that he will attend the neighborhood theatre, the present night being Friday. The clinician, however, knows in addition to these facts that Professor A has recently broken his leg. This single fact is sufficient to change the probability of .90 to a probability of approximately zero.

Broken legs occur rarely, but when they do they are highly informative. These kinds of cues, Meehl conjectured, might give the clinician a distinct advantage since they wouldn't appear in a statistical algorithm, but knowing them, a clinician might be able to make a better guess. Meehl was hopeful that a niche for clinical judgment might be sought out, even if the twenty or so studies that existed at the time still favored the actuarial method.

Unfortunately, Meehl's cautious optimism wasn't borne out. In the subsequent decades, over one hundred studies amassed, clearly favoring simple formulas to intuitive judgment in a wide range of decisions under uncertainty. Four decades later Meehl wrote, "As the evidence accumulated beyond the initial batch of research comparisons, it became clear that conducting an investigation in which informal clinical judgment would perform better than the equation was almost impossible." He added that "in around two fifths of the studies [clinical versus actuarial] methods were approximately equal in accuracy, and in around three fifths the actuarial method was significantly better." Interestingly, adding longer interviews with patients, a rich source of narrative information that can't easily fit into an equation, actually made the clinician *worse*. Given these consistently pessimistic findings, Meehl suggests that simple rules and models ought to replace intuitive judgment in many domains of expertise. For instance, psychiatric diagnoses should depend on following a checklist of symptoms rather than the therapist going off her gut feeling. In the areas where calculations reliably outperform intuition, this could improve decision-making accuracy. In areas where the clinician equals the algorithm, it could save enormous costs, given that the status quo usually involves lengthy deliberation by highly paid experts, whereas simple models can be calculated effectively with only a little bit of data entry into a spreadsheet. The clinicians Meehl studied offer a marked contrast from skilled poker players, who until the recent advance of deep learning and supercomputer-fueled algorithms could edge out even sophisticated poker software.

Why does the clinician perform so poorly compared to simple calculations? One hypothesis is that intuition works much like the weighted-sum approach used by the actuary, but it is simply less accurate. In this account, the psychiatrist making parole decisions is unconsciously doing the same sort of weighing of evidence from different factors, but she is simply less precise than the formulas, which leads to her difficulties. Testing that hypothesis, researcher Eric Johnson reviewed the transcripts of hospital staff making decisions about which graduate students to admit into their residency programs while they were asked to talk through their thoughts as they occurred. "Rather than being fallible approximations to a linear model, these judges seem to use information in quite a different manner," Johnson remarked. Instead, judges seemed to make use of highly specific information that is unlikely to show up frequently enough to be represented in the statistical approach. To use Meehl's example, it is as if intuitive experts mostly looked around for broken legs and ignored more mundane considerations, such as the fact that the professor tends to go to the movies on Fridays.

To see how intuitions that work by constructing a story can break

down, consider a famous failure of intuition demonstrated by Daniel
Kahneman and Amos Tversky. First, read a brief passage about Linda:

> Linda is 31 years old, single, outspoken, and very bright. She
> majored in philosophy. As a student, she was deeply concerned
> with issues of discrimination and social justice, and also participated
> in anti-nuclear demonstrations.

Now ask which of the following propositions is more likely:

1. Linda is a bank teller.
2. Linda is a bank teller and is active in the feminist movement.

Many people feel the second response is more likely, but it is strictly
less probable than the first. The set of people who are bank tellers active
in the feminist movement is a subset of the set of people who are bank
tellers. Imagined as a Venn diagram, one wholly contains the other,
so the probability of the first must be greater or equal to the second
as a matter of logic. Nonetheless, our intuition often gives the opposite answer because Linda's description makes her seem more similar
to a bank teller who is active in the feminist movement. Subjective
judgment tends to underperform statistical calculations because our
intuition is a great storyteller, able to construct a highly vivid picture
based on past experience, but fails to aggregate mundane information
even if it is more predictive.

Intuitive Expertise: Skill or Hubris?

In chapter 4, we discussed the incredible power of expertise to make
knowledge invisible and seemingly arrive at a good decision without
much reflection. Now we're considering situations where expertise
barely outperforms a simple tally. Which is it? Is expertise real or
fake? Are quick judgments reliably accurate or overconfident bluster?
Such questions were put to Gary Klein and Daniel Kahneman in

their collaborative paper, "Conditions for Intuitive Expertise: A Failure to Disagree." Klein, whose work was discussed in chapter 4, worked with firefighters in naturalistic scenarios, finding that they often made rapid-fire decisions that were eerily prescient. Kahneman, in contrast, has a devoted a research career to the study of intuitive judgment and its frequent failings. Despite research programs that put them on opposite sides of a debate over the merits of expert intuition, the duo found that they largely agreed on the conditions that were necessary for genuine expertise to develop:

> [T]wo conditions must be satisfied for an intuitive judgment (recognition) to be genuinely skilled: First the environment must provide adequately valid cues to the nature of the situation. Second, people must have an opportunity to learn the relevant cues.

Expert judgment tends to do more poorly than statistical approaches when the power of prediction comes from combining a lot of different cues that are each individually weak. "Where simple and valid cues exist, humans will find them if they are given sufficient experience and enough rapid feedback to do so," Klein and Kahneman write. "Statistical analysis is more likely to identify weakly valid cues, and a prediction algorithm will maintain above-chance accuracy by using such cues consistently." In other words, when there are stable, highly predictive features of the environment when making a decision, expert intuition tends to do fairly well. In contrast, when making sound decisions requires consistently adding up a lot of features that are only poorly correlated with outcomes, simple rules tend to do better.

Of course, expertise does not need to be limited to intuitive judgments. Poker players develop a recognition-primed intuition, derived from the experience of playing tens of thousands of hands. But good players also know the math, able to overrule a tempting intuition if the odds simply don't allow it. Recognizing where intuitions may be limited can be a powerful advantage for a genuine expert who wants an edge over her competition, as she can appropriately defer to the data when that makes sense. Today bank loans are given out based on actuarial formulas, not the intuitions of lenders, and the banking profession is better for it. Using formulas hasn't removed the need for loan officers, but it has reduced a potential source of bias and error in the bank's policies.

Can We Tame Wicked Learning Environments?

Poker, while possessing greater uncertainty than chess or checkers, nonetheless has many of the features that Klein and Kahneman argue make for a learner-friendly environment. Cues are highly valid, feedback is instantaneous, and we have strong mathematical theories for interpreting outcomes. Most of the skills we'd like to master are not nearly so favorable. Many of us are in the situation more closely studied by Meehl, where a lifetime of experience has led to considerable confidence, but lackluster predictive power. Given this contrast, it might be worth asking whether our practice can be made a little bit more like poker and a little bit less like professionals in Meehl's studies.

Predicting the future of major political events is certainly a task with a wickedly difficult learning environment. Events have complex causes—no single cause or factor is sufficient to explain what happens. History doesn't repeat itself—there's no chance to experience the same situation, multiple times, learning from our mistakes. Small changes can amplify to big effects. Who could have predicted that a Tunisian fruit vendor's act of protest would trigger the Arab Spring? Or that a viral outbreak in Wuhan, China, would lead to American high school students taking their exams at home a year later? Despite the difficulties, prediction is also incredibly important. Politicians, business leaders, stock traders, and pundits all depend on being able to see the future a little more clearly.

Given this immense importance, but fiendish difficulty, how well do experts do? This was the question posed by psychologist Philip Tetlock in his decade-spanning Expert Political Judgment Project.

Experts of various stripes were asked to participate, offering to rate the probability of various events (that had yet to happen): the fall of apartheid in South Africa, the dissolution of the Soviet Union, or whether the province of Quebec would separate from Canada. Experts did manage to do better than chance, but just barely. While expertise conferred enormous confidence, that self-assuredness did not translate into more accurate predictions. Tetlock writes that there was "a curious inverse relationship between how well forecasters thought they were doing and how well they did." Consistent with other research on expertise under uncertainty, experts performed better than novices (they impressively beat psychology undergraduates at the University of California, Berkeley), but decidedly failed against simple models that extrapolated past trends. Experts in Tetlock's study even managed to underperform compared to smart nonexperts who were answering questions outside their field.

Although the typical expert didn't score much better than chance, Tetlock was able to identify subsets of forecasters who managed to make surprisingly good predictions. In particular, a major difference between the good forecasters and the lousy ones was how able they were to integrate multiple, conflicting perspectives. Bad forecasters tended to fit every situation into a single, overarching worldview. This confidence and coherence may help in writing forceful opinion essays and well-cited academic papers, but it tends to do poorly when trying to grapple with the complexity of the real world. Good forecasters, in contrast, tended to be more like the experts Harry Truman complained about when he said he was tired of "one-handed economists"—people who constantly said, "Well, on the one hand . . ." That equivocation may be annoying, but it resulted in those forecasters being better able to hedge diverse perspectives and resulted in more accurate forecasts. While intellectual confidence may attract followers, it appears intellectual humility is better associated with being right about future events.

Building on his research on expert political judgment, Tetlock wanted to see if good forecasters could be identified and trained.

Competing in a massively funded forecasting tournament put on by the Intelligence Advanced Research Projects Activity (IARPA) to find better ways to improve the political predictions of the United States intelligence community, Tetlock's superforecasting team managed to beat the control group by 60 to 78 percent, even out-predicting teams that had access to classified data. Throughout his project, Tetlock identified a few strategies that allowed his forecasters to deliver useful predictions:

1. **Break larger judgments into smaller ones.** Intuitions often work by swapping the question being asked with a similar-sounding question that's easier to answer. Good forecasters resisted this temptation by breaking it down into smaller parts. When asked to predict the detection of a radioactive poison in Palestinian politician Yasser Arafat's remains, a naive forecaster might substitute that with her opinion on the likelihood that he was poisoned by Israeli spies. However, a smart forecaster would begin by breaking it down into parts: How does the poison decay? How likely would it be to be detected after many years? What are the possible ways it could be found in his body? By dissolving a complex question into multiple parts, good forecasters resisted the temptation to swap the question with one that "feels right."

2. **Make use of base rates.** A major reason simple formulas exceed the power of human intuitions is that people overweight the presence of highly vivid information, and comparably neglect the more mundane cues. Tetlock's superforecasters worked against that tendency by explicitly trying to figure out the overall probability for events of a similar type. How often do military coups succeed? How often does the NASDAQ close at a higher value one year later? By comparing to common reference classes, we ensure our answers start out in the right ballpark before we make finer adjustments.

3. **Form discussion groups for constructive disagreement.**
   Tetlock found that teams of forecasters did better than those
   alone. In particular, when groups of people are allowed to
   debate and share information, it is possible to aggregate more
   perspectives and reduce leaping to conclusions from a single
   viewpoint.

4. **Keep score and calibrate.** Predicting on a precise probability
   scale is unnatural. Even for pundits who regularly make
   predictions, it can still be unusual to make claims about the
   future with a percentage likelihood attached. Tetlock draws an
   illustrative comparison: "Imagine a world in which people love
   to run, but they have no idea how fast the average person runs,
   or how fast the best could run, because runners have never
   agreed to basic ground rules—stay on the track, begin the
   race when the gun is fired, end it after a specified distance—
   and there are no independent race officials and timekeepers
   measuring results. How likely is it that running times are
   improving in this world? Not very." Only by escaping the
   vague verbiage of typical pronouncements can forecasters gain
   valuable feedback and calibrate future decisions.

Tetlock's superforecasters are not prophets. Even good forecasters
can't predict much a decade out. The world may simply be too unpredictable for learning to occur, even with enhanced feedback and
a disciplined method for avoiding intuitive overconfidence. However,
Tetlock's experiment suggests that we may be able to partly tame some
of the wickedness of many learning environments, allowing us to
develop genuine, if imperfect, expertise.

Strategies for Learning Under Uncertainty

Raw experience doesn't guarantee genuine expertise. Even the relatively
learner-friendly environment of a poker game can lead to superstitions

and bad judgments if it isn't properly disciplined with a good understanding of probability and calibrated feedback. In less precise domains, the result can be disastrous. Despite decades of hands-on experience, so-called experts can fail to outperform simple tallies. Nonetheless, as Tetlock's forecasting experiments indicate, the situation is not hopeless. We can think and decide better, provided we adopt the right approach. Let's look at four different strategies for learning better under uncertainty.

Strategy #1: Use a Model

The most obvious strategy for avoiding the weaknesses of intuitive judgment is simply not to use it. There's no point feeling out whether a bet seems appropriately sized or not when you can simply calculate the odds of making your hand, and compare it to the odds needed to bet based on the size of the pot. Similarly, in many professional domains, our expertise would likely be enhanced if we could substitute intuitive guessing for models based on statistics. The models don't need to be complicated. Counting the factors for or against a decision isn't complicated, but it often outperforms subjective judgment. Put the information into a spreadsheet and you can easily get a weighted sum for the best fit to the data.

Even if you don't use the model as the final arbiter of your decisions, it can still provide a good starting point for further analysis. As mentioned, human intuition tends to grasp on to rare features of the environment but often fails to appropriately aggregate lots of weakly predictive information. A model, then, can do the work of getting you a good starting point as a guess, which you can adjust upward or downward if you believe you have additional information that could be relevant.

Strategy #2: Get More Than Just Outcome Feedback

Outcome feedback is often not enough to develop accurate intuitions. The difference between a bet that is 55 percent in your favor, or against, may require hundreds of hands before the correct choice becomes obvious. However, such a slight edge is not inconsequential—it can be the difference between a winning and losing poker player in the long run. Similarly, the outcome feedback in many professions is spotty. Hiring managers pat themselves on the back for the great talent they scouted out. But how often do those same managers reflect on the gems they turned away after a lackluster interview? Research shows that simply providing forecasters with outcome feedback is not sufficient to improve performance—in one experiment, people even got worse after more experience.

To improve, we need to enhance the quality of our feedback. That starts by keeping track of our decisions, so our fallible memories can't distort what actually happened. Next, we need to calibrate our confidence. Tetlock's forecasters were judged not just on the directionality of their decisions (that is, did the things they thought would happen in fact happen more often than not?) but also on how appropriately confident they were (for example, did the category of events they thought would occur with 99 percent probability actually occur 99 percent of the time?). Whether it's predicting patient outcomes, future sales, or world events, getting feedback on our calibration matters because overconfidence can lead to decisions that don't leave room for error in the presence of future mistakes.

Strategy #3: Build a Brain Trust

More minds are better than one. Joining into groups that allow for friendly debate has two distinct advantages in improving the quality of your decisions. The first is that it allows you to aggregate more information. Francis Galton first attested the power of this effect when he observed a guessing game to estimate the weight of an ox at a county fair. None of the people guessing got the right answer, but the *average* of their guesses was nearly perfect. Holding debates allows you to put together information you might not have initially considered when making a decision. The second advantage is that debate sharpens your thinking. The sociologists Dan Sperber and Hugo Mercier have argued that human reasoning itself is adapted more for the social act of justifying one's actions and beliefs than for the individual art of finding true answers to problems. In an intriguing experiment, psychologists David Moshman and Molly Geil gave individuals the Wason four-card task discussed in chapter 6. Consistent with the tricky nature of the task, only 9 percent of participants got the question right. Things changed, however, when groups were allowed to discuss the question together. The success rate for small groups jumped to 75 percent. Were discussion simply a process of averaging, as with Galton's ox weighers, this would mean that after debate the wrong answer that was picked most often would eventually win out. Placing the question in the context of a group, the people who found the correct solution could usually convince others, even if they were in the minority. Interestingly, in the experiment by Moshman and Geil, some groups arrived at the correct answer even when no individual member had initially suggested it. As the authors report, "[these] results suggest that levels of understanding that are difficult to elicit in situations of individual performance may emerge in the context of collaborative reasoning."

While discussion doesn't guarantee a convergence to the correct answer—ideology, groupthink, and domineering group members can derail debate—it's more likely than when we think entirely in isolation. By forming a group of fellow practitioners, from different perspectives, to hash over tough problems, you'll be more likely to embody the nimble, multiperspective thinking style Tetlock found was key to his successful forecaster's accurate judgment.

Strategy #4: Know When (and When Not) to Trust Your Gut

Perhaps the most valuable lesson of the research on intuition is to delineate the situations where it is likely to succeed, and those places where it is likely to be overconfident. Intuition works best when discernible cues reliably predict events, and performers have the ability to learn from quick feedback. When these favorable conditions are absent, we need to proceed more cautiously. Genuine expertise here requires going beyond gut feelings and relying more on simple estimates based on past data and explicit reasoning that can avoid the tempting bait-and-swap maneuver our intuition often uses to change a hard question into an easy one.

Experience and Reality

Feedback plays a role in calibrating our judgments. But it plays an even more important role in many dynamic skills. Interacting with the environment, both physical and social, is an essential part of ensuring that the practice we engage in ends up mastering the skills that are actually used in real practice.

CHAPTER 10

Practice Must Meet Reality

We learn how to behave as lawyers, soldiers, merchants or what not by being them. Life, not the parson, teaches conduct.

—*Oliver Wendell Holmes Jr.*

- How important is realistic practice?
- Why do classroom skills often fail to translate to real-life proficiency?
- How can you gain access to the situations where a skill is actually used?

Fog rolled in from the hills surrounding Los Rodeos Airport on the island of Tenerife in the late afternoon of March 27, 1977. Dutch pilot Jacob Veldhuyzen van Zanten was eager to get back in the air. His stop at Los Rodeos had not been scheduled. The original destination was Gran Canaria, part of the Canary Islands, a Spanish territory located just off the coast of Morocco. Canarian separatists had detonated a bomb at Gran Canaria Airport, diverting all traffic to the nearby island of Tenerife. After hours of waiting, Gran Canaria Airport reopened and Veldhuyzen van Zanten moved his plane onto the runway to take off and resume their journey.

The Dutch pilot pulled on the throttle when his first officer reminded him that they had not yet been given clearance for takeoff. "No, I know that" was his frustrated reply. The fog might thicken at any moment, putting visibility below the mandated minimum for takeoff, potentially keeping Veldhuyzen van Zanten, his crew, and all 235 passengers stuck on Tenerife overnight. "Go ahead, ask," he ordered. The first officer radioed the tower saying that they were "ready for takeoff." The traffic control tower radioed back, "OK . . . stand by for takeoff, I will call you." At this exact moment, another flight, Pan Am 1736, was using the same radio frequency to respond to the tower, "No . . . uh, we're still taxiing down the runway." As a result, the cockpit of the Dutch flight heard only "OK" from the traffic control tower followed by a squelch of interference. Mistakenly believing they had been authorized, an impatient Veldhuyzen van Zanten resumed his acceleration down the runway. By the time he spotted the taxiing Boeing 747 he was going too fast to stop. He pulled hard to lift his plane into the sky, scraping the tail along the tarmac. But his last-second maneuver wasn't enough. The two planes collided, killing 583 people. To this day, it remains the worst aviation accident in history.

The disaster at Tenerife was a tragedy. But to learn from it, we first need to consider a different question: Why is flying in a plane generally so safe? Catastrophic accidents involving planes absorb our attention, in part, because flying is so routine. Per mile traveled, you're far more likely to be harmed while driving a car, taking a bus, or riding a train. Flying wasn't always this way. The early pilots faced grave danger as they took to the skies. Our safety today owes much to the quality of pilot training, and the man who found the way to teach it.

The Man Who Taught the World to Fly

For good or ill, many new technologies prove themselves on the battlefield. The invention of the stirrup transformed European society, enabling aristocratic knights to dominate over a peasant infantry. Gunpowder cannons allowed the Ottomans to sack Constantinople, ending the reign of the last Roman emperor, fifteen hundred years after the death of Julius Caesar. The airplane was no exception. From the moment of its invention, a new arms race began over who would dominate the sky. The world would not have to wait long to see the new technology in action. Just over a decade after Orville and Wilbur Wright's legendary flight, the Great War in Europe had begun.

England had long relied on its powerful navy to protect its shores and control overseas colonies. Yet in the battle for the skies, they were losing. Some of this disadvantage was technical. Germany had gained the upper hand with the introduction of Anthony Fokker's *Eindecker* plane, whose innovative synchronization gear enabled a pilot to fire a machine gun directly through the spinning propeller blades. Earlier attempts to mount guns on the wings were wildly inaccurate, and armor plating designed to protect the propeller from the hail of bullets exposed the pilot to the risks of ricochet. The new invention allowed planes to serve not only as tools for reconnaissance but also as weapons in their own right. Aerial dogfighting became a necessity to take command of the skies, and the British were far behind. By 1916, over a third of pilots in the Royal Flying Corps were lost, one of the highest casualty rates in all the British armed forces.

Technical superiority was only a small part of Germany's advantage. The greater contributor to Britain's shortfall was lousy training. The curriculum, formulated during peacetime, emphasized the mechanical operation of the aircraft, its construction, and the theory of flight. In contrast, experience actually flying the plane was often sorely lacking. Instructors would take students up for test flights to show the operation of the controls. When a second seat was lacking, this often meant the student had to hold on to the wing spars during the demonstration. In theory, when the student was deemed ready, the two would switch places, with the pupil taking the pilot's seat. In practice, however, many instructors were reluctant to allow the student to fly the plane, fearing a crash. The result was that many pilots were sent to the front lines never having actually flown the planes they were certified to operate. During

April 1916 alone, Hugh Trenchard, commander of the Royal Flying Corps, wrote six letters to the Air Ministry and War Office to complain about the poor training. Another officer wrote in early 1916 that he had just received his third pilot that week who had "never flown any of the type of aircraft I have in this country." Many new recruits died in their first flights.

A fierce critic of this situation was Major Robert Smith-Barry. A survivor of a crash in 1914 that broke both his legs and left him with a permanent limp, he was an advocate for the undertrained pilots. "They've only seven hours flying sir—and it's bloody murder," he wrote in 1916. "They've barely learned to fly, let alone fight." Smith-Barry wrote a series of letters to Trenchard, complaining that with current training methods, the new recruits were little more than "Fokker fodder." An impatient Trenchard replied, "[D]on't worry us anymore with your complaints. If you think you can do better, go and do it," putting Smith-Barry in charge of training at the facilities in Gosport.

Smith-Barry radically redesigned the training program. He introduced dual-control systems that allowed pupils to steer the plane with backup controls for instructors to use in emergencies. Instead of smooth flying under ideal conditions, instructors deliberately put the plane in spins or dives and forced pupils to recover. In-flight communication was facilitated by the "Gosport tube"—a hose that connected student headphones to a funnel strapped over the instructor's mouth. This enabled the trainers to provide instructions over the otherwise deafening noise of the aircraft. Smith-Barry also revised the classroom curriculum, cutting down on theoretical lessons in favor of more flying time. Smith-Barry believed students should "always be in the pilot's seat." The best way to learn to fly a plane was by flying one, and Smith-Barry had found the means for teaching it safely.

Smith-Barry's reforms were an amazing success. Prior to the Gosport system, nearly one in ten training flights ended in a crash. Smith-Barry reduced this to around 3 percent, while increasing the difficulty of the maneuvers being taught to students. Enhanced training led to greater survival rates by pilots. The offensive buildup in 1918 led to a 354 percent rise in the size of the aircraft fleet, but only a 65 percent rise in casualties. Combat flying had gotten safer, even as the British pushed the offensive into German territory. Accidents, when they did occur, were less severe. Prior to Smith-Barry's training reforms, the "majority of crashes were fatal and the result of grievous pilot error," historian Robert Morley documents. In contrast, later accidents "occurred almost entirely during landings and tended to be nonfatal. In many cases, they were not severe enough to destroy the aircraft."

Following the war, Smith-Barry's reforms for pilot training were widely adopted throughout English-speaking countries. "The dual-control aircraft and the pupil-first philosophy remain bedrock principles of both civilian and military pilot training to this day," writes Morley. Despite his early annoyance with Smith-Barry, Trenchard later recognized his contributions to pilot training, calling Smith-Barry "the man who taught the air forces of the world how to fly."

The Aftermath of Tenerife

Steady improvements in both aircraft engineering and pilot training have made flying in a commercial jet one of the safest forms of travel. Yet these advances also meant that "raw flying skill no longer played a significant part in aviation accidents," write pilot and educator Timothy Mavin and professor Patrick Murray. At the time of the accident, Jacob Veldhuyzen van Zanten was the chief pilot instructor for KLM, with over eleven thousand hours of flight experience. In the immediate aftermath of the disaster, KLM executives even suggested tasking Veldhuyzen van Zanten with conducting the investigation, not realizing that it had been his flight that caused the collision.

Tenerife caused a shift in thinking about pilot training. Beyond individualistic pilot skill, training began to emphasize the interpersonal aspects of flying. Investigators placed the blame for the accident on communication failures. The Dutch copilot's "ready for takeoff" and air traffic control's reply, "OK," were both nonstandard and ambiguous, leading to mutual misunderstanding. The Pan Am flight had failed to clear the runway at the exit indicated, leading to confusion about their location. Above all, the accident was blamed on Veldhuyzen van Zanten's disastrous decision to take off without confirming clearance. Although the Dutch captain had maintained a collegial attitude with his crew, his authority within the company likely made it harder for the copilot to assert his doubts that they were clear to depart. Following the incident, pilot education stressed standardized communication protocols that left no room for misunderstanding and interpersonal training to encourage lower-ranking pilots to assert themselves when they perceived risks.

As Smith-Barry's experience showed, piloting a plane is something you can really only learn in a cockpit, not a classroom. A chief reason for this is that piloting skills are dynamic—the thinking that operates when flying a plane is a constant dialogue between pilot and aircraft, one that cannot be effectively practiced in isolation. At the same time, the disaster at Tenerife shows the perils of training that omits essential elements of that interaction. Piloting a plane is not just the dialogue between man and machine, but between a pilot and the surrounding social environment. As Veldhuyzen van Zanten's case illustrates, one can achieve high levels of proficiency operating an aircraft, and still have dangerous blind spots.

How Important Is Realistic Practice?

Realistic practice may be necessary for learning dynamic skills, but it doesn't always come easily. Pilot instructors prior to Smith-Barry's reforms might have been negligent, but they weren't irrational. It must not have been comforting to hand the throttle to a student who had a one-in-ten chance of crashing the plane. Cost cannot be ignored either. Extensive classroom preparation may not have led to proficient pilots, but it did effectively ration scarce aircraft. None of these problems are limited to aviation. Doctors face the same dilemma. The lack of qualified medical personnel owes more to a shortage of residency slots in teaching hospitals than it does to a lack of seats in classroom auditoriums. In many countries, English proficiency is prized, but access to native speakers is hard to come by. The result is that the immersive strategy that works so well for toddlers is impractical for many language learners. Given that realistic practice is often dangerous, costly, or scarce, many researchers have sought to understand when it is necessary. One area that's received considerable attention in aviation training is flight simulators.

Flight simulators were invented shortly after the airplane was developed. The Antoinette trainer, an early model, was constructed with a barrel sawn in half lengthwise that students could sit in. Instructors would shake the plane to simulate flight and have the student respond by adjusting controls attached to pulleys. But the flight simulator didn't take off as an industry until 1929, when Edward Link developed the Link Trainer. Concerned about the cost of flight instruction, Link developed the simulator using compressed air and bellows from his father's factory. Link originally marketed the device as a coin-operated toy. It was only when the United States military realized its potential for training pilots and began buying the device by the thousands that simulators became big business. Today flight simulators are a multibillion-dollar industry, with realistic computer graphics, cockpit replicas, and motion controls.

How useful are flight simulators? Research paints a consistent picture. Simulators tend to do better than actual aircraft at the earliest stages of learning to fly. After some experience, time in a simulator is still helpful, but less so than additional time in the pilot's seat. Given that a simulator is usually in the range of 5 to 20 percent of the cost of an actual aircraft, however, even the reduced efficiency can be cost-effective. In some studies, time spent in a simulator eventually becomes harmful, as students learn to rely on features of the simulator that aren't present in an actual aircraft. Stanley Roscoe, a psychologist who specialized in applications of flight simulators to aviation training, hypothesized that the benefit of further simulator training would appear as a decelerating curve. Commenting on the state of simulators in 1971, he wrote that "the first hour of instruction in a ground trainer can save more than one hour in pre-solo flight training. The fifteenth hour in a ground trainer surely would not."

Follow-up research supports the overall shape of his curve, even if there are questions about the exact numbers. A 1990 meta-analysis by John Jacobs, Carolyn Prince, Robert Hays, and Eduardo Salas found that over 90 percent of the studies reviewed favored simulator-plus-aircraft training to aircraft-only training. Similarly, a 1998 review by Thomas Carretta and Ronald Dunlap found that simulators helped, but that this benefit diminished after twenty-five mock sorties. A 2005 analysis by Esa Rantanen and Donald Talleur found a similar curve, with the benefits of simulators being greater than equal time in the pilot seat for the first few hours, being less effective (but still helpful) after that, and eventually becoming unhelpful compared to time in the pilot seat.

Why might simulated practice be more useful than a real plane? In the beginning, flying is overwhelming and stressful. The simplifications created by the simulator may make it easier to understand the basics of flying. Researchers William and Brian Moroney write, "Despite the emphasis on high fidelity and 'realism,' *simulators are not realistic*. In a sense, the lack of realism may contribute to their effectiveness." Evidence for the beneficial effects of simplification for beginners comes from a 1990 study that trained landing procedures in a simulator. One group trained with crosswinds and one without. Despite the test occurring with crosswinds, it was the group that trained without them that actually performed better. It seems the distortion created by the crosswinds made it harder to understand how the controls influenced the motion of the plane.

The kind of realism matters too. New pilots often want an experience that matches closely with being in the air, but researchers find that the functional correspondence between the simulator and the actual plane matters more. William and Brian Moroney write, "Precise replication of the control, display, and environmental dynamics is based on the unsupported belief that higher fidelity simulation results in greater transfer of training from the simulator to the actual aircraft." Instead of fancy graphics, what matters is that the information used to make decisions and the actions taken inside the simulator are analogous to those that should be made on a real plane.

As we've seen, however, flying a plane is more than just manipulating the controls. The surrounding social environment cannot be ignored. As hard as it is to simulate a mechanical plane, it is nearly impossible to simulate a workplace culture. Standard operating procedures can be taught, but how they are actually used is always a process that emerges organically from people practicing the craft. Becoming proficient requires navigating a social world that both facilitates learning and restricts access.

Situated Cognition and the Culture of Learning

Just as the aviation industry was awakening to the importance of broader interactions in the performance of piloting skill, some psychologists were beginning to question their discipline's detachment from thinking in everyday life. Ulric Neisser, whose book *Cognitive Psychology* heralded the revolution in the new science of thinking, wrote a follow-up book, *Cognition and Reality*, attacking many of the tenets of the new approach to psychology. In particular, he was concerned that studies of problem solving and list learning in the rarefied air of the laboratory might be overlooking important aspects of real thinking. Situated cognition began as a movement focused on not just how people think as individuals, but how that thinking is constrained and facilitated by the physical and social world that surrounds them.

A straightforward example of situated cognition is learning to catch a fly baseball. The exact trajectory of the ball is difficult to compute. It requires understanding differential equations that take into account gravity, wind, and even the spin of the ball itself. Calculating exactly where the ball will land is a feat outside most human's mental abilities. So how do we play baseball? The answer is that we can use a shortcut. By running after the ball and maintaining a constant angle between you and the traveling projectile, you can catch up to where it will land without needing to know calculus. The skill requires a constant feedback loop between you and the environment in order to make a successful catch. The would-be physicist can practice calculating the ball's trajectory in a classroom, but the outfield catcher cannot.

Supporters of situated cognition argue that these interactive crossovers, where thinking requires constant feedback from the outside world, are not just limited to catching balls and piloting planes. The car mechanic who runs the engine to listen to a strange sound, the entrepreneur who builds a test product before ramping up production, and the chef who tastes the sauce before deciding whether to add more spices are all engaged in a process of improvisation. According to this view, we cannot understand what the mechanic, entrepreneur, or chef knows without considering the environment they practice in. The knowledge in their head may be less like the physicist's trajectory and more like the outfielder's trick—leaning on the world rather than an explicit theory.

The process of improvisation extends to our interaction with other people. When an insurance claims processor has to decide whether a tricky case deserves coverage, she consults her peers. Over time, these conversations become a collective interpretation of how to apply the protocols. When a new processor joins the team, she must adapt not only to the standard operating procedures, but to the interpretation of those procedures by her more senior colleagues. This process occurs in all professions, from scientists who must submit to the judgment of their peers before their findings are declared a fact, to the lawyers who negotiate the meaning of ambiguous terms such as what standard of behavior accords with a "reasonable person." The embedded nature of this knowledge often makes it hard to extract from the contexts in which it was generated.

Legitimate, Peripheral Participation

Anthropologist Jean Lave, in collaboration with her student Etienne Wenger, proposed a theory of legitimate, peripheral participation for the process by which people become encultured in a community of practice. Drawing upon her fieldwork with West African tailors, Lave found that apprentices rarely learned through explicit instructions given by a master. Instead, the gradual introduction to the real work of the craft allowed them to become, "with remarkably few exceptions, skilled and respected master tailors."

Legitimacy and transparency are central to this process. Legitimacy refers to the acceptance, by members of the community, of the path taken to full participation. An uncredentialed research assistant and a doctoral student may perform similar work in a laboratory, but only the latter is on a legitimate path to becoming a scientist. Similarly, no amount of legal knowledge can make up for lacking a law degree in the eyes of a court. Credentials, however, are only a particularly visible manifestation of legitimacy. The company that has an informal policy of only promoting from within is making an implicit claim about the legitimacy of alternative paths to management.

Transparency refers to the ability to observe and understand the cultural practices present in the community. In an illustrative case, Lave and Wenger document how meat cutters in a grocery store were positioned at a wrapping station, while the more experienced butchers worked in a separate part of the facility. One apprentice butcher remarked, "I'm scared to go in the back room. I feel so out of place there. I haven't gone back there in a long time because I just don't know what to do when I'm there." Without a window onto actual practice, the apprentices only had access to their formal instruction, which often emphasized skills that were seldom used on the job.

Lave and Wenger argue that the process of learning can't be seen as something that takes place entirely inside our heads. Instead, learning is a communal activity, encompassing both the enculturation of new members and the evolution of practices sustained by interactions both within the group and the outside world. Following this line of reasoning, they argue that apprenticeship makes more sense as a path to practice than extensive schooling.

Pitfalls in Informal Learning

It's easy to romanticize learning by doing. But learning in practice has just as many drawbacks as detached classroom exercises. As we've seen before, experts often make lousy teachers, as they are often unable to articulate the basis for the skills they perform. Even when they can explain themselves, they often don't have time to teach. Interns at big companies are often exploited for a cheap source of labor, rather than provided an opportunity to slowly work their way into a profession. Existing members of a high-status group may erect barriers to new entrants. These barriers work to limit competition and sustain the prestige of the existing members. They also tend to raise prices and restrict access to essential services the profession provides. Economists Morris Kleiner and Evgeny Vorotnikov estimate that the burden of professional licensing costs the United States economy between $183 billion and $197 billion per year. As George Bernard Shaw observed wryly in his 1906 play *The Doctor's Dilemma*, "All professions are conspiracies against the laity."

The informal culture that emerges from communal interactions is not always benign. Bullying and harassment are just as likely outcomes as mutual teamwork and support. Sloppy communication norms and a hierarchical cockpit culture led to Jacob Veldhuyzen van Zanten's disastrous decision at Tenerife. Improvements came about as a result of a greater reliance on formal pilot training, not simply a hope that the culture of aviation would fix itself.

Despite these concerns, it seems clear that the social world cannot be ignored, neither for novices who wish to enter a practice, nor for the authorities and educators who want to ensure that those practices serve the common good. As new entrants, we need to pay attention not only to the content of the skills we wish to master but also to the social environment that enables access to practice. As educators and employers, we must also recognize that formal lessons and standard operating procedures will only emerge in practice after a process of negotiation and accommodation by the people who eventually perform the work.

Lessons for Learning in Real Life

Situated learning suggests a potent need for real practice. Classroom lessons and simulations may be essential in the beginning, but eventually all skills must be sustained by engagement in the real world. Here are some lessons to consider when navigating the social and physical obstacles to practice.

Lesson #1: Study How Entry into Practice Really Works

Legitimacy constrains the possible paths to engaging in a practice. In some cases, these restrictions are highly visible—such as the degree required to become a doctor, or the army officer who must become a major before becoming a general. In other cases, the pathway to full participation is obscured. Jason Brennan, a tenured philosopher at Georgetown University, reviewed data on who makes it in academia in his book *Good Work If You Can Get It*. He finds that academic rank trumps nearly all other considerations in choosing where to study:

> If you want to succeed in academia, go to the best graduate program with the best job placement you can. This trumps almost everything else, including fit, whether you share the same research interests as the faculty there, the size of the graduate stipend or the location of the university.

Brennan advises against focusing too much on teaching: "The grad students who spend the most time 'perfecting their teaching' often fail out of their programs and never get careers as teachers. It may not be fair, but it's how it is." He also stresses the importance of a prestigious academic advisor. "A good rule of thumb: You can't get any job your advisor couldn't get. If your advisor wouldn't be competitive for a job at Princeton, then neither will you."

Brennan's advice applies to academia, but similar stories could be told about entry into almost any elite profession. Acting, entrepreneurship, journalism, music, and executive management all have surprisingly narrow paths to success. If you want to be one of the few who make it, you need to do your homework and figure out how the field actually works. You may not always like what you hear, but you can't work around an obstacle you can't even see.

Lesson #2: Separate Skills from Signals

Since opportunities for genuine practice are often scarce, it's natural to want to restrict them to the best possible applicants. This creates a tension, however, when the skills needed to get the job aren't the skills needed to perform the job. The signaling theory of education argues that a lot of our extensive and expensive schooling is not to build useful workplace skills or build more conscientious citizenry, but to act as a filter so that limited slots for good positions and on-the-job training go to the best applicants.

Bryan Caplan wrote a spirited defense of signaling theory in his book *The Case Against Education*. Caplan argues that economic data better fit the theory of signaling than the alternative theories of human capital (the idea that school teaches useful skills and knowledge, and thus make us more productive) and ability bias (the idea that smart people go to school, and so they would be high earners even if they were college dropouts). One source he draws upon is sheepskin effects, where the return to an extra year of college goes up dramatically for students in their graduating year. If we believed the human capital story, we should expect students to get gradually more productive (and thus earning higher wages) with each added year of schooling. Instead, if we believe that schooling is mostly about showing off smarts, work ethic, or social conformity, then most of the value of a college education is obtained with the degree. Another source of evidence comes from General Education Development diplomas. Students with those credentials ought to have the same academic skills as high school graduates, yet the premium for having a GED is much weaker than a high school diploma.

Completely useless activities that have a value in signaling generic abilities are an extreme. In practice, most opportunities for improvement are a mixture of enhancing proficiency as well as credibly communicating talent. The programmer who gets a certificate for a new technology may learn the same amount as the person who studies informally, but only the former can put it on her resume. Similarly, the manager who leads his team to success on a major project may have acquired some useful ideas about leadership, but the visibility of his success matters more for eventual promotion. The theory of signaling means that it's not enough to get good: you need to find a way to show it.

Lesson #3: Learn the Lore of the Tribe

In chapter 4, we discussed how lore, or informal knowledge held in communities, is often needed for performing a skill. Lore also serves a different function, providing signals of membership to particular groups. Bernard Brodie, the father of pharmacology, discussed the heuristic he used when deciding what research to pay attention to in the emerging field of neurotransmitters. "When the experiments were good, we called it sero*tonin*," Brodie recalled. "When I heard it pronounced se*rot*onin, I knew the experiments were bad and I stayed home."

Educational theorist E. D. Hirsch argued that acquiring the lore of educated society is a major function of schools. Educated publications like the *New York Times* or the *Atlantic* presume a minimum degree of cultural knowledge. This background knowledge smooths communications among educated people, since they can assume that readers will know what the Emancipation Proclamation is or why the Magna Carta mattered. Lacking this lore, the informal discussions that take place are often impenetrable. Lore, however, is not simply a property of general education as every specialization develops a unique argot for facilitating conversations.

With written texts, one solution for dealing with novel jargon is simply to read slowly and look up every word or phrase you're unsure of.

This approach may be painstaking at first, but eventually you'll acquire enough of the basic concepts that you can read new material fluently. In interpersonal settings, being the person who asks silly questions about what words mean might be embarrassing at first, but it is often a short-term cost that needs to be paid so you can understand the work.

Integration with real-life practice is necessary, but it's rarely sufficient for mastery. Improvement requires correcting our mistakes and misconceptions. In the next chapter, we'll look at the importance of feedback not just in learning new things, but in unlearning bad habits and faulty ideas.

CHAPTER 11

Improvement Is Not a Straight Line

Wisdom doesn't consist in knowing more that is new, but less that is false.

—*Henry Wheeler Shaw*

- When do we first need to get worse, before getting better?
- What are the risks of unlearning?
- Why does progress eventually stall without corrective feedback?

F ew athletes have dominated their sport as Tiger Woods has dominated golf. At ten months old, Woods climbed down from his
high chair to imitate his father's golf swing with a plastic club. At
age two, he made his national television debut, lobbing balls for the in-
credulous audience of *The Mike Douglas Show*. At fifteen, he was the
youngest-ever US Junior Amateur champion. He then went on to win it

three times in a row. After dropping out of Stanford to turn pro, he won the Masters tournament by a record-breaking twelve strokes. Following this meteoric rise, Woods did something few could have expected: he decided to completely change the way he swung a golf club.

Known for his long, powerful drives, Woods had relied on a whip-like action to make the ball reach speeds of up to two hundred miles per hour at impact. To produce the force, his hips rotated so fast that his arms couldn't always keep up. This delayed action meant Woods's clubface was pointed outward. Uncorrected, this would fire the ball out to the right, far off the fairway. Woods's kinesthetic intuition allowed him to correct this discrepancy in the middle of the swing—twisting his hands slightly to turn the clubface and hit the ball squarely whenever his arms got "stuck." Yet this improvisation depended on luck and precision. "I won with perfect timing," Woods remarked when analyzing his record win at the Masters. "[I]f I don't have that, I've got no chance." In theory at least, by changing his golf swing Woods could add consistent execution on top of athletic genius.

Yet the decision to rebuild wasn't without risks. Other golfers had their professional ambitions shattered after attempts to alter their swing. David Gossett was seen as a golf prodigy, winning the US Amateur at nineteen. After reaching the pros, he decided his swing wasn't good enough. The botched change scuttled his career. "Chasing the almighty, great swing is not real," he later told reporters. Chip Beck won four PGA Tour events, but felt he needed a new movement to hit the ball higher. A few years later, he quit golf to become an insurance salesman. David Duval, Ian Baker-Finch, and Seve Ballesteros all decided they needed to redesign their swings. None ever played competitively again. "Long grooved into the frontal lobes of golf's conventional wisdom is the notion that every person has a 'born,' or 'natural,' swing," writes sports journalist Scott Eden, and "to meddle with your natural swing is to meddle with your soul." For Woods to contemplate such a radical move, not in the face of stiffened competition but after record-breaking success, was seen as bordering on insanity. One commentator argued it was as if Michael Jordan decided to switch to shooting jump shots left-handed, just for fun.

Despite the risks, Woods wanted no half measures. Instead of gradually introducing the modifications suggested by his swing coach, Butch Harmon, he wanted to implement all of them at once. "It's not going to be easy for you to make this change and still play through it," cautioned Harmon. "I don't care," was Woods's reply. He wanted to be the best golf player of all time. If that meant rebuilding from scratch, so be it. After eighteen months of grinding practice and a tournament season where he underperformed due to the unfamiliar swing, Woods found his groove with the new motion. The year after, he posted eight tournament wins, a feat that hadn't been accomplished since 1974. In the following years, he became the youngest golfer to complete a Career Grand Slam, winning all of the major golf tournaments and firmly securing his number one position in golf.

Since his golden years working with Harmon, Woods has made major changes to his swing at least three times. Some critics argue that these frequent transformations robbed Woods of years during his athletic prime, keeping him from overtaking Jack Nicklaus's untouched career record of eighteen major tournament wins (Woods has fifteen). An alternative view is that Woods's ability to change his game preserved his longevity in the sport. The lithe, corkscrew motion of his teenage swing wouldn't have worked as a well-muscled thirty-year-old, and progressively worsening knee and back injuries made significant adjustments unavoidable. Whether you view Woods's changes as a help or a hindrance—a sign of unhealthy perfectionism or the confidence to take risks—none can question Woods's track record as one of the greatest golfers of all time.

Unlearning: Getting Worse to Get Better

While few of us will face the level of public scrutiny and performance pressure as Tiger Woods, life often confronts us with situations that require us first to get worse, before getting better. The career change that promises financial stability, but comes at the cost of working up from the bottom in a new industry. The search for a satisfying relationship that means breaking up the one that has hit a dead end. The strategy to ward off an upstart rival that requires winding down your old business. In each case, reaching a new peak requires descending from our spot on the current hill, and creates the risk that we may never rise up from the valley below.

The difficulty of unlearning is easy to see with motor skills. In 1967, psychologists Paul Fitts and Michael Posner proposed an influential theory for how we develop movement proficiency. They argued that learning occurs in three phases:

1. **The Cognitive Phase.** In this phase, the performer tries to understand the task, what is required, and how to perform the skill. Conscious, deliberate control of movements is often used as the learner tries to figure out the correct technique.

2. **The Associative Phase.** After a basic understanding of the skill has been reached, the performer tries different things out. It's in this phase that major errors are gradually eliminated and performance becomes smoother.

3. **The Autonomous Phase.** Finally, when errors have been weeded out, skill becomes increasingly effortless. By this stage, the explicit instructions used in the first phase may even be forgotten. The skill may become almost reflex-like, not relying on conscious control.

For a new golfer, her swing is still in the cognitive phase. A good coach can guide her to the approximate movement she needs to create. At this stage, she's likely to be thinking about explicit rules guiding her performance, trying to remember to avoid looking up too soon after hitting the ball or making sure to rotate her body enough in the backswing. As she practices in varying conditions, she enters the associative phase. Movements get calibrated to different conditions, so she knows how to swing both woods and irons and adjusts her force to shoot accurately from both the fairway and the rough. Finally, as the movement becomes repeatedly practiced, the details recede from conscious awareness. Once this occurs, internally focused thoughts on the nature of bodily movements can interfere with the autonomous skill. Instead, best performance is achieved by having an external focus on the goal of the movement, not the mechanics for executing it.

Fitts and Posner's theory helps make sense of the risks involved in Woods's major swing change. By making significant adjustments, he was regressing to the cognitive phase of skill acquisition. To be successful, he would need to move the skill back through the associative phase, weeding out errors in varied playing conditions, and repeating it enough so that the new movement would be sufficiently automatic that his old swing wouldn't spontaneously emerge, especially under the added pressure of a tournament.

Yet the phases of skill acquisition also point out why major changes can often be necessary. No skilled movement is repeated with machine-like precision. Were that the case, athletic performance would be impossible. A change in wind, grass, or the firmness of the ground would change a golfer's movements so much that hitting a ball consistently would be impossible. All skills involve a certain degree of flexibility, which enables the performer to adapt to changing conditions. However, this flexibility isn't unlimited. A person can go from hunting and pecking on a large keyboard to a smaller one, but no amount of practice with that motion will eventually transform that person into a touch typist. Finding a new way to perform a skill requires more than just tweaking an existing motor program, but building a new one from scratch.

Einstellung and Functional Fixedness: Does Old Knowledge Interfere with New Ideas?

Motor skills aren't the only aspects of learning where previous abilities can interfere with new performances. Abraham Luchins studied the problem of how past successes in problem solving could inhibit future results. In one puzzle, he asked subjects how to fill a bucket of water using only jars of specific volumes. For example, a puzzle might ask a subject to obtain twenty liters of water, using only a twenty-nine-liter jar and a three-liter jar. The answer is to pour in twenty-nine liters, and then remove three liters, three times. For these puzzles, Luchins presented a sequence of problems that could all be solved by repeating a pattern of adding the second jar, and removing the first jar and two times the third jar. Following multiple repetitions of this pattern, he then gave subjects a puzzle that could be solved with the more complicated pattern they had learned (that is, B - A - 2C) or with a simpler solution (A - C). In their initial experiment, none of the subjects noticed the simpler solution. Luchins called this perseveration of a habitual mode of problem-solving *Einstellung*, or the mindset "which predisposes an organism to one type of motor or conscious act."

Nor is the perseveration of old habits of thinking limited to problem-solving steps. Gestalt psychologist Karl Duncker coined the term *functional fixedness* to describe how perceiving an object in one role can make it hard to think of alternative uses. In a famous experiment, he gave subjects the problem of affixing candles to the side of a wall. In one condition, the subjects were given boxes, candles, and tacks. In another condition, the materials were the same, but the boxes were filled with the tacks. In the first condition, all of the subjects managed to figure out the solution, which was to use the tacks to fix the boxes to the walls, which, acting like little platforms, could support the candles. In contrast, less than half of the subjects figured this out when the boxes were initially filled. Seeing the box as a container, rather than as a potential platform, strongly influenced how subjects perceived the problem.

Figure 11

Subjects were given a box of tacks and a candle with the aim of affixing the candle to a wall. When tacks were put inside the box, fewer subjects considered the solution of using the box as a platform.

The need to unlearn faulty ways of thinking about a problem is a major issue in education. Subjects like economics, physics, and psychology confront students with radically different ways of thinking about everyday subjects. Research shows, however, that many students do not successfully export the reasoning they learn in classrooms to problems from everyday life. Physics students learn to calculate force and momentum like Newton, but continue to think like Aristotle outside the classroom. Economics students learn theories of welfare-enhancing trade, but continue to think like mercantilists when evaluating public policy. And as we saw in chapter 6, the folk psychological idea that the mind is like a muscle is widely believed, even though considerable evidence weighs against it.

In some cases, what has to be unlearned may be a popular misconception. The idea that people have different learning styles (for example, visual, auditory, or kinesthetic) and that they will learn best when instruction matches their preferred style doesn't have much evidence to support it, yet the idea continues to float around in popular culture. In such cases, it's unlikely that someone spontaneously arrived at the learning styles theory. Instead, it's probably just an idea that persists because it seems intuitively plausible and few people are familiar with the research against it.

In other cases, however, misconceptions are likely deeper. They may reflect a more basic, intuitive module for dealing with the world that develops outside of instruction and may be harder to overcome. Impetus theories of motion don't make for very good physics. But they may be useful approximations in our high-friction environment for everyday purposes. Would-be physicists don't replace their original folk intuition with the formal system derived from science, but learn the more rigorous system in parallel. Eventually, if their expertise deepens enough, they can successfully suppress naive intuitions when encountering problems that require physics knowledge. Yet the road to expertise is a twisting one. In one experiment, researchers showed a simulated "race" of two balls going down different tracks. The two tracks began and ended at the same heights as each other, but had different shapes of dips and hills. In one simulation, one of the two balls sped up as it climbed a hill, catching up to the other ball. Few physics-naive students picked this motion as realistic. Distressingly, however, those who had taken the college class frequently said this unusual motion was realistic! They erroneously justified it by invoking conservation of mechanical energy, which, although it requires that the two balls have the same speed when they reach the final height, does not require that the balls arrive there at the same time. Physics novices can apply ideas they've learned in class, but they sometimes have difficulty knowing exactly when they apply. Like a well-ingrained golf swing, it takes considerable effort to supplant the intuitions nature has encouraged us to cultivate all our lives.

Nip Bad Habits in the Bud

The easiest way to deal with the problem of unlearning is to not need it in the first place. Learning the correct technique, from the start, prevents the need to go back and make changes later. Access to a good coach or tutor early on can prevent bad habits forming that may become entrenched. And, in many cases, once the best method has been learned, no retraining is required.

The importance of learning the best method can be seen in the process of children learning math procedures, like multi-digit subtraction. Cognitive scientists John Seely Brown and Kurt VanLehn found that many of the mistakes children make when learning this algorithm work like buggy computer code—children don't fully understand how the algorithm works, so they use a procedure that's different from the correct one. For instance, a common buggy algorithm in subtraction problems is to always subtract the larger number from the smaller one. Consider a student using this buggy algorithm on the question, "22-14 = ?" Instead of following the proper procedure of borrowing one from the tens column to solve "12-4 = 8," the student would simply swap the digits and put the answer "4-2 = 2" in the ones column. Extra practice may not be helpful for students with buggy algorithms, as they may further ingrain the incorrect procedure. A more successful approach would be for a teacher to stop the student, explain the mistake, and ensure that the technique proceeds on the best footing. Corrective feedback can be essential to avoid falling into bad habits early on.

For many skills, there is no "correct" procedure, but there are better ones. Experienced teachers can guide their students to more successful ways to write code, swing a baseball bat, or structure an essay. If those methods get more practice, they'll eventually become automatic. If alternative methods that don't work as well take root, they may require more significant unlearning later. Given the heroic efforts that are often required, it's better to begin with the right approach.

But completely avoiding unlearning is often impossible. While using the correct technique in subtraction problems is simply a matter of following instructions, many other skills don't emerge from a flawless foundation. English-speaking children go through a regular sequence when learning to use the past tense. Initially, they begin using the irregular verbs they hear from adults (for example, "I went there," "I did it"). With some exposure, they start to learn the rule that they can attach -*ed* to many verbs to make them past tense. This leads to a period of overregularization—where the rule applies even though that particular case is an exception (for example, "I goed there"). Finally, children learn which words are irregular (for example, *go/went, do/did*) and correctly use both the irregular forms and regular past-tense endings. This kind of transition is non-monotonic, as children actually become less grammatical in their speaking at first, before getting better. Young children are also frequently impervious to correction, as many parents have witnessed when trying to adjust a toddler's pronunciation.

Children learn grammar automatically, and don't require instruction to speak properly except in unusual circumstances. All that's needed is exposure and opportunities to interact. However non-monotonicity has been observed in other domains of learning. Vimla Patel, a psychologist specializing in medical cognition, notes that medical students' reasoning frequently goes through similar changes in quality. For instance, both early medical students and medical experts tend to make few elaborations when thinking about patient problems. In contrast, intermediate students tend to draw far more inferences and dredge up more medical information than either beginners or seasoned clinicians. This so-called intermediate effect occurs because novice students have little knowledge to recall, and so they fail to elaborate much when they get stuck on problems. Experts, in contrast, don't elaborate for a different reason: they know the likely answer and so they focus on only critical information pertinent to the problem, ignoring irrelevant aspects of the problem. In a similar vein, developmental psychologist Robert Siegler argues for a "moderate experience hypothesis" that says people have the greatest variety of strategies (good and bad) with intermediate levels of experience in a field. At this stage, we know enough to have multiple ways to tackle a problem, but not so much that the optimal method has suppressed all alternatives. Non-monotonicity means that the path to mastery is not always a straight line. It invariably has dips and detours along the way.

In other cases, unlearning is necessary because the best method simply isn't available when we're starting out. The new crop of doctoral students may be more likely to lead a revolution in a scientific field, because they're not as burdened by calcified ways of thinking about old problems. Max Planck, one of the physicists who led the quantum revolution, noted astutely that "science proceeds one funeral at a time." Often, the old guard who spent a lifetime growing accustomed to a particular paradigm find it difficult to switch to a new perspective, even after the evidence has become overwhelming. Albert Einstein fought bitterly against the nondeterministic aspects of quantum mechanics, despite winning his Nobel Prize for discoveries that led to it. Keeping up with new developments in our professional lives often requires uncomfortable adjustments.

Confronting Faulty Ways of Thinking

How do we avoid getting stuck in our ways? One method for unlearning involves confronting the flaws in our thinking with direct feedback. Anders Ericsson argued that a key to deliberate practice, his model for how elite experts get so good, was the presence of immediate feedback and guided practice sessions with the help of a coach. In his theory, the problem of stagnation in our skills results from the transition to Fitts and Posner's autonomous mode of processing. The "deliberate" part of deliberate practice refers to the need for the performer to shift back to the cognitive phase, where aspects of the skill are under direct, conscious supervision. By combining this effortful mode of processing with immediate feedback from the environment, the performer can make conscious efforts to adjust. In this case, Woods fits the model of deliberate practice perfectly. Not only was he famous for his work ethic to practice relentlessly, but he approached many aspects of his swing from a deliberate perspective—thinking through and consciously adopting adjustments based on feedback.

Feedback can also be used to confront misconceptions in academic subjects, such as physics. Traditional instruction often focuses on mastery of equations in well-defined problem types. While this kind of training is certainly necessary for mastering the subject, it may fail to directly confront a student with the inadequacy of her intuitive conceptions. Physics Nobelist Carl Wieman argues that we should introduce more hands-on physics simulations. These would allow students to make predictions about the movement of objects in idealized experiments and make the correct mental model of the physical process more salient. Other researchers have found that interactive simulations can improve conceptual knowledge over traditional instruction alone. Pure play with simulators is unlikely to produce a scientific level of understanding of a subject. But combined with more traditional exercises working with equations, an expanded set of activities may help to counteract the disconnect many students have between the physics they learn in the classroom and how they reason about objects moving in everyday life.

Unfortunately, direct feedback about mistakes with a familiar strategy may not be enough to fix it. One reason for this is that unless the replacement strategy is sufficiently practiced, it may still be too effortful to compete with the old pattern. This is one reason golfers have so much difficulty switching to a new swing, and they often regress to old habits under pressure. Even if they may know, at some level, that they have mistakes in their performance, the new way of doing things may not work much better! Similarly, many physics novices may continue to use their intuitive mode of reasoning outside the classroom, because reasoning with physics is effortful and error-prone. In contrast, their intuitive system is fast and easy, even if it doesn't always lead to the correct answer. Experts are far more likely to lean on their training, not simply because they are aware that everyday intuitions can't be trusted, but also because the training is so well practiced that it doesn't take nearly as much effort to execute. To unlearn lousy strategies we need to not only confront our mistakes, but also ensure that we can fluently apply a viable alternative.

Strategies for Unlearning

Unlearning isn't easy. It requires not only the investment to practice new strategies until they can compete with old habits, but also the emotional punch of accepting a decline in your temporary performance. Despite these difficulties, we often face situations where unlearning is necessary. Bad habits may have taken root early in practice that require correcting; a change in the environment, industry, or our own bodies may require doing things differently than we're used to and sometimes the path to proficiency itself takes non-monotonic detours in performance, as we stumble through the awkward transition between naivety and mastery. Here are a few tactics to make unlearning more successful.

Tactic #1: Introduce New Constraints

Old habits of thinking can exert a gravity on your performance. You fall back into routines, even if you're trying to do something original. You can prevent that backsliding by changing the task constraints so performing the skill in the old way is impossible. Sometimes these constraints can take the form of prohibitions against certain kinds of actions—writing an essay without using any adverbs or trying to paint a picture without using color. In other cases, the constraints can be requirements for action. Hitting a tennis shot using an undersize racquet face forces you to hit balls in the center. Constraints are a hallmark of good design practices, in part because the space of possible useful solutions is so large that absent any restrictions, stale ideas may overwhelm the search for original options.

Designed by a coach, constraints can be chosen to counteract an unwanted tendency in your performance. Deliberate instruction on how to move your body, by moving you back to the cognitive phase of learning, can have unwanted side effects in the fluency of your performance. In golf, the "yips" are a common phenomenon where excessive attention on one's own movements can ruin a golf swing. Good constraints, in contrast, can push a performer away from their bad habits without focusing attention on them.

Tactic #2: Find a Coach

A weakness of self-directed efforts at improvement is that it's often impossible to simultaneously monitor your own performance and actually use the skill. "Feel is not real" is a piece of golf-improvement lore that points to the fact that performers frequently have misconceptions about how their own body is moving during a swing. A putter may think he's barely holding on to the grip, but he's actually strangling the club. A golfer teeing off may imagine he's rotating all the way through, but instead is only bringing the club halfway to where it needs to be. Our distorted self-image makes improvement difficult.

Coaching and tutoring can make a major difference, even if the person you're hiring isn't better than you are. Tiger Woods worked extensively with coaches who were much worse golfers than he was. Because they can observe what you're doing, without actually needing to devote the mental bandwidth to perform the skill themselves, they can offer insights into your performance.

Tactic #3: Renovate Rather Than Rebuild

Ultimately, complete overhauls of a well-learned skill are probably the exception, rather than the rule. Few golfers could have performed at elite levels had they made such frequent revisions to their basic movements. It's a testament both to Woods's athletic skill and his work ethic that he was able to overcome those odds. In most cases, we're probably better off augmenting or modifying the foundation we've built upon, rather than tearing things down and starting from scratch. Whether it's a golf swing or a scientific worldview, the safest option is usually to make changes smoothly—seek the ridge between mountains rather than recklessly climb down to the valley below. Like the ship of Theseus, whose wooden planks were replaced one by one until none of the original ship remained, radical shifts in perspective are easier to make by adjusting one piece at a time, rather than threatening to demolish the entire foundation.

The need for unlearning isn't limited to intellectual ideas or athletic abilities. Ultimately, our emotions often provide the biggest barriers to making improvements. Fears and anxieties hold us back from learning. Feedback matters not just for correcting misconceptions, but for testing out our own apprehensions.

CHAPTER 12

Fears Fade with Exposure

One of the major weaknesses of all psychological theories is the assumption that people are highly vulnerable to threats and stress. The theories are designed for creatures more timorous than human beings.

—*Stanley Rachman, psychologist*

- Why do many of the steps we take to avoid anxieties make them worse?
- How do we get outside our comfort zone?
- Is courage the same as fearlessness?

n the years before the Second World War, as conflict with Germany came to be seen as inevitable, leaders began to confront the possibility of a new kind of danger: planes were likely to drop bombs over major populated centers. Air raids during the First World War had been limited. Only three hundred tons of bombs had dropped on London in the entirety of the conflict. In the interwar decades, technology advanced, bringing with it a new scale of destruction. Planners anticipated Germany might begin with a sudden blitzkrieg, dropping 3,500 tons in the first twenty-four hours of an assault, with hundreds more dropped daily for weeks. Casualties were predicted to be in the hundreds of thousands. Whole cities might be destroyed after only a few weeks.

Beyond the physical devastation, politicians, leaders, and psychologists all agreed that massive panic was inevitable. Addressing the House of Commons, former British prime minister Stanley Baldwin articulated these fears: "I think it is well also for the man in the street to realize that there is no power on earth that can protect him from being bombed. Whatever people may tell him, the bomber will always get through." In a public speech, Winston Churchill projected that three to four million people might flee major metropolitan centers in the aftermath of an attack. Tens of thousands of police officers were requested to prevent surging crowds from trampling each other in the inevitable exodus. A group of esteemed psychiatrists in London prepared a report arguing that psychological casualties were likely to exceed physical casualties three to one. The expert consensus was expressed best when the well-known director of a London medical clinic said it was "clear to everyone that there must be an immediate inundation with cases of neurosis on the declaration of war—and certainly after the first air raid."

Yet as war began and bombs fell, no mass panic actually occurred. "To the considerable surprise of almost everyone, the psychological casualties were few, despite the death and destruction caused by the attacks," writes psychologist Stanley Rachman. In one report, of the 578 casualties hospitalized after a period of heavy bombing, only two were suffering primarily from psychological symptoms. In another, only fifteen of 1,100 patients in a medical clinic showed obvious psychological disorders. Far from being inundated with traumatized neurotics, the number of patients admitted to mental hospitals in 1940 was actually less than in 1938, with a further decrease in 1941. "One point emerges very clearly," writes psychologist Irving Janis: "there was a definite decline in overt fear reactions as the air blitz continued, even though raids became heavier and more destructive."

Witnesses to daily life during the Blitz lends further support to the resiliency of ordinary people. Philip Vernon, who surveyed dozens of doctors and psychologists working during the war, observed that "[n]ear the beginning of the war the mere sounding of the sirens was enough to send large numbers to shelters." However, as the bombings intensified, "Londoners were generally taking no notice of sirens at all, unless accompanied by the noise of planes, gunfire, or bombs, and in some areas it is a social faux pas to mention the fact that they have sounded." Another observer at the time noted, "The calm behavior of the average individual continues to be amazing. Commuting suburbanites, who up to yesterday had experienced worse bombardments than people living in Central London, placidly bragged to fellow passengers on the morning trains about the size of bomb craters in their neighborhoods, as in a more peaceful summer they would have bragged about their roses and squash."

Britain's stoic reactions were hardly unique. Survivors of the atomic bombings of Hiroshima and Nagasaki also experienced surprisingly low rates of mental disturbance. Similar reports came from bombed German cities, where a plurality of respondents to one survey indicated they felt less afraid after successive bombings. In a more recent example, Philip Saigh happened to be conducting a study on anxiety in Beirut, Lebanon, shortly before the ten-week siege by Israeli forces in 1982. Following up with the study participants, he found no difference in anxiety levels before and after the invasion. In addition, those who had not been evacuated showed a marked decline in fear reactions to war-related stimuli. Hysterical panic during disasters is more common in popular imagination than in reality. As Lee Clark reviews in his article "Panic: Myth or Reality?" the Hollywood image of people stampeding over each other in an emergency isn't based in fact. "After five decades of studying scores of disasters such as floods, earthquakes, and tornadoes, one of the strongest findings is that people rarely lose control."

The experience of Britons during the Blitz illustrates an important psychological principle: fears tend to diminish with exposure. Experiencing fear, without suffering direct harm, reduces fear in similar future situations. Even faced with the terror of nightly bombing raids, the typical response was not escalating anxiety, but adaptation.

Learning Fear and Safety

Fear often looms larger than any intellectual difficulty in our efforts at improvement: The person who spends years studying French but doesn't feel comfortable conversing during a trip to Paris. The student with test anxiety who feels his stomach churn before opening the practice exams. The job candidate who turns down a work opportunity she doesn't feel "ready" for—even when she's completely qualified. How many of us completely avoid entire skills or subjects because the thought of practicing them fills us with dread? Despite these difficulties, we often fail to understand our fears. More importantly, we fail to see how the strategies we use to reduce anxiety frequently make it worse.

The origin of our anxieties has long been a popular source of speculation within psychology. Sigmund Freud famously claimed anxieties were infantile impulses, repressed in the subconscious. William James believed fears were innate, ripening with appropriate experience. The father of behaviorism, John Watson, argued that fears came from a simple process of conditioning. In his infamous experiment with Little Albert, he repeatedly showed the eleven-month-old a white rat while striking a steel bar behind the boy to produce a loud sound. As the fright of the noise became associated with the rat, the child came to fear not only mice, but all sorts of white, furry things. The conditioning theory of fear helps explain a divergence in reactions to bombings during the Blitz. Those who experienced a "near miss"—being inside a building that was bombed or witnessing a fatal injury—often had their fears resurge temporarily. In contrast, those who experienced a "remote miss"—hearing the distant rumble of explosions but facing no personal harm—were more likely to have their fears diminish. Whether fears worsened or alleviated with exposure depended, in part, on how direct the danger was.

The conditioning theory of fear, however, isn't without difficulties.

Echoing William James, psychologist Martin Seligman argued we are predisposed to acquire some fears, but not others. Far more people have phobias of snakes than electrical outlets, even though more people have had a shock than a snakebite. Similarly, fears can arrive without an obvious episode of conditioning. Fears of air raids were highest in Britain before the war—when no one had yet experienced an attack. While some phobias and anxieties can be linked to a particularly traumatic experience, others seem to develop without provocation. Fears can be acquired vicariously, through watching someone else's fearful reaction, and through verbalization, such as when we fear being mugged in a particular part of town after being warned it is dangerous. Avoiding danger is an evolutionary imperative. It makes sense that we would have multiple pathways to fear, beyond those that require direct experience. An animal that could only learn about a danger after a brush with death wouldn't stick around long enough to have many offspring. Modern theories of anxiety place the blame on a mixture of factors, including specific experiences, general stressors, and innate predispositions.

While the conditioning theory of fears doesn't offer a tidy explanation for how fear originates, it does provide a useful starting point in considering what sustains our anxieties. According to Orval Mowrer's influential two-factor theory, irrational anxieties persist because we try to avoid them. When we encounter a perceived threat, the natural response is to find a way to neutralize it. The person who feels anxious about giving speeches finds an excuse to get out of presenting at work. The student who feels queasy around equations avoids taking classes with mathematics. The anxious introvert stays home from parties. Escaping from fear, however, has two side effects that make anxiety harder to eradicate. The first difficulty is that by avoiding the potentially dangerous stimuli, we can't get any new information about whether the imagined threat is significant in reality. By avoiding feedback, the conditioned association between a feared stimulus and danger cannot be extinguished. Like an insect trapped in amber, our fears are preserved because we don't allow ourselves to encounter disconfirming evidence about them. The second difficulty is that avoidance becomes self-reinforcing. Imagine a situation that makes you anxious (for example, an exam, speech, or job interview). In worrying about it, you take some action to reduce the perceived threat (for example, drop the class, find someone else to present your work, or pass up the job opportunity). The anxiety is now gone and you feel relieved. Yet that relief can act as a psychological reward, strengthening avoidance behavior in the future. This type of conditioning is known as negative reinforcement, as it's the removal of a potential pain that acts as a positive signal to your central nervous system. Avoidance perpetuates anxiety.

Avoidance doesn't only include a literal escape. Obsessive-compulsive disorder is characterized by engaging in complex rituals to avoid feared consequences. Washing your hands when they get dirty is good, but washing them every fifteen minutes is excessive. In this case, the ritualized handwashing acts like an avoidance behavior: the person feels anxiety about being unclean, immediately washes their hands multiple times, and the perceived threat subsides. The handwashing behavior is reinforced in the future and the person is prevented from experiencing feedback that would show it was unnecessary. Of course, not all avoidance behaviors are unhelpful. The same process is at work when we feel anxious about a big exam and respond by studying harder. A person who avoids standing too close to the edge of a cliff may be entirely reasonable, rather than suffering from acrophobia. Anxiety and avoidance aren't defects of our design, but profoundly useful features. Avoidance behaviors only become a problem when they interfere with our lives. When you take steps that do little to neutralize the danger, or when the cost of taking preventative measures is completely out of proportion with the actual risks, anxiety is disruptive rather than adaptive.

Exposure diminishes anxiety through processes of extinction and habituation. The term *extinction* comes from animal learning research. Ring a bell with food and a dog will learn to salivate from the bell alone. However, if you ring the bell enough times without bringing food, eventually the original learned response extinguishes. Similarly, according to the conditioning theory of fear, our anxieties are learned associations between signals and danger. By exposing ourselves to the signal, without experiencing danger, we revise our expectations. As a result, the original fear learning is suppressed. The second mechanism for exposure is through habituation. This occurs when a stimulus that naturally evokes a particular response has a diminishing impact as you experience it more often. A loud sound may cause you to jump instinctively, but as you hear the same loud sound over and over, your jumpiness fades. To understand the distinction between extinction and habituation, consider overcoming a fear of doing stand-up comedy by going to an open-mic night. Extinction would mean going onstage and realizing that, contrary to expectations, being humiliated wasn't actually so likely. Habituation would mean that after being booed off-stage a dozen times, you aren't so bothered by bombing during your comedy routine.

Exposure to fear without actual danger results in learning safety. A tempting assumption would be that the learned safety works by erasing the original fear conditioning. In this way, just as learning to fear a neutral stimulus can be seen as a conditioning process, extinguishing that fear might be seen as a gradual "forgetting" of the original association. Unfortunately, this doesn't appear to be the case. Instead, learning safety appears to be a process of building a new memory, using distinct neural circuitry, that inhibits the original fear response. Evidence for the two-memory view comes from research showing that, while exposure does indeed reduce fears, acquired fears appear to be more general and durable than learned safety. The result is that fears that have been extinguished can return, either when we face the fear in a new context, as time elapses between the episodes of exposure, or even just from general stressors that have nothing to do with the original fear. Consistent with this theory, Vernon observed that fear of air raids tended to return after a prolonged reprieve from bombings, as if the inoculation against anxiety had partly worn off. Exposure works better when it is provided in a broad variety of contexts and refreshed periodically. Some research even suggests that occasional reinforcement—where feared consequences sometimes *do* occur during exposure—results in more durable benefits than exposure where danger is always absent, as this makes the learning of safety more robust to an unlucky, aversive experience.

Is Exposure Enough to Overcome Fears?

The therapeutic benefits of exposure have long been appreciated, even if they haven't always been understood. The English philosopher John Locke prescribed a regimen of gradually escalating encounters to deal with an animal phobia in his treatise *Some Thoughts Concerning Education*. Likewise, the German poet Johann Wolfgang von Goethe overcame a youthful fear of heights by repeatedly standing atop a small ledge in a local cathedral. After completing these exercises, he was able to enjoy mountain climbing and ascend tall buildings without trepidation. Yet it wasn't until Joseph Wolpe introduced his protocol of systematic desensitization in the 1950s that exposure became a regular part of the clinical treatment for anxiety.

Wolpe worked with patients to help develop a fear hierarchy. This was an ordered list of situations starting with those that caused mild discomfort, progressing all the way to those provoking extreme terror. By gradually experiencing these situations, along with relaxation techniques, patients' fears diminished. Wolpe's theory was that relaxation and anxiety inhibited each other, so by using breathing techniques to relax the patient while they faced stressful stimuli, this would counteract the stressful association. Despite the usefulness of the protocol, the theory of reciprocal inhibition wasn't borne out. Subsequent research found that relaxation, while potentially helpful, was not necessary to get the required effect. Exposure still worked even if stress levels remained high throughout.

Around the same time as Wolpe's development of systematic desensitization, flooding and implosive therapies also applied exposure for treating fear. Instead of gradually ramping up the exposure, flooding presented a patient with their most-feared situation from the outset and prevented them from escaping. A person with a phobia of dogs might be locked in a room with a barking dog, unable to leave until their fear subsided. Implosive therapy was similar to flooding, although usually done with highly vivid fantasy scenarios, guided by a therapist, rather than real-life exposure. Both theories operated under the assumption that fully activating a fear was necessary to refute it, and that milder forms of exposure might fail to have the full therapeutic effect. Once again, scrutinizing research upheld the general value of exposure within these treatments, but extreme fear reactions were not necessary. Exposure came to be seen as the active ingredient, with the debate between diving or wading into fear shifting to the periphery.

As cognitive approaches came to overtake behaviorism in psychology departments, therapies based on examining thoughts and beliefs eclipsed purely behavioral techniques. Cognitive therapy emphasized not just the behaviors of patients using the language of stimulus and response, but the contents of patients' thinking. A social phobic's aversion to parties, for instance, is not just habitual avoidance, but also depends on a distorted worldview, such as the belief that social rejection is likely. Despite its theoretical foundation and appeal to common sense, evidence for the additional efficacy of cognitive therapy beyond exposure has often been weak. Cognitive-behavioral therapies, which usually include both exposure as well as talk therapy, tend not to outperform therapies based on exposure alone. More recently, mindfulness-based approaches to anxiety have gained in popularity, but it remains to be seen whether they can outperform simple exposure.

An explanation for the surprising lack of effectiveness of therapies that seek to change beliefs, induce relaxation, or alter thinking patterns without exposure is that threats are processed by different neural circuitry than those that underlie our consciously accessible memories and beliefs. "Talk therapy requires conscious retrieval of memories and thinking about their origins and/or implications and thus depends on working memory circuits of the lateral prefrontal cortex. By contrast, therapies involving exposure depend on medial prefrontal areas that contribute to extinction, the process on which exposure is modeled," explains neuroscientist Joseph LeDoux. "[T]he fact that medial frontal areas connect with the amygdala, whereas the latter areas do not, might account for why it is easier and faster to treat fears, phobias and anxiety with exposure-based approaches." Dissecting your beliefs, in other words, may not be helpful if anxiety is being sustained by neural circuitry in a different part of your brain. Despite this neuroanatomical distinction, LeDoux notes that the relationship between exposure as practiced in therapeutic contexts and the extinction studies done with animals is a complicated one. Encouraging someone to expose themselves to a feared situation generally requires talking. It may turn out that the explanation for the efficacy of exposure does depend on consciously accessible beliefs and expectations, but that the best way to change those is through direct experience rather than discussing them. Adjusting consciously held beliefs may also be useful for sustaining the therapeutic benefits of exposure, helping to protect against relapse. Nonetheless, in keeping with the view that fear is driven in part by unconscious neural circuitry, researchers have found that subliminal exposure, when the feared stimulus is masked so it cannot be perceived consciously, can result in reduced avoidance behaviors. Simply talking about your anxieties is rarely sufficient to overcome them.

Despite the difficulties in finding consistent enhancements to exposure, the basic protocol remains remarkably successful. A meta-analysis looking at the use of exposure treatment for specific phobias found large effect sizes compared to both placebo and no-treatment conditions. In addition, the authors found that therapies incorporating exposure outperformed alternative therapies that did not. Other meta-analyses draw similar conclusions with social phobias, generalized anxiety, panic, and obsessive-compulsive disorder—with effect sizes roughly equal to those seen from pharmacological interventions. Exposure has even been successfully used to treat post-traumatic stress disorder, which is notable in light of the widespread belief that exposure makes trauma worse. Patients aren't more likely to drop out of therapies involving exposure and many patients find them to be credible and effective. Despite the strong experimental evidence for the benefits of exposure, researchers Jonathan Abramowitz, Brett Deacon, and Stephen Whiteside report that "the majority of patients with any anxiety disorder do not receive evidence-based psychotherapy; indeed, psychodynamic therapy is received as often as [cognitive-behavioral therapies]." Exposure works, even if it remains underused.

Fear and Mastery

Fear deals a double blow to the learning process. First, because the natural impulse to anxiety is avoidance, we often fail to practice skills that scare us. The timid driver, unsure presenter, or math-phobic often go out of their way to avoid situations that might use those abilities. But failing to get enough practice also ensures that these skills remain disfluent and effortful—compounding the rationale for avoiding using them. Worse, anxiety crowds out space in our mind for thinking about a problem. Complex skills are harder to learn when we're highly agitated because distracting worries fill up our limited working memory capacity.

Overcoming anxiety isn't easy, but exposure at least suggests an escape route. If we can expose ourselves to our apprehensions, in situations where the risks are modest, the fear reaction will eventually subside. Reducing fear, we find practice easier. Practice improves our performance and reduces the effort needed, further expanding the range of situations where it makes sense to use the skill. What was previously a self-reinforcing pattern of anxiety and avoidance can be replaced with increased confidence and enthusiasm.

The difficulty, of course, is in switching from the pattern of avoidance toward the enthusiastic mindset of the person willing to face their fears. While the process of exposure can be daunting, I think fully accepting and understanding its theoretical rationale can help shift the decision to engage in it. Fears seem totally objective when we're caught in their grasp. Public speaking simply *is* scary, rather than being a subjective response to an ambiguous situation. From such a position, it's hard to fully appreciate how easy and natural it would be if we simply got onstage enough times.

Accepting the logic of exposure doesn't remove the need for bravery. As we've seen, talking through fears doesn't usually eliminate them. However, if we appreciate how even objectively terrifying situations, like the wartime bombing of the Blitz, could become normal through repeated exposure, perhaps we can have the courage to take steps in confronting the far milder fears that hold us back.

Strategies for Surmounting Fear

Courage isn't just the province of combat survivors. Life challenges us with countless mundane fears and anxieties. In those situations, we have a choice about how we can respond to them—seeking out experiences to test the reality of our fears, or shying away and leaving them forever in the dark. Overcoming fear requires feedback. Not just an intellectual understanding that your worries are overblown, but the visceral feedback from direct experience.

Let's look at some strategies for applying exposure to test our fears.

Strategy #1: Construct Your Fear Hierarchy

Wolpe's practice of having patients construct a fear hierarchy is still used in cognitive-behavioral treatments of anxiety today. While the debate over flooding versus gradual exposure was rendered theoretically irrelevant, there may still be practical reasons to prefer going step-by-step. One reason is simply that if a fear is too strong, you might not be able to go through with exposure to it! This may be truer with self-guided exposure, when the authoritative voice of a therapist isn't there to push you forward.

Abramowitz stresses the need to mirror the situational, cognitive, and physiological aspects of the fear as closely as possible. "The importance of closely matching hierarchy items to the patient's fear cannot be overemphasized: a person afraid of dogs must confront the types of dog he or she is frightened of. Someone afraid of germs from hospitals must confront items *in a hospital*. Someone afraid of starting a fire because she has left a light on in her house must turn many lights on and leave the house, and so on." Matching the situational aspects of exposure means identifying exactly which scenarios the person anticipates feeling afraid of. Exposure to situations that are superficially similar but don't elicit fear won't work.

Creating a fear hierarchy can also be a first step in questioning the reasonableness of some of the assumptions they are built upon. Just as even the most terrifying nightmare can often feel silly when we say it out loud, the basis of our fears may seem less plausible when we write down what we fear and what we expect to happen. While we've already seen that belief change alone is probably insufficient to overcome our unconscious threat-detection circuitry, it can help encourage exposure. The moderate efficacy of cognitive therapy without exposure may partly be due to people engaging in self-exposure after being confronted about the validity of their beliefs about threats.

Strategy #2: Don't Say "Everything Will Be Okay"

Faced with worry, it's natural to seek reassurance. Unfortunately, this can have exactly the same problem as the avoidance behaviors we discussed earlier. "It is important to note that the purpose of exposure therapy is not to persuade or reassure the patient that he or she is absolutely safe or that the feared consequences are out of the question whatsoever," writes Abramowitz, later adding, "Under no circumstances should the therapist reassure the patient that 'everything will be okay.'" The presence of a therapist can, paradoxically, make exposure less effective if the person learns that they are safe, so long as they have their therapist with them.

Just as making a list of fears can be helpful, so can making a list of common avoidance behaviors. These can involve actual avoidance, such as the person who excuses himself from speaking at meetings because of social anxiety, or they can involve crutches that increase the feeling of safety. A person who worries about embarrassment from sweating too much might obsessively use strong antiperspirants. Although this behavior "works" to reduce the anxiety, it can make the person reliant on the safety behavior, even when it is impractical.

Going to a party with the intention of sweating as much as possible would work better to disconfirm the belief that visible sweating will lead to strong negative social judgments.

Ultimately, the process of exposure is about testing our fearful expectations. We can't do that if we undermine the experiment by finding ways to neutralize any potential threat. A person who is afraid of speaking in public might get embarrassed onstage. The aim of exposure isn't to prove that humiliation is impossible, but to recognize that it is probably less likely than we think it is, and even if it does occur, we will be better able to cope than we imagine. Testing fears requires engaging in acceptable risks, rather than the extremes of both recklessness and vainly trying to eliminate all possible danger.

Strategy #3: Face Fears Together

Courage is more likely in communities than in individuals. "There is consistent evidence that membership in a small, cohesive group can play an important part in controlling fear," writes psychologist Stanley Rachman; "most people appear to be more susceptible to fear when they are alone." Having a social purpose served to inoculate firefighters, rescue workers, and nurses from some of the worst psychological effects of the Blitz. Vernon argues that it was the people who lived alone who were more likely to worsen after repeated bombings. Part of the explanation for the remarkable resilience of people seen during disasters might be that they did not face their fears in isolation.

Fear of public speaking likely matters more than rhetorical skill for the presenting ability of most people. Yet most of us get few opportunities to practice. With limited, infrequent exposure, stage fright usually remains high. Organizations like Toastmasters can help, since in addition to providing ample exposure to public speaking opportunities, they do so within a supportive, communal atmosphere. Joining studying groups for mathematics or conversation clubs for practicing a language can have a similar benefit: providing exposure to the anxiety-provoking situation in the presence of other people.

Strategy #4: Distinguish Courage from Fearlessness

Courage is not the same thing as acting without fear. "Fear is not a lump," explains Rachman. Instead, he argues that fear can best be seen as at least three different interacting components: a physiological component of arousal (for example, a higher heart rate, sweating palms), a subjective component of beliefs and feelings, and a behavioral component of avoidance and safety seeking. While these three systems generally point in the same direction, they are not identical. People regularly find themselves in situations where physiological and subjective states of fear are quite high, yet they manage to persist in their tasks. Courage is not action without fear, but action in spite of fear.

Exposure itself is unlikely to generalize broadly to many different fears. As we've discussed, the learning of safety tends to be more specific than learning fear, and so exposure is needed in multiple contexts with regular refreshers to be sustained. However, seeing courage as an attitude and philosophy of life may be more defensible. "Fearful people have a strong tendency to overestimate how frightened they will be when they encounter a fear-provoking object or situation," Rachman explains. He reviews evidence from multiple domains showing that people overpredict their fearful reactions to events, and underestimate their ability to maintain composure. Ultimately, the information we gain from facing our fears isn't just about the reality of danger, but the reality of ourselves.

The Path to Improvement

Seeing examples, doing practice, and getting feedback are key to getting better at anything. But learning is more than just an intellectual process. Emotions, from fear to enthusiasm, play at least as large a role in determining which skills we end up improving. In the conclusion, we'll synthesize the various perspectives discussed so far in the book, and end with some practical wisdom for charting the path to improvement.

Practice Made Perfect

T here's an old tale about a woodcutter who was given an axe and three hours to chop down a large tree. The woodcutter decided to spend the first two and a half hours sharpening the axe. In a similar way, we spend countless hours of our lives on things we want to do well. We want to be better parents, professionals, artists, and athletes. In comparison to all this chopping, we often spend only a small fraction of the time actively trying to sharpen our axe. I began writing this book with a particular reader in mind: You're someone who cares about how learning works. You want to improve at something yourself, whether that is getting an A on your exams, becoming an expert at your work, or feeling confident in a sport or hobby. Or perhaps you're more interested in helping others get better. You're a coach, teacher, employer, or parent looking to see how you can help those around you acquire valuable skills. While it's a professional hazard to make blanket statements about one's audience as an author, I feel fairly confident that if you've made it this far, you care about sharpening the axe.

Throughout this book, I've shared stories and research about how learning works. We've seen the importance of examples and how our problem-solving efforts build on the knowledge of others, examined the mind's bottleneck and how it constrains the path to mastery, considered the importance of building skills from a successful foundation, and seen how to extract knowledge from experts who often forget what it was like to be a beginner. We've dug into the power of practice: the importance of progressive problem solving and fine-tuning the difficulty in our training, why the mind is not like a muscle and how we should be more precise in our attempts at improvement, the value of variability in creating flexible skills, and why accomplishments at the frontier of creativity correlate so closely with overall productivity. Finally, we've examined the critical role of feedback: why many expert estimations are overconfident in environments of uncertainty, how the physical and social environment shapes the skills we need to master, the role of unlearning in eventual mastery, and how we can overcome our fears and anxieties when leaving our comfort zones to learn something new. In each of these chapters, I tried to synthesize a prominent perspective given by the research and suggest a few practical take-aways. The science of learning is diverse and often contentious. While I'm certain that not everyone will agree with all of my conclusions, I hope the citations listed in the endnotes can be a jumping-off point for serious readers to engage with some of the ideas for themselves.

In this chapter, I'd like to step back from the research to try to pull all these diverse perspectives together and offer some general advice. My main focus will be on you as the learner. How can you get better at the things you care about? As a secondary consideration I'll also try to reflect on what this research says about how we can be better teachers, coaches, and mentors to those who depend on us.

Three Questions for Mastery

The economist and author Tyler Cowen likes to ask people, "What is it you do to train that is comparable to a pianist practicing scales?" Those without a good answer to this question, he argues, are perhaps not so serious about improving at their craft. The world is changing rapidly. Skills that could have sustained a profession for a lifetime may become obsolete as new technologies can do them automatically. Life-long learning isn't just a feel-good slogan, but a necessity. Given its importance, I think it's useful to ask yourself three questions about the pursuits you care about.

Question One: How Can I Improve the Way I Learn from Others?

Examples, as we've seen, play a critical role in learning complex skills. The ability to learn from others is a distinguishing characteristic of our species. We see further by standing upon the hard-won problem-solving insights of those who came before us. When seeking out learning materials:

1. **Find examples that include all of the steps needed to solve the problem.** While we can easily observe the physical actions of another person performing a skill, mental actions are invisible. Indeed, the danger of learning from experts is that their fluency with a skill causes them to skip over intervening steps. A good worked example should break down the problem-solving steps to a level so that each action is comprehensible to the person who is studying it.

2. **Make sure you've learned enough background knowledge so the examples make sense.** Understanding is not an all-or-nothing property, so we must use judgment. Too little explanation and the problem is a memorized answer without any generality. Too much and we can fall down a rabbit hole of endless elaboration.

3. **Seek out varied examples to generalize the problem-solving patterns.** The ability to form abstract concepts and analogies from concrete instances is central to our flexibility as thinkers. Yet novices to a field tend to perceive problems more in terms of superficial features than deep principles. Offering

multiple examples that exhibit a broader range of variation makes it easier to extract what they have in common. It's also often helpful to present counterexamples: similar-seeming situations that don't work for a subtle reason to prevent overgeneralization.

The obvious first place to start looking for examples is in well-structured courses. These have the advantage of sequencing examples, making sure background knowledge is made available and in revealing otherwise invisible mental steps performed by experts. As we've seen in chapter 3, beginning with a successful foundation can make a big difference for mastery and motivation. In-person classes, massive open online courses, textbooks, and even YouTube videos can provide a good starting place for many skills. If you can afford it and help is available, getting one-on-one tutoring is also particularly helpful—especially if off-the-shelf materials are lacking.

As we gain experience in a domain, classes replete with worked examples tend to be less common. This is partly a matter of economics. Most people are beginners to a skill, so the largest market exists to serve those just starting out. Additionally, knowledge tends to branch and specialize as skill progresses. This makes it much harder to reliably cover everything that matters as you make more progress. Being more advanced does not imply learning from examples is pointless, however. Recall from chapter 1 that Andrew Wiles, despite being a PhD-holding specialist in the area of mathematics needed to solve Fermat's Last Theorem, nonetheless spent two years reading everything he could in preparation for the proof. Instead, it is simply the case that as we move beyond the examples neatly laid out in courses we must lean on more informal resources.

Joining communities that practice the skill you are trying to master can be essential for making continued progress, past the stage covered by beginner resources. This is particularly true for professional skills, where good examples are often hard to find without access to the working environment. For professions that depend on cutting-edge knowledge, such as in science or technology, access to communities working at the frontier can be critical if you want to make a novel contribution. Even for professions that don't depend on generating new knowledge, access to an environment with rigorous standards and varied work problems can be instrumental in pushing your skills further. Management consultants face a wider range of problems in working with multiple firms than do those who work in a single company. One study even found that consultants did better than restaurant managers when being asked business problems concerning a restaurant, despite similar levels of overall education. Mapping out a pathway to participation in these accelerated learning environments doesn't guarantee access, but it is an important first step.

Being in the same room as skilled practitioners isn't usually enough, however. Extracting knowledge from experts can be a tricky business, but we can take lessons from cognitive task analysis. Asking them to solve problems in front of you, listening to their stories with attention to the timeline of events, or simply asking whom they find knowledgeable about specific issues can begin to reveal what experience has hidden.

Question Two: How Can I Make My Practice More Effective?

Access to high-quality examples is just the first step in learning effectively. Mastering anything requires a lot of practice. Unfortunately, our intuitions are unreliable guides to what kind of practice is most effective. Desirable difficulties from techniques such as retrieval, spacing, or interleaving tend to be rated as ineffective by students, even when students learn better by using them. Even if the right kind of practice is rarely obvious, we can use the principles covered so far to fine-tune our efforts.

A first consideration is complexity. Working memory is limited, but the cognitive load for a given task depends heavily on our prior experience with it. This means the most effective kind of practice is always changing in the process of learning. Early on, we benefit from more guidance, repetition, and studying examples over problem solving. As we build experience, however, this advice flips, and we benefit from less structured problems, varied practice, and progressively harder challenges. One way to think about this tension is that, in the beginning, the key challenge is getting knowledge into your head. While it is possible to learn through direct experience, the potentially vast spaces of problem-solving search and the extraneous cognitive load of means-ends analysis often result in studying examples being more efficient. However, once the knowledge is in your head, the problem flips to getting it out at the right time! This requires practice, as you sort out when the problem-solving patterns you learned initially apply to ambiguous situations. One way we can avoid the pitfalls of either failing to get the right knowledge into our head, or failing to get it out at the right time, is by constructing a practice loop. By combining seeing an example, doing a practice attempt, and getting feedback, we can start to assimilate the patterns of expert performance.

Another consideration is the grain size of practice. Should your practice loop be focused on a specific component skill—say vocabulary flash cards, tennis serves, or math puzzles? Or should it be broader— say, full conversations, tennis games, or applying math in a real-life situation? Advocates of the former tend to focus on the value of part-task practice to reduce cognitive load, benefiting learners who might otherwise struggle with complete tasks. Drills may also be easier to compress into a practice session. A basketball player can shoot a lot more layups during a practice session than during a game. Advocates for whole-task practice point out that repeating a drill until it becomes completely automatic does not always translate into fluent performance during the complete task. A person who drills flash cards for vocabulary may recognize them instantly but still slow down when hearing them in the context of a conversation. Whole-task practice is also more meaningful, as the actions are understood in their useful context. As with the tension between seeing examples and solving problems for yourself, I believe both drills and realistic practice are important.* Drills can iron out tricky spots in a complex skill and reduce cognitive load for handling tough situations. Yet we also need a lot of practice with complete tasks so that those skills are well integrated and meaningfully understood. We can resolve the tension by working back and forth, a loop between drills and realistic practice on top of our basic practice loops that combine seeing, doing, and feedback.

As a final consideration, we should also be clear-eyed in thinking about what a skill is. The mind is not a muscle, so vaguely described abilities such as being a better problem solver, strategic thinker, or being more creative probably aren't things that can be improved or practiced in general. Instead, we become better problem solvers by accumulating more strong methods for specific kinds of problems. We become better strategic thinkers by learning particular strategies and mental models that apply to particular situations. We become more creative by accumulating useful knowledge and giving ourselves a secure environment to explore them in unfamiliar ways. There's nothing wrong with having broad goals for improvement. Becoming completely fluent in all aspects of a language is a fine aspiration. But it's also the case that achieving this goal consists of accumulating a lot of individual words and phrases, and separately practicing skills of pronunciation, reading, writing, and listening. Grand ambitions to be better communicators, programmers, investors, writers, or artists must proceed from a recognition that this is achieved by building up and integrating a lot of specific skills and knowledge. A symphony can only be performed by playing the notes.

---

* For further summaries on the research literature comparing the benefits of part-task and whole-task practice, I point the interested reader toward reviews by Wickens et al.; Wightman and Lintern; and Fabiani. I also recommend James Naylor and George Briggs's influential theory, which argued that tasks benefit more from part-task practice as they become more complex, and benefit more from whole-task practice as they become more integrated.

Question Three: How Can I Enhance the Quality of My Feedback?

Finally, obtaining high-quality, realistic feedback is essential. Some feedback is really just an example, presented after the fact. If you get the answer wrong on a mathematics exam, your instructor might give you the solution in the form of a worked example, showing you what you should have done. This kind of feedback is particularly valuable, because it combines the advantages of seeing an example with the fact that, having recently gotten the question wrong, you're more likely to pay attention to and study it. This works well when there is a single, correct answer and it's relatively easy to make a comparison between what you did and the canonical response.

However, most domains aren't like this. There are many ways to write an essay, design a building, lead a team, or give a speech—even if some ways are better than others. Corrective feedback in these cases can still be quite valuable. A knowledgeable teacher, mentor, or coach can offer adjustments from the approach you actually used, instead of simply comparing it to a single correct answer. The informational value of feedback is obvious, but getting feedback from another person introduces social and motivational consequences that aren't always positive. Corrective feedback is often blended with evaluative judgments. The letter grade you get on an essay isn't just a nudge for better writing, but also a score that determines whether you'll pass the class and graduate. Feedback can demotivate, as we all know from a particularly harsh response to something we worked hard on. But positive feedback can demotivate too. Research finds that bulk praise—"You're so smart!"—also diminishes effort, since it encourages people to think they have no need to improve. These social and motivational considerations can easily wipe out the expected benefit of feedback. A good feedback environment is one where feedback is used to assist learning, not reward or punish performance, focused on making corrections to the task rather than judging the individual, based on a relationship of mutual trust and respect.

What about skills where there isn't a right answer, or a teacher who can easily guide us to a better one? As we saw in chapter 9, extensive experience doesn't guarantee expertise. If the learning environment is uncertain, and we get inconsistent feedback, we may end up both overconfident and mediocre. Enhancing the quality of the feedback that the environment naturally provides is important for developing genuine skill. Some strategies for enhancing feedback include:

1. **Keep score and track performance.** For skills where outcomes are highly variable, we can easily mislead ourselves about the long-run accuracy of our decisions. Keeping score can be ego-bruising if we realize we're not as proficient as we believe, but it's necessary to calibrate our approach. Numbers don't tell the whole story, but they do keep us honest.

2. **Conduct after-action reports.** As discussed in the opening chapter, after-action reports were essential for the Top Gun fighter pilots to learn from feedback about their simulated sorties. A major difficulty of learning from experience is that when our working memory capacity is devoted to performing a skill, we have almost no space to reflect or evaluate our performance. Making a record of your practice attempt that you can analyze afterward can suggest improvements that you might have missed in the moment.

3. **Form a brain trust.** Individuals have many cognitive blind spots. While aggregating individuals doesn't automatically solve these problems, it can reduce them. Joining a group where members can dissect and discuss each other's work is a powerful tool for highlighting weaknesses you might have otherwise missed.

Feedback is not just the correction of mistakes. Life is dynamic and involves a continuing interaction between ourselves and the physical and social world around us. Realistic practice becomes increasingly important as we make progress, because the feedback generated from contact with the environment becomes incorporated into our skills. The social environment also plays an important role, as practices emerge informally in the ongoing activity of groups who work together, often unstated and frequently diverging from the stated practice described in books and classrooms. This doesn't imply that the most realistic practice is always best. Cognitive load, cost, access, and enhanced feedback can all make simulations more efficient than the real thing. But genuine mastery is nearly impossible to achieve without direct engagement in the environments where a skill is actually applied.

Apprehensions and fears are also shaped by feedback. Our anxieties about learning a new language, studying math, standing onstage, or working in a new field are often bigger determinants of our ability to make progress than memory or reasoning. Yet it's difficult to rationalize our fears away. Instead, it's the exposure to the feedback signal from the environment that a particular threat is overstated that adjusts not just our beliefs, but also our emotions.

Some Final Reflections on Getting Better

The process of getting better can be both exhilarating and frustrating. The feeling of finally "getting" a subject, skiing down a hill without falling down, completing a painting that looks good, speaking another language, or publishing something that's respected by your colleagues—few things can compete with the sensation of getting a grasp on a difficult skill. But learning can also be frustrating. We can spend years practicing something and still not feel particularly confident. We give up on hobbies, sports, professional opportunities, and paths of study because we don't feel capable of learning them. My enduring interest in learning as a subject is, in part, because our experiences trying to get better encompass both extremes.

When I began working on this book, I had already spent nearly two decades writing and thinking about learning. My writing career began as a college student, publishing studying tips on a personal blog. After graduating, I dove headlong into yearlong projects learning programming, languages, drawing, and more. The successes and stumbles in those projects formed the backdrop for my previous book, *Ultralearning*. At the time, I had thought I had said nearly everything I could about the topic, and was prepared to move on to new subject matters. However, two things pulled me back into doing the research for this book. The first was encountering the *Tetris* story in the introduction. While *Ultralearning* had documented impressive individual achievements in learning skills, the story of *Tetris* was not about any particular player but a surrounding culture making improvement possible. This got me interested in various systems for learning, from the artistic apprenticeship of the Renaissance, informal practice of jazz musicians, and writing workshops among science fiction novelists to the training of pilots and phonics instruction in learning to read. In this book I wanted to move beyond the stories of a few impressive people learning something quickly, and focus on the basic factors that underpin learning in general.

The second factor that led to writing this book was an unresolved question from my previous book. In *Ultralearning*, I had written about some of the often-disappointing research on transfer of learning—that is, how much improvement in one skill leads to improvement in another. The implication that seemed obvious to me at the time was that if transfer is less than we think, we ought to spend more time practicing exactly the skills we intend to improve. As is often the case in learning more on a topic, my original intuition was neither confirmed or denied, but complicated. As I review in chapter 6, there is considerable research showing that skills tend to be relatively specific. However, the science also pointed away from the idea that simply practicing the exact skill we wish to learn would invariably lead to improvement. John Sweller's work on cognitive load theory, Albert Bandura's theory of social learning, and the success of Direct Instruction highlighted the importance of having good examples and clear explanations. Paul Meehl's work on clinical intuition complicated the belief that years of experience necessarily led to accurate judgments. The need to learn from others complicates my original intuition, because even if skills are relatively specific, we may not have easy access to the perfect mentor to teach us exactly what we need to know. The final form of this book was, in many ways, trying to reconcile those two competing constraints—the need to learn from others, along with the importance of specific knowledge and practice in getting better.

In *Ultralearning*, I wrote that preparing that book had mirrored its subject matter: an intensive self-directed learning project to write a book about intensive self-directed learners. I feel the same way about this book. Writing this book was a process of delving into cloistered communities of experts—trying to make sense of divergent findings and theories. Both trying to make sense of what experts who have studied these issues their entire lives think about the questions (and why they frequently disagree), but also making up my own mind, reflecting on my own experience learning different skills and subjects. I hope I was able to showcase some of the diversity of views, as well as broad areas of agreement, while still presenting a coherent point of view. I leave it to the reader to decide whether or not I have succeeded.

A Little Further on the Road to Mastery

Mastery can be daunting. There is always far more to learn than we will ever have time to approach in our lifetimes. This is something I was consistently reminded of while researching this book. For every question I felt I had answered satisfactorily, a dozen new ones popped up in their place. The pursuit of mastery can be self-defeating. It recedes as you approach it. Each summit reached only shows you how many more peaks there are to climb.

Seen from the perspective of world-class talents, most of us will not master anything in our lives. We will never be as savvy an investor as Warren Buffett, as skillful a musician as Miles Davis, or as clever a mathematician as Andrew Wiles. If the aim of mastery is to reach the apex of proficiency, then it is an aspiration that dooms nearly all of us to failure. But reaching for mastery and failing to grasp it is a good way to fail. For even when we can't become the best, we can still be a little better at the things that matter most to us. A little better is often enough.

ACKNOWLEDGMENTS

This book would not have been possible without the help of many people. I'd like to thank my agent, Laurie Abkemeier, who shepherded this book through its original conception (and many subsequent changes in direction); my editor, Hollis Heimbouch, for her confidence in me and her guidance; and the entire team at Harper Business who worked hard to turn the book into a reality. I'd like to thank Vatsal Jaiswal, Megan Young, Barbara Oakley, Cal Newport, Tristan de Montebello, and Kalid Azad for many helpful conversations as the ideas were taking shape. I'd also like to thank the many scientists and researchers who discussed their work with me, helping me to make sense of the formidable research literature: Paul Kirschner, John Sweller, Carl Bereiter, Vimla Patel, Fred Paas, Stephen Reed, Jeffrey Karpicke, Richard Mayer, Arthur Reber, Robert Bjork, Pedro de Bruyckere, Richard Clark, David Perkins, Alan Schoenfeld, Richard Nisbett, Bruce Rawlings, Halszka Jarodzka, David Klahr, Manu Kapur, Robert DeKeyser, John Shea, Philip Tetlock, David Moshman, Jose Mestre, Carl Wieman, Dean Simonton, and Jeroen van Merriënboer. Any mistakes I've made in reporting the science are certainly my fault and not theirs. I'd like to thank my parents, Marian and Douglas Young, both educators, who taught me that learning is its own reward. Last, but certainly not least, I'd like to thank my wonderful wife, Zorica, for her infinite support, patience, and guidance. I could not have done it without you.

NOTES

Introduction: How Learning Works

2   Joseph Saelee fired up a game of *Tetris*: Joseph Saelee, "284 Lines (Full Video)," YouTube, February 15, 2020, 11:19, https://www.youtube.com/watch?v=L7SRuMG6AJc.

2   managed to reach level 34: Joseph Saelee, "First Ever Level 34 in NES Tetris," YouTube, February 15, 2020, 3:19, https://www.youtube.com/watch?v=rWMUYBinriw.

3   first documented "max-out": Cornelius, *Ecstasy of Order*.

3   During the same tournament: Schonbrun, "A New Generation."

3   How does a game: I am indebted to John Green for first sharing this story. John Green, "Why Are Humans Suddenly Getting Better at Tetris?" YouTube, October 18, 2018, 3:50, https://www.youtube.com/watch?v=twS0SrDg-fc.

3   Russian computer scientist Alexey Pajitnov: Gaming Historian, "The Story of Tetris," YouTube, February 2, 2018, 59:30, https://www.youtube.com/watch?v=_fQtxKmgJC8.

3   "you play the best Tetris": Cornelius, *Ecstasy of Order*.

4   hallucinate falling blocks: Goldsmith, "Brain on Tetris."

5   had invented the technique: Cornelius, *Ecstasy of Order*.

5   in a 2010 documentary: Cornelius.

5   Such a gap in knowledge: Cornelius.

7   "The secret of our species' success": Henrich, *Secret of Our Success*, 2.

7   a modified version of the same task is given to five-year-olds: Rawlings, "After a Decade of Tool Innovation."

7   The clear exception was in social learning: Herrmann et al., "The Cultural Intelligence Hypothesis."

8   Many alchemists worked: Jan Baptista van Helmont, for instance, made careful measurements of weight in his some of his trials, first demonstrating that the weight of a tree does not come from the soil in one experiment and showing that the mass of sand does not change when it is turned into glass in another. Principe, *Secrets of Alchemy*.

9   "Alchemy's primary sources": Principe, *Secrets of Alchemy*, 2.

9   Robert Boyle's experiments: Boyle, *New Experiments Physico-Mechanicall*.

9   "There's not a single person in the world": Friedman, *Free to Choose*.

10   researchers observed the brain activity: Haier et al., "MRI Assessment of Cortical Thickness."

11   Retrieval beats review: Rowland, "The Effect of Testing versus Restudy on Retention."

11   Yet students prefer: Clark, "Antagonism between Achievement and Enjoyment."

12   Despite performing the skill three thousand times: Thorndike, *Human Learning*.

12   the concept of deliberate practice: Ericsson, Krampe, and Tesch-Römer, "The Role of Deliberate Practice."

12   researchers found that the quality of medical care: Choudhry, Fletcher, and Soumerai, "The Relationship between Clinical Experience and Quality of Health Care."

13   a sixfold improvement: Ericsson, *Development of Professional Expertise*, 49.

13   experiment run with foreign exchange traders: Ericsson, 49.

13   invention of paper was decried by Socrates: Plato, *Phaedrus*.

13   roughly 60 percent of the jobs: Autor et al., "The Origins and Content of Work."

Chapter 1: Problem Solving Is Search

21   "Whenever one cannot go": Duncker, "On Problem Solving."

21   Euler begged a friend: Singh, *Fermat's Last Theorem*, 49.

21   fooled the mathematicians Augustin Cauchy and Gabriel Lamé: Singh, 126.

22   Paul Wolfskehl put up a prize: Singh, 136.

23   "It looked so simple": Singh, 23.

23   Gerhard Frey suggested an unexpected link: Singh, 203.

24   "It seemed to be exactly what I needed": Singh, 241.

24   "it involved a lot of sophisticated machinery": Singh, 246.

24   "Nothing I ever do again": Singh, *Fermat's Last Theorem* (BBC documentary).

25   Scientists search through a problem space: Klahr, Exploring Science.

26   over forty-three quintillion configurations: Kiersz, "Rubik's Cube."

26   "Perhaps the methods I needed": Singh, *Fermat's Last Theorem*, 240.

27   Seventy years later, mathematicians proved: Davis, Matijasevič, and Robinson, "Hilbert's Tenth Problem."

27   belong to this class of problems: Computer scientists study the complexity of problems by determining whether efficient algorithms exist to solve them. A Rubik's Cube, for instance, is easy to solve (provided you know how), and the standard 3x3x3 cube only requires twenty moves at most. Sudoku and Tetris, in contrast, are NP-complete, which suggests no efficient algorithm exists (assuming the widely believed P≠NP conjecture is correct). Chess is even worse, belonging to the class EXP, for which we know there are no efficient procedures for finding a solution.

28   the mutilated chessboard: As posed by Max Black in 1946.

29   Simon and Newell called these weak methods: Langley et al., *Scientific Discovery*.

30   "I want to take my son": Newell and Simon, Human Problem Solving, 416.

33   Psychologists André Tricot and John Sweller argue: Tricot and Sweller, "Domain-Specific Knowledge."

35   the Gestalt psychologists also explored problem solving: Examples include Duncker, "On Problem Solving," and Wertheimer, *Productive Thinking*.

35   they can view the answer: Solution to the Nine-Dot Puzzle:

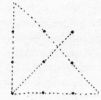

Figure 12

Solution to the Nine-Dot Puzzle on page 35. Solving the problem requires the insight that lines may extend beyond the dots.

36   "I could best describe my experience": Singh, *Fermat's Last Theorem* (BBC documentary).

Chapter 2: Creativity Begins with Copying

38   "Rules are not the fetters": Aristides, *Classical Drawing Atelier*.
38   This more than doubled: Pogrebin and Reyburn, "Painting Sells for $450.3 Million."
39   "Know that there ought not": Cennini, *Il libro dell'arte*.
39   First was copying masterworks: Aristides, *Classical Drawing Atelier*.
40   "Of the order of learning to draw": Da Vinci, *Notebooks*, 290.
40   Poetry and philosophy were the proper study: Efland, *A History of Art Education*, 8.
40   "When the artist rose": Efland, 26.
41   "So I shall take good care": As quoted in Efland, 53.
41   "Cižek has been compared": Efland, 197.
41   "In our arts climate": Aristides, *Classical Drawing Atelier*.
41   "A first principle not recognized": Skinner, "A Case History in Scientific Method."
42   "running an experiment on problem solving": Sweller, "Story of a Research Program." The experiment referenced comes from Sweller, Mawer, and Howe, "Consequences of History-Cued."
42   "Perhaps we should be showing": Sweller, "Story of a Research Program."
43   a series of experiments: Sweller and Levine, "Effects of Goal Specificity"; Sweller, Mawer, and Ward, "Development of Expertise"; and Owen and Sweller, "What Do Students Learn?"
43   results weren't even close: Owen and Sweller, "What Do Students Learn?"
44   when a novel question format was presented: Cooper and Sweller, "Effects of Schema Acquisition."
44   "Most of the field leapt": Sweller, "Story of a Research Program."
44   "I have been persecuted": Miller, "Magical Number Seven, Plus or Minus Two."
45   modal model of human memory: Baddeley, *Human Memory*.
46   Anders Ericsson and Walter Kintsch proposed: Ericsson and Kintsch, "Long-Term Working Memory."

46   Subjects read a story: Kintsch, *Comprehension*.

47   central distinction in cognitive load theory: A third type of load, germane load, was proposed to account for experiments where greater effort leads to greater learning (but only if students have capacity to spare). However, more recently Sweller and some other cognitive load theorists have suggested this third category is theoretically unnecessary, perhaps being better described as a kind of intrinsic load. Kalyuga, "Cognitive Load Theory."

48   "Redundancy is anything but harmless": Sweller, "Story of a Research Program."

49   Studies with eye-tracking software: Jarodzka et al., "Conveying Clinical Reasoning."

49   "each time one prematurely teaches": Piaget, "Piaget's Theory."

49   David Klahr and Milena Nigam examined this question: Klahr and Nigam, "The Equivalence of Learning Paths."

50   breaking apart worked examples into subgoals: Catrambone, "The Subgoal Learning Model."

50   engage in self-explanations of examples: Chi et al., "Self-Explanations."

51   Da Vinci's notebooks are filled: Da Vinci, *Notebooks*.

52   The expertise-reversal effect: Kalyuga, "Expertise Reversal Effect."

52   the fallacy of confusing epistemology: Kirschner, "Epistemology or Pedagogy."

Chapter 3: Success Is the Best Teacher

56   "It is the duty of a student": Kelly, "Advice I Wish I Had Known."

56   would celebrate two birthdays: Hermann, *Helen Keller*, 208.

56   At only nineteen months old: Hermann, 9.

57   "Sometimes I stood": Hermann, 13.

57   "The most important day": Keller, *Story of My Life*, 24.

57   "I was at once interested": Keller, 25.

57   "I left the well-house": Keller, 26.

58   including Leonard Dowdy: Hermann, *Helen Keller*, 342.

58   Haben Girma: Girma, *Haben*.

58   as few as fifty people: Hermann, *Helen Keller*, 11.

58   reading ability is closely linked: Keith Stanovich was the first to propose this theory on the connection between reading and subsequent development of intelligence. Stanovich, "Matthew Effects in Reading."

58   measured the reading abilities and intelligence scores: Ritchie, Bates, and Plomin, "Does Learning to Read Improve Intelligence?"

59   "complete tasks that require comparing": US Department of Education, NCES, "Adult Literacy in the United States."

59   less than 15 percent scored in the highest two levels: US Department of Education, NCES, "What PIAAC Measures."

59   almost a third fewer books: Jones, "Americans Reading Fewer Books."

60   Phonological awareness: Adams, *Beginning to Read*, 70.

60   "By an overwhelming margin": Adams, 69.

61   pay attention to the letter combinations: Adams, 223.

61   particularly good at pronouncing pseudowords: Adams, 178.

61   compared the word recognition abilities: Juel and Roper-Schneider, "Influence of Basal Readers."

63   the strong benefit that one-on-one tutoring: Bloom, "The 2 Sigma Problem."

63   Mastery learning breaks the curriculum: Guskey, *Implementing Mastery Learning*.
63   central assumption of mastery learning: Bloom, "Learning for Mastery."
65   Systematic meta-analyses find that mastery learning: Hattie, *Visible Learning*, 170.
65   A related approach, Direct Instruction: Hattie, 205.
65   DISTAR: Adams, *Beginning to Read*.
66   a calculation of expected benefits: Atkinson and Birch, *Introduction to Motivation*, 16.
66   borders on circular reasoning: Bandura, *Social Learning Theory*, 4.
66   Bandura helped to clarify the issue: Bandura, 78.
68   "Performance accomplishments provide": Bandura, 81.
70   extensively tutored by George Starkey: Newman and Principe, *Alchemy Tried in Fire*.
70   received tutelage from Paul Erdős: Bernstein, "The Mind of a Mathematician."
72   expert readers fixate nearly every word: Adams, *Beginning to Read*, 176.

Chapter 4: Knowledge Becomes Invisible with Experience

73   "We know more": Polanyi, *The Tacit Dimension*.
75   "It's just like snot!" Maddox, *Rosalind Franklin*, 161.
75   "among the most beautiful x-ray photographs": Maddox, 14.
75   The model they had suggested: Maddox, 169.
75   when the world-renowned chemist: Maddox, 203.
76   defined the term "tacit knowledge": Polanyi, *The Tacit Dimension*.
77   "The sterile combinations": Poincaré, *Science and Method*, 181.
78   elite chess masters to weekend club players: De Groot, *Thought and Choice in Chess*.
78   players did not differ much in terms of depth of search: Modern studies in chess expertise conducted by Neil Charness, using larger sample sizes than de Groot and a wider range of skill levels, have found differences in search depth. But it appears as if depth of search levels off at an intermediate level of skill, making it ill-suited to explain the power of stronger players. Ericsson and Smith, *General Theory of Expertise*, 44.
78   typically show little enhanced ability: Chi, Glaser, and Farr, *Nature of Expertise*, xvii.
78   replicated and extended de Groot's work: Chase and Simon, "Perception in Chess."
78   Experts in medicine, programming, electronics, athletics, and music: For examples in medicine, athletics, and music: Ericsson and Smith, *General Theory of Expertise*; programming: Chi, Glaser, and Farr, *The Nature of Expertise*; electronics: Egan and Schwartz, "Chunking in Recall of Symbolic Drawings."
79   "nothing less than recognition": Simon, "What Is an 'Explanation' of Behavior?"
79   field research with experienced firefighters: Klein, Calderwood, and Clinton-Cirocco, "Rapid Decision Making on the Fire Ground."
79   the first move generated: Klein et al., "Option Generation in Chess."
80   "Often I cannot explain": Farndale, "Magnus Carlsen."
80   Adaptive expertise requires: Hatano and Inagaki, "Two Courses of Expertise."
80   pick better moves: Ericsson and Smith, *General Theory of Expertise*, 43.

80   unconsciously creating multiple, conflicting representations: Ericsson and
      Smith, General Theory of Expertise, chapter 12.
80   Construction-Integration model: Kintsch, *Comprehension*.
81   was clear to Franklin: James Watson was a biologist and claimed he avoided
      studying chemistry after nearly burning down the organic chemistry labora-
      tory while in university. Watson, *The Double Helix*, 29. Francis Crick, a phys-
      icist, once embarrassed himself in front of the biochemist Erwin Chargaff
      when he forgot the chemical structure of the nucleic acids in DNA—the basic
      components of the very molecule they were trying to analyze. Watson, 111.
81   naturally omits information: Grice, "Logic and Conversation."
82   the textbook they were using was simply wrong: Watson, *The Double Helix*,
      157.
82   injected harmless bacteria: Watson, 23.
83   always seemed eerily close: Watson, 108.
83   equally insistent that Chargaff's results were incorrect: Watson, 111.
83   studies where cytosine was absent: Watson, 179.
83   more than half had worked: Zuckerman, *Scientific Elite*, 113.
84   "becomes more valuable": Beth, Klein, and Hoffman, *Working Minds*, 167.
84   One review lists: Beth, Klein, and Hoffman, 11.
85   "self-report methods assume": Beth, Klein, and Hoffman, 14.
85   Critical Decision Method: Beth, Klein, and Hoffman, 71.
85   PARI method: Zsambok and Klein, *Naturalistic Decision Making*, 136.
86   examples over explicit instructions: LeFevre and Dixon, "Do Written Instructions
      Need Examples?"
86   Sociogrammetry is another method: Beth, Klein, and Hoffman, *Working
      Minds*, 229.
86   "On the receipt of an inquiry": Simon, *Administrative Behavior*, 243.

Chapter 5: The Difficulty Sweet Spot
91   "This is a fundamental truth": Ericsson and Pool, *Peak*.
91   receive a MacArthur "genius" grant: Consuela, *Octavia Butler*, ix.
92   "Honey, negros can't be writers": Canavan, *Octavia E. Butler*, 37.
92   "didn't really have anyone to help me": Consuela, *Octavia Butler*, 3.
92   "I had no examples": Consuela, 52.
92   "not being able to stop at all": Butler, "Positive Obsession."
92   "because with white-collar work": Consuela, *Octavia Butler*, 221.
92   "I had an extra typewriter": Consuela, 137.
93   "the things I had been learning": Consuela, 53.
93   "finish some short stories": Consuela, 20.
94   most commercially successful work: Canavan, *Octavia E. Butler*, 84.
94   young children often write with expert-like fluency: Bereiter and Scardamalia,
      The Psychology of Written Composition.
95   "The short stories I submitted": Consuela, *Octavia Butler*, 52.
95   "No, it's work": Consuela, 37.
95   "are all apprentices": While this version of the quote circulates widely, I was
      not able to locate an exact source. Hemingway reportedly said as much in an
      interview in the now-defunct *New York Journal-American* in 1961. However, an
      early biographer, Charles Andrew Fenton, reports a conversation where Hem-

ingway expressed a similar, albeit less artfully worded, sentiment to a friend, where the great writer said, "I'm apprenticed out at [writing] . . . until I die. Dopes can say you mastered it. But I know nobody ever mastered it, nor could not have done better." Fenton, *The Apprenticeship of Ernest Hemingway.*

96   "Frustrating. Frustrating": Consuela, *Octavia Butler*, 3.

96   more difficult practice leads to greater improvement: Bjork and Bjork, "Desirable Difficulty."

96   strengthens memory more than repeat viewing: Roediger III and Butler, "Critical Role of Retrieval Practice."

97   desirable difficulty is spaced practice: Dempster, "The Spacing Effect."

97   understood as a rational adaptation: Anderson, *Learning and Memory*, 239.

98   "This is not about imitating": Consuela, *Octavia Butler*, 77.

98   tend not to study worked examples: Carroll, "Using Worked Examples."

98   "Whatever you wrote": Consuela, *Octavia Butler*, 53.

99   ought to be a "three strikes rule": Mayer, "Should There Be a Three-Strikes Rule?"

99   "After a half century of advocacy": Kirschner, Sweller, and Clark, "Why Minimal Guidance During Instruction Does Not Work."

99   "Nothing flies more in the face": Anderson, Reder, and Simon, "Applications and Misapplications."

100   has argued that the "productive failure" paradigm: Kapur, "Productive Failure."

100   2021 meta-analysis conducted by Kapur: Sinha and Kapur, "Evidence for Productive Failure."

100   argue for allowing students to invent their own methods: Schwartz and Martin, "Inventing to Prepare for Future Learning."

100   compared the two sequences of instruction: Ashman, Kalyuga, and Sweller, "Problem-Solving or Explicit Instruction?"

100   "a worked example is more effective": Glogger-Frey, "Inventing a Solution and Studying a Worked Solution."

101   "learned and transferred relatively well": Matlen and Klahr, "Sequential Effects of High and Low Instructional Guidance."

101   a zone of proximal development: Oxford Reference, "Zone of Proximal Development."

101   for a zone of learnability: Kintsch, *Comprehension*, 324.

101   texts with poorer organization: McNamara and Kintsch, "Learning from Texts."

101   the expertise reversal effect proposed: Kalyuga, "Expertise Reversal Effect."

102   "A workshop is a way": Consuela, *Octavia Butler*, 217.

102   "getting a rejection slip": Butler, "Positive Obsession."

103   completion problems help: Merriënboer and Paas, "Automation and Schema Acquisition."

104   "People may not believe this": Bereiter and Scardamalia, *The Psychology of Written Composition.*

Chapter 6: The Mind Is Not a Muscle

105   "Strengthening muscle in one task": Singley and Anderson, *Transfer of Cognitive Skill*, 26.

106   "perform better at work and in school": Federal Trade Commission, "Lumosity to Pay $2 Million."

106 "improves performance in school": Federal Trade Commission, "Stipulated Final Judgment."

106 Intellectual ability is correlated: Ritchie, *Intelligence.*

106 "no evidence was found for transfer": Owen et al., "Putting Brain Training to the Test."

106 Another study looked at ninth graders: Watrin, Hülür, and Wilhelm, "Training Working Memory for Two Years."

106 "failed to observe generalizable performance improvements": Noack et al., "Cognitive Plasticity in Adulthood and Old Age."

106 "working memory training programs appear": Melby-Lervag, Redick, and Hulme, "Working Memory Training Does Not Improve Performance."

107 nonetheless quicken the mind: Plato, *Plato's Republic,* 298.

107 the general improvement of mental faculties: Locke is frequently claimed as the intellectual forefather of formal discipline. For instance see Dewey, *Democracy and Education.* However, Locke's actual views on education were more complicated. See Hodge, *John Locke and Formal Discipline.*

107 conducted a series of experiments: Woodworth and Thorndike, "The Influence of Improvement."

107 geometry and Latin didn't assist: Thorndike, "Mental Discipline."

107 learned to estimate the size: Thorndike, *Educational Psychology,* 90.

107 Children who practiced discriminating: Thorndike, *The Principles of Teaching,* 240.

107 ability to detect English verbs: Thorndike, 241.

107 "the mind is so specialized": Thorndike, 246.

108 cognitive benefits of chess and music instruction: Sala and Gobet, "Does Far Transfer Exist?"

108 "The rationale for teaching computer programming": VanLengen, "Does Instruction in Computer Programming Improve Problem-Solving Ability?"

108 "learning to drive a nail": Meikeljohn, "Is Mental Training a Myth?"

109 subjects who practiced the first task: Woodworth and Thorndike, "The Influence of Improvement."

109 in experiments with mathematical equations: Thorndike, "The Effect of Changed Data upon Reasoning."

109 Charles Judd had boys practice throwing darts: Judd, "The Relation of Special Training and General Intelligence."

109 the Gestalt psychologist Max Wertheimer showed: Wertheimer, *Productive Thinking.*

111 atomic units called production rules: Anderson and Lebiere, *The Atomic Components of Thought.*

112 gave students the rule for integration: Anderson, *Learning and Memory,* 323.

112 students who practice generating: DeKeyser, "Beyond Explicit Rule Learning."

112 Research has shown that French-immersion students: Swain, "Communicative Competence."

112 some of the more general production rules: Anderson, *Rules of the Mind,* 195.

112 Connectionist systems model skills: McClelland and Rumelhart, *Parallel Distributed Processing.*

112 schema theories represent: Brewer, "Bartlett's Concept of the Schema."

113 exemplar-based accounts: Logan, "Instance Theory."

113 an experiment conducted by Mary Gick and Keith Holyoak: Gick and Holyoak, "Analogical Problem Solving."

113 the Wason four-card task: Singley and Anderson, *Transfer of Cognitive Skill,* 23.

114   subjects do not seem to perform better: Cheng et al., "Pragmatic versus Syntactic Approaches."

115   an ability to detect rule violations: Cheng et al.

115   students who had taken an algebra class: Reed, Dempster, and Ettinger, "Usefulness of Analogous Solutions."

115   lamented the problem of "inert knowledge" in education: Whitehead, "Aims of Education."

115   students taught statistical heuristics: Fong, Krantz, and Nisbett, "Effects of Statistical Training."

116   superficial variations of the Tower of Hanoi puzzle: Singley and Anderson, *Transfer of Cognitive Skill*, 23.

116   Research on physics experts finds: Chi, Feltovich, and Glaser, "Representation of Physics Problems."

116   is not widely appreciated by students: Karpicke, "Metacognitive Control."

116   controlled experiments repeatedly demonstrate: Karpicke and Blunt, "Retrieval Practice."

118   in the context of an algebra class: Bassok and Holyoak, "Pragmatic Knowledge and Conceptual Structure."

118   compensated for by faster learning: Anderson, Reder, and Simon, "Situated Learning and Education."

119   built out of knowledge: Greg Ashman proposed this metaphor for the mind: "Rather than see the mind as a set of library shelves and knowledge as the neatly ordered books that fill those shelves, perhaps we should see the mind as a set of tools *made out of* knowledge. Knowledge is what you think with. Knowledge is the mind." Ashman, *Explicit Teaching*, 12.

120   "but it never cheats": Thorndike, *The Principles of Teaching*, 247–48.

Chapter 7: Variability Over Repetition

121   "I used to think": Berliner, *Thinking in Jazz*, 20.

122   "you brought your horn": Davis and Troupe, *Miles*.

122   "Play something different, man": Berliner, *Thinking in Jazz*, 390.

122   "After an introduction to the choir": Berliner, 57.

123   Charlie Parker improvised multiple unique solos: Owens, *Bebop*, 12.

123   extent of his improvisational prowess: Berliner, *Thinking in Jazz*, 305.

123   "Energized by its vitality": Berliner, 20.

123   "Jazz is not just": Berliner, 99.

123   "scream in the middle of a peaceful street": Berliner, 155.

123   "My teacher would have you improvise": Berliner, 165.

124   "I never get tired": Berliner, 242.

124   "exhaust all the possibilities": Berliner, 239.

124   learning to play in all keys: Berliner, 248.

124   "somewhat paradoxical principle": Battig, "Facilitation and Interference."

125   extended Battig's early observations: Shea and Morgan, "Contextual Interference Effects."

125   benefits of a randomized practice schedule are higher: Magill and Hall, "A Review of the Contextual Interference Effect."

125   training engineering students to troubleshoot: Merriënboer, de Croock, and Jelsma, "The Transfer Paradox."

126 found in second language learning: Pan et al., "Interleaved Practice."

126 Japanese learners of English grammar: Nakata and Suzuki, "Mixed Grammar Exercises Facilitates Long-Term Retention."

127 the teacher would hit iron poles: Berliner, *Thinking in Jazz*, 240.

127 make mistakes in the beginning: Berliner, 141.

127 "feel where the chords": Berliner, 115.

127 "essential ingredient in learning": Berliner, 120.

128 "Discovering that certain": Berliner, 207.

128 "Charlie Parker licks": Berliner, 155.

128 medical students studying electrocardiogram readings: Hatala, Brooks, and Norman, "Practice Makes Perfect."

128 molecules in organic chemistry: Eglington and Kang, "Interleaved Presentation."

128 painting styles by different artists: Kang and Pashler, "Learning Painting Styles."

128 species of birds and butterflies: Birnbaum et al., "Why Interleaving Enhances Inductive Learning."

128 seemingly different examples: Goldstone, "Isolated and Interrelated Concepts."

128 the successful teaching methodology: Engelmann and Carnine, *Theory of Instruction*, 123.

129 "The more ways you have of thinking": Berliner, *Thinking in Jazz*, 214.

129 "knew what notes didn't fit": Berliner, 232.

129 Bartz struggled during jam sessions: Berliner, 232.

129 "It was not until he was immersed": Berliner, 166.

130 "the discovery of scales": Berliner, 236.

130 "E-flat major arpeggio": Berliner, 238.

130 "Suppose you have two theories": Richard Feynman, "Knowing vs Understanding," YouTube, 5:36, https://www.youtube.com/watch?v=NM-zWTU7X-k.

131 number scrabble: Newell and Simon, *Human Problem Solving*, 59.

131 "There is nothing so practical": Marrow, *The Practical Theorist*, viii.

133 complex motor skills: Wulf and Shea, "Principles."

133 English learners with more experience: Gao et al., "Effects of Speaker Variability."

133 practice variability in mathematics: Likourezos, Kalyuga, and Sweller, "The Variability Effect."

134 developed an unusual fingering technique: Berliner, *Thinking in Jazz*, 159.

134 reportedly retreated into lengthy practice sessions: Walk That Bass, "Bebop Explained," YouTube, May 24, 2019, 17:54, https://www.youtube.com/watch?v=gEwWjJ7c0u4.

135 "In research on firefighters": Beth, Klein, and Hoffman, *Working Minds*, 134.

136 "I would go to the library": Davis and Troupe, Miles, 61.

137 participants generally believed: Kornell and Bjork, "Learning Concepts and Categories."

Chapter 8: Quality Comes from Quantity

139 "Well, you just have lots of ideas": Pauling, "Crusading Scientist."

140 1,093 patents in his lifetime: History.com, "Thomas Edison."

140 When Edison died in 1931: Josephson, "Edison," 401.

141 fewer than two dozen works: Heydenreich, "Leonardo da Vinci."

141 thirteen thousand original paintings: Brown, "Famous Picasso Paintings."

141 earliest investigators to consider this question: Quetelet, *Treatise on Man*.

141   personal productivity and social creativity are highly correlated: Dean Simonton, personal communication.

141   "This ratio of hits to total shots": Simonton, *Greatness*, 184.

142   potential for world-changing impact: Originally Simonton proposed an equal-odds "rule," but has since updated it to an equal-odds baseline to reflect more recent analyses of the historical data. The equal potentiality of creative success is most evident in fields that have a standard "least-publishable unit," such as a scientific paper, as opposed to fields where contributions can differ significantly in scope (for instance, a poem versus an opera).

142   scholarly output of a given field: Price, *Little Science, Big Science.*

142   the most highly cited scientists: Zuckerman, *Scientific Elite*, 145.

142   neurosurgeons with the most citations: Davis, "Creativity in Neurosurgical Publications."

143   "'thinking writ large'": Simon, "How Managers Express Their Creativity."

143   "refinement of everyday thinking": Einstein, "Physics and Reality."

144   reviewed 76 famous composers: Hayes, "Cognitive Processes in Creativity."

144   "My refuge": Josephson, *Edison*, 35.

145   "a birth of time": Bacon, *Novum Organon.*

145   the long and surprising list of multiple discoveries: Ogburn and Thomas, "Are Inventions Inevitable?"

146   Merton counts eighteen instances: Merton, "Singletons and Multiples."

146   creativity cannot be judged: Sternberg, *Handbook of Creativity*, chapter on "Implications of a Systems Perspective for the Study of Creativity," 313–35.

146   Computer analyses of musical compositions: Simonton, *Greatness*, 110.

147   "Anything that won't sell": Edison Innovation Foundation, "Famous Quotes."

147   "My main purpose in life": Edison Innovation Foundation.

147   native beasts of burden: Diamond, *Guns, Germs, and Steel.*

147   "The common belief": Csikszentmihalyi, "Creativity and Genius."

148   creative thinking can be understood: Campbell, "Blind Variation."

148   long history of accidental inventions: Greenwald, "30 Life-Changing Inventions."

148   "Le principe de l'invention": Souriau, *Théorie de l'Invention*, 45.

148   "In experimenting, I find": Josephson, *Edison*, 235.

149   "Why, man, I've got a lot of results": Josephson, 345.

149   "If Edison had a needle": Josephson, 199.

149   originally developed for diabetes: Henderson, "Semaglutide."

149   originally developed to treat hypertension: Ghofrani, Osterloh, and Grimminger, "Sildenafil."

150   six-year-old Carl Gauss: Wertheimer, *Productive Thinking.*

150   creative as a gambler: Sternberg, *Handbook of Creativity*, 10.

151   "did not have ennui": Josephson, *Edison*, 79.

151   contact with an inventor prior: Howes, "Age of Invention."

152   "Midnight! Is that so": The actual story is somewhat less dramatic, as it appears Edison left his wedding to work on a problem in the lab, but Edison himself recalls coming back around dinnertime. Josephson, *Edison*, 87.

152   one hundred hours per week: Simonton, *Greatness*, 139.

152   developed stomach problems: Isaacson, *Einstein*, 217.

152   his eighty-five novels: Simonton, *Greatness*, 139.

152   with few vacations: Simonton, 139.

152   the hard-charging "Type A" profile: Matthews, Helmreich, and Beane, "Pattern A."

153   "genius is one percent inspiration": Josephson, *Edison*, 364.
153   organize the writing of new episodes: Armstrong, *Seinfeldia*, 191.
154   "had almost a sixth sense": Kanigel, *Apprentice to Genius*, 190.
155   study of Nobel laureates: Zuckerman, *Scientific Elite*, 229.
156   feigning irresponsibility: Feynman, *"Surely You're Joking."*
156   one's "deep work": Newport, *Deep Work.*

Chapter 9: Experience Doesn't Reliably Ensure Expertise

161   "True intuitive expertise": Kahneman, "Don't Blink!"
161   the youngest-ever winner: World Series of Poker, "2007 World Series of Poker Europe."
162   winning more money: PokerListings, "Best Poker Moments."
162   while having a piece of tape: Imir, "Annette Obrestad."
162   Obrestad got her start: Annette Obrestad, "My Story," YouTube, October 18, 2018, 18:37, https://www.youtube.com/watch?v=mk-0CmsIVFg.
162   Obrestad had won over $3.9 million: Hendon Mob, "Norway All Time Money List."
163   bragged about his swindling exploits: Magyar, *Greatest Stories in Poker History*, 18.
163   "The common belief": Magyar, 22.
163   "There are few things as unpardonably neglected": Twain, *Life as I Find It.*
163   Roosevelt regularly played stud games: Magyar, *Greatest Stories in Poker History*, 44.
163   fund part of an early congressional campaign: Kiger, "Nixon's WWII Poker Game."
163   "A man's true feelings": Brunson, *Super System.*
164   a $39 online tournament: PokerListings, "About Chris Moneymaker."
164   "A guy like Doyle Brunson": Negreanu, "Daniel Negreanu Teaches Poker."
167   three thousand parole decisions: Grove and Meehl, "Comparative Efficiency."
168   "we are trying to predict": Meehl, *Clinical versus Statistical Prediction*, 24.
168   "two fifths of the studies": Grove and Meehl, "Comparative Efficiency."
169   transcripts of hospital staff: Chi, Glaser, and Farr, *Nature of Expertise*, chapter on "Expertise and Decision Under Uncertainty."
170   famous failure of intuition: Kahneman, Tversky, and Slovic, "Judgements."
171   "conditions must be satisfied": Kahneman and Klein, "Conditions for Intuitive Expertise."
172   Expert Judgment Project: Tetlock, *Expert Political Judgment.*
173   do better than chance: Tetlock, xx.
173   "a curious inverse relationship": Tetlock, xi.
173   "one-handed economists": Quote Investigator, "One-Handed Economist."
174   beat the control group by 60–78 percent: Tetlock and Gardener, *Superforecasting*, 18.
174   forecasters resisted this temptation: Tetlock and Gardener, 278.
175   teams of forecasters: Tetlock and Gardener, 200.
175   "running times are improving": Tetlock and Gardener, 14.
175   good forecasters can't predict: Tetlock and Gardener, 243.
177   simply providing forecasters with outcome feedback: Benson and Önkal, "The Effects of Feedback."

177   Francis Galton first attested: Yong, "Real Wisdom of the Crowds."

178   social act of justifying one's actions: Mercier and Sperber, *Enigma of Reason*.

178   Molly Geil gave individuals: Moshman and Geil, "Collaborative Reasoning."

Chapter 10: Practice Must Meet Reality

180   "We learn how to behave": Holmes, *The Essential Holmes*, 45.

181   "Go ahead, ask": Aviation Safety Network, "ASN Accident Description."

181   accidents involving planes: NSC Injury Facts, "Deaths by Transportation Mode."

181   invention of the stirrup: White, *Medieval Technology and Social Change*.

182   Gunpowder cannons allowed: Crowley, "The Guns of Constantinople."

182   battle for the skies: Morley, "Earning Their Wings."

182   attempts to mount guns: Morley, 53.

182   over a third of pilots: Morley, 81.

182   hold on to the wing spars: Morley, 44.

183   wrote six letters: Morley, 73.

183   "never flown any": Morley, 72.

183   A survivor of a crash: Morley, 94.

183   "They've barely learned to fly": McKenna, "Robert Smith-Barry."

183   "Fokker fodder": Morley, "Earning Their Wings," 95.

183   "[D]on't worry us anymore": Morley, 95.

183   "always be in the pilot's seat": Morley, 97.

183   Prior to the Gosport system: Morley, 111.

184   65 percent rise in casualties: Morley, 111.

184   "occurred almost entirely during landings": Morley, 117.

184   "The dual-control aircraft": Morley, 118.

184   "the man who taught": McKenna, "Robert Smith-Barry."

184   "raw flying skill": Mavin and Murray, "Simulated Practice."

184   KLM executives even suggested: Reijnoudt and Sterk, *Tragedie Op Tenerife*.

185   shortage of residency slots: Boyle, "Medical School Enrollments Grow."

186   Antoinette trainer: Wise, Hopkin, and Garland, *Handbook of Aviation Human Factors*, 440.

186   developed the Link Trainer: Wise, Hopkin, and Garland, 440.

186   military realized its potential: US Air Force, "Link Trainer."

186   better than actual aircraft: Wise, Hopkin, and Garland, *Handbook of Aviation Human Factors*, 443.

186   "first hour of instruction": Roscoe, "Incremental Transfer Effectiveness."

187   favored simulator-plus-aircraft training: Jacobs et al., "Flight Simulator Training Research."

187   twenty-five mock sorties: Carretta and Dunlap, "Transfer of Training Effectivness."

187   found a similar curve: Rantanen and Talleur, "Incremental Transfer."

187   "emphasis on high fidelity": Wise, Hopkin, and Garland, *Handbook of Aviation Human Factors*, 442.

187   trained with crosswinds: Lintern, Roscoe, and Sivier, "Display Principles."

187   "Precise replication of the control": Wise, Hopkin, and Garland, *Handbook of Aviation Human Factors*, 441.

189   insurance claims processor: Wenger, Communities of Practice.

189   "reasonable person": Spaeth, "What a Lawyer Needs to Learn."

189   legitimate, peripheral participation: Lave and Wenger, *Situated Learning*.

190   "remarkably few exceptions": Lave and Wenger, 30.

190   "scared to go in the back room": Lave and Wenger, 78.

191   burden of professional licensing: Kleiner and Vorotnikov, "At What Cost?"

191   "All professions are conspiracies": Spoken by Sir Patrick in Shaw's play *The Doctor's Dilemma*.

192   "succeed in academia": Brennan, *Good Work*, 56.

192   "The grad students who": Brennan, 67.

192   "You can't get any job": Brennan, 68.

193   a GED is much weaker: Heckman, Humphries, and Kautz, *The Myth of Achievement Tests*.

194   "When the experiments were good": Kanigel, *Apprentice to Genius*, 99.

194   lore of educated society: Hirsch, *Cultural Literacy*.

Chapter 11: Improvement Is Not a Straight Line

196   "Wisdom doesn't consist": Quote Investigator, "It Is Better to Know."

196   climbed down from his high chair: Eden, "Stroke of Madness."

196   his national television debut: Dethier, "Tiger Woods' First-Ever TV Appearance."

197   relied on a whiplike action: Harmon and Eubanks, *The Pro*, 161.

197   "I won with perfect timing": Harmon and Eubanks, 163.

197   shooting jump shots left-handed: Eden, "Stroke of Madness."

198   "It's not going to be easy": Eden.

198   eighteen months of grinding practice: Harmon and Eubanks, *The Pro*, 166.

199   proposed an influential theory: Fitts and Posner, *Human Performance*.

200   having an external focus: Wulf, Lauterbach, and Toole, "The Learning Advantages."

200   machinelike precision: Bernshteĭn, *Co-ordination and Regulation of Movements*.

200   how past successes: Luchins, "Einstellung."

201   coined the term *functional fixedness*: Duncker, "On Problem Solving."

202   do not successfully export: Gardener, *Unschooled Mind*.

202   Aristotle outside the classroom: DiSessa, "Unlearning Aristotelian Physics."

202   Economics students learn: Voss et al., "Informal Reasoning."

202   different learning styles: Willingham, Hughes, and Dobolyi, "The Scientific Status of Learning Styles Theories."

202   intuitive module for dealing: Kubricht, Holyoak, and Lu, "Intuitive Physics."

203   unusual motion was realistic: Thaden-Koch, Dufresne, and Mestre, "Coordination of Knowledge."

203   buggy computer code: Brown and VanLehn, "Repair Theory."

204   teacher to stop the student: Rosenshine and Stevens, *Handbook of Research on Teaching*.

204   go through a regular sequence: Marcus et al., "Overregularization in Language Acquisition."

204   learn grammar automatically: Pinker and Morey, *The Language Instinct*.

204   medical students' reasoning frequently: Patel and Groen, "Developmental Accounts."

205   "moderate experience hypothesis": Siegler, *Emerging Minds*.

205   "science proceeds one funeral": Planck, *Scientific Autobiography*.

205   Einstein fought bitterly: Britannica, "Albert Einstein's Perspective."

205 a key to deliberate practice: Ericsson and Pool, *Peak*.

206 stagnation in our skills: Ericsson, *Development of Professional Expertise*, 417.

206 hands-on physics simulations: Wieman and Perkins, "Transforming Physics Education."

206 interactive simulations can improve: Jimoyiannis and Komis, "Computer Simulations in Physics."

207 many physics novices: Kahneman, *Thinking, Fast and Slow*.

208 the "yips": Masters and Maxwell, "The Theory of Reinvestment."

Chapter 12: Fears Fade with Exposure

210 "One of the major weaknesses": Rachman, *Fear and Courage*, 38.

210 raids during the First World War: Titmuss, *Problems of Social Policy*, 4.

211 a sudden *blitzkrieg*: Titmuss, 6.

211 "man in the street to realize": Stanley Balwin, "A Fear for the Future," speech before the House of Commons of the United Kingdom, November 10, 1932.

211 three to four million people might flee: Titmuss, *Problems of Social Policy,*, 9.

211 inevitable exodus: Titmuss, 19.

211 "clear to everyone": Titmuss, 20.

211 "To the considerable surprise": Rachman, *Fear and Courage*, 20.

211 only fifteen of 1,100 patients: Vernon, "Psychological Effects of Air-Raids."

211 patients admitted to mental hospitals: Stokes, "War Strains and Mental Health."

211 "One point emerges very clearly": Janis, *Air War and Emotional Stress*, 112.

212 "generally taking no notice": Vernon, "Psychological Effects of Air-Raids."

212 "calm behavior of the average individual": Panter-Downes, London War Notes.

212 Survivors of the atomic bombings: Janis, Air War and Emotional Stress, 65.

212 bombed German cities: Janis, 112.

212 those who had not been evacuated: Saigh, "Pre- and Postinvasion Anxiety in Lebanon."

212 "After five decades": Clark, "Panic."

213 believed fears were innate: James, *Principles of Psychology*, vol. 2, 704.

213 experienced a "remote miss": Janis, *Air War and Emotional Stress*, 123.

214 argued we are predisposed: Seligman, "Phobias and Preparedness."

214 theories of anxiety place the blame: Mineka and Zinbarg, "A Contemporary Learning Theory."

214 influential two-factor theory: Mowrer, *Learning Theory and Behavior*.

216 Evidence for the two-memory view: Bouton, "Context, Ambiguity and Unlearning."

216 fears that have been extinguished can return: Vervliet, Craske, and Hermans, "Fear Extinction and Relapse."

216 air raids tended to return: Vernon, "Psychological Effects of Air-Raids."

217 results in more durable benefits: Craske et al., "Maximizing Exposure Therapy."

217 regimen of gradually escalating encounters: Locke, *Thoughts Concerning Education*, 109.

217 youthful fear of heights: Marks, Fears, Phobias, and Rituals, 457.

217 his protocol of systematic desensitization: Wolpe, *Psychotherapy by Reciprocal Inhibition*.

217 research found that relaxation: Marks, *Fears, Phobias, and Rituals*, 459.

217 flooding and implosive therapies: Abramowitz, Deacon, and Whiteside, Exposure
      Therapy, 15.

218 the active ingredient: Marks, *Fears, Phobias, and Rituals* 459.

218 tend not to outperform: Foa et al., "A Comparison of Exposure Therapy";
      Ramnerö, "Is There Room for Cognitive Interventions?"; Feske and Chambless,
      "Cognitive Behavioral versus Exposure Only Treatment"; Marks, *Fears, Phobias,
      and Rituals.*

218 mindfulness-based approaches to anxiety: Hofmann and Asmundson,
      "Mindfulness-Based Therapy."

218 "medial frontal areas": LeDoux, *Anxious*, 259.

219 does depend on consciously accessible beliefs: Hofmann, "Cognitive Processes
      During Fear."

219 cannot be perceived consciously: Siegel and Warren, "Less Is Still More."

219 treatment for specific phobias: Wolitzky-Taylor et al., "Treatment of Specific
      Phobias."

219 similar conclusions with social phobias: Gould et al., "Treatment for Social
      Phobia."

219 generalized anxiety: Gould et al., "Generalized Anxiety Disorder."

219 panic: Gould, Otto, and Pollack, "Panic."

219 obsessive-compulsive disorder: Balkom et al., "Obsessive Compulsive Disorder."

219 treat post-traumatic stress disorder: Van Etten and Taylor, "Comparative
      Efficacy of Treatments."

219 aren't more likely to drop out: Abramowitz, Deacon, and Whiteside, *Exposure
      Therapy*, 353. Data on attrition can also be seen in meta-analyses previously
      cited.

219 "majority of patients with any anxiety disorder": Abramowitz, Deacon, and
      Whiteside, 351.

221 "The importance of closely matching": Abramowitz, Deacon, and Whiteside,
      87.

222 "It is important to note": Abramowitz, Deacon, and Whiteside, 82.

222 "Under no circumstances": Abramowitz, Deacon, and Whiteside, 115.

222 presence of a therapist: Abramowitz, Deacon, and Whiteside, 119

223 "membership in a small, cohesive group": Rachman, Fear and Courage, 59.

223 people who lived alone: Vernon, "Psychological Effects of Air-Raids."

224 "Fear is not a lump": Rachman, *Fear and Courage*, 7.

224 "Fearful people have a strong tendency": Rachman, 225.

Conclusion: Practice Made Perfect

226 "What is it you do to train": Cowen, "Learn Like an Athlete."

227 superficial features than deep principles: Chi, Feltovich, and Glaser, "Repre-
      sentation of Physics Problems."

229 consultants did better than restaurant managers: Barnett and Kowslowski,
      "Adaptive Expertise."

230 value of part-task practice: Ayres, "Impact of Reducing Cognitive Load."

230 translate into fluent performance: Carlson, Khoo, and Elliot, "Component
      Practice."

232 bulk praise: Kluger and DeNisi, "The Effects of Feedback Interventions."

BIBLIOGRAPHY

Abramowitz, Jonathan S., Brett J. Deacon, and Stephen P. H. Whiteside. *Exposure Therapy for Anxiety: Principles and Practice*. New York: Guilford Press, 2011.

Adams, Marilyn Jager. *Beginning to Read: Thinking and Learning About Print*. Cambridge, MA: Bradford Books, 1994.

Anderson, John. *Learning and Memory: An Integrated Approach*. New York: Wiley, 2000.

———. *Rules of the Mind*. New York: Psychology Press, 2014.

Anderson, John, and Christian J. Lebiere. *The Atomic Components of Thought*. New York: Psychology Press, 2014.

Anderson, John, Lynne Reder, and Herbert Simon. "Applications and Misapplications of Cognitive Psychology to Mathematics Education." 1999. Accessed June 26, 2023. https://files.eric.ed.gov/fulltext/ED439007.pdf.

———. "Situated Learning and Education." *Educational Researcher* 25, no. 4 (1996): 5–11.

Aristides, Juliette. *Classical Drawing Atelier: A Contemporary Guide to Traditional Studio Practice*. New York City: Watson-Guptill, 2011.

Armstrong, Jennifer Keishin. *Seinfeldia: How a Show About Nothing Changed Everything*. New York: Simon & Schuster, 2017.

Ashman, Greg. *The Power of Explicit Teaching and Direct Instruction*. Thousand Oaks, CA: Corwin, 2020.

Ashman, Greg, Slava Kalyuga, and John Sweller. "Problem-Solving or Explicit Instruction: Which Should Go First When Element Interactivity Is High?" *Educational Psychology Review* 22 (2020): 229–47.

Atkinson, John William, and David Birch. *Introduction to Motivation*. 2nd ed. New York: Van Nostrand, 1978.

Autor, David, Caroline Chin, Anna M. Salomons, and Bryan Seegmiller. "New Frontiers: The Origins and Content of Work 1940–2018." *NBER Working Paper Series*, 2022.

Aviation Safety Network. "ASN Accident Description." Accessed June 27, 2023. http://aviation-safety.net/database/record.php?id=19770327-0.

Ayres, Paul. "Impact of Reducing Cognitive Load on Learning in a Mathematical Domain." *Applied Cognitive Psychology* 20, no. 3 (2006): 287–98.

Bacon, Francis. *Novum Organon.* 1620.

Baddeley, Alan. *Human Memory: Theory and Practice.* Hove, UK: Psychology Press, 1997.

Balkom, Anton J. L. M. van, Patricia van Oppen, Alexander W. A. Vermeulen, Richard van Dyck, Mary C. E. Nauta, and Harne C. M. Vorst. "A Meta-Analysis on the Treatment of Obsessive Compulsive Disorder: A Comparison of Antidepressants, Behavior, and Cognitive Therapy." *Clinical Psychology Review* 14, no. 5 (1994): 359–81.

Bandura, Albert. *Social Learning Theory.* Englewood Cliffs, NJ: Prentice-Hall, 1977.

Barnett, Susan M., and Barbara Kowslowski. "Adaptive Expertise: Effects of Type of Experience and the Level of Theoretical Understanding It Generates." *Thinking & Reasoning* 8, no. 4 (2002): 237–67.

Bassok, Miriam, and Keith Holyoak. "Pragmatic Knowledge and Conceptual Structure: Determinants of Transfer Between Quantitative Domains." In *Transfer on Trial: Intelligence, Cognition, and Instruction*, edited by Douglas Detterman and Robert Sternberg, 68–98. Norwood, NJ: Ablex, 1993.

Battig, William. "Facilitation and Interference." In *Acquisition of Skill*, edited by Edward Bilodeau, 215–45. New York: Academic Press, 1966.

Benson, P. George, and Dilek Önkal. "The Effects of Feedback and Training on the Performance of Probability Forecasters." *International Journal of Forecasting* 8, no. 4 (1992): 559–73.

Bereiter, Carl, and Marlene Scardamalia. *The Psychology of Written Composition.* Mahwah, NJ: Erlbaum, 1987.

Berliner, Paul. *Thinking in Jazz: The Infinite Art of Improvisation.* Chicago: University of Chicago Press, 2009.

Bernshteĭn, Nikolaĭ Aleksandrovich. *The Co-ordination and Regulation of Movements.* New York: Pergamon Press, 1967.

Bernstein, Mark F. "The Mind of a Mathematician." *Princeton Alumni Weekly*, November 13, 2019. Accessed June 26, 2023. https://paw.princeton.edu/article/mind-mathematician.

Beth, Crandall, Gary Klein, and Robert R. Hoffman. *Working Minds: A Practitioner's Guide to Cognitive-Task Analysis.* Cambridge, MA: MIT Press, 2006.

Birnbaum, Monica, Nate Kornell, Elizabeth Bjork, and Robert Bjork. "Why Interleaving Enhances Inductive Learning: The Roles of Discrimination and Retrieval." *Memory & Cognition* 41 (2013): 392–402.

Bjork, Robert, and Elizabeth Bjork. "Desirable Difficulty in Theory and Practice." *Journal of Applied Research in Memory and Cognition* 9 (2020): 475–479.

Bloom, Benjamin. "Learning for Mastery." *Evaluation Comment* 1, no. 2 (1968).

———. "The 2 Sigma Problem: The Search for Methods of Group Instruction as Effective as One-to-One Tutoring." *Educational Researcher* 13, no. 6 (1984): 4–16.

Bouton, Mark. "Context, Ambiguity and Unlearning: Sources of Relapse After Behavioral Extinction." *Biological Psychiatry* 52, no. 10 (2002): 976–86.

Boyle, Patrick. "Medical School Enrollments Grow, but Residency Slots Haven't Kept Pace." Association of American Medical Colleges, September 3, 2020. Accessed June 27, 2023. https://www.aamc.org/news/medical-school-enrollments-grow-residency-slots-haven-t-kept-pace.

Boyle, Robert. 1662. *New Experiments Physico-Mechanicall, Touching the Spring of Air, and Its Effects.* Oxford: H. Hall, Printer to the University, for T. Robinson.

Brennan, Jason. *Good Work If You Can Get It: How to Succeed in Academia.* Baltimore: Johns Hopkins University Press, 2020.

Brewer, William F. "Bartlett's Concept of the Schema and Its Impact on Theories of Knowledge Representation in Contemporary Cognitive Psychology." In *Bartlett, Culture and Cognition*, edited by Akiko Saito, 69–89. London: Psychology Press, 2000.

Britannica. "Understand Albert Einstein's Perspective of Disagreement About the Element of Uncertainty of Quantum Theory." Accessed June 27, 2023. https://www.britannica.com/video/186825/indeterminacy-element-interpretation-quantum-mechanics-objections-Niels.

Brown, Forrest. "Famous Picasso Paintings: 7 Works That Captured Our Imagination." CNN, February 3, 2020. Accessed June 27, 2023. https://www.cnn.com/style/article/famous-picasso-paintings/index.html.

Brown, John Seely, and Kurt VanLehn. "Repair Theory: A Generative Theory of Bugs in Procedural Skills." *Cognitive Science* 4, no. 4 (1980): 379–426.

Brunson, Doyle. *Doyle Brunson's Super System: A Course in Power Poker.* Las Vegas, NV: B&G, 1978.

Butler, Octavia. "Positive Obsession." In *Bloodchild and Other Stories*, 125–35. New York: Seven Stories Press, 2005.

Campbell, Donald. "Blind Variation and Selective Retention in Creative Thought as in Other Knowledge Processes." *Psychological Review* 67, no. 6 (1960): 380–400.

Canavan, Gerry. *Octavia E. Butler.* Urbana: University of Illinois Press, 2016.

Caplan, Bryan. *The Case Against Education: Why the Education System Is a Waste of Time and Money.* Princeton, NJ: Princeton University Press, 2018.

Carlson, Richard A., Boo Hock Khoo, and Robert G. II Elliot. "Component Practice and Exposure to a Problem-Solving Context." *Human Factors: The Journal of the Human Factors and Ergonomics Society* 32, no. 3 (1990): 267–86.

Carretta, Thomas, and Ronald Dunlap. "Transfer of Training Effectivness in Flight Simulation 1988 to 1997." United States Air Force Research Laboratory, 1998.

Carroll, William. "Using Worked Examples as an Instructional Support in the Algebra Classroom." *Journal of Educational Psychology* 86, no. 3 (1994): 360–67.

Catrambone, Richard. "The Subgoal Learning Model: Creating Better Examples So That Students Can Solve Novel Problems." *Journal of Experimental Psychology: General* 127, no. 4 (1998): 355.

Cennini, Cennino. *Il libro dell'arte.* Translated by Daniel V. Thompson. New York: Dover, 1954.

Chase, William, and Herbert Simon. "Perception in Chess." *Cognitive Psychology* 4, no. 1 (1973): 55–81.

Cheng, Patricia W., Keith Holyoak, Richard Nisbett, and Lindsay Oliver. "Pragmatic versus Syntactic Approaches to Training Deductive Reasoning." *Cognitive Psychology* 18, no. 3 (1986): 293–328.

Chi, Michelene, Miriam Bassok, Matthew W. Lewis, Peter Reinmann, and Robert Glaser. "Self-Explanations: How Students Study and Use Examples in Learning to Solve Problems." *Cognitive Science* 13, no. 2 (1989): 145–82.

Chi, Michelene, Paul Feltovich, and Robert Glaser. "Categorization and Representation of Physics Problems by Experts and Novices." *Cognitive Science* 5, no. 2 (1981): 121–52.

Chi, Michelene, Robert Glaser, and Marshall Farr. *The Nature of Expertise.* Hillsdale, NJ: Erlbaum, 1988.

Choudhry, Niteesh K., Robert H. Fletcher, and Stephen B. Soumerai. "Systematic Review: The Relationship Between Clinical Experience and Quality of Health Care." *Annals of Internal Medicine* 142, no. 4 (2005): 260–73.

Clark, Lee. "Panic: Myth or Reality?" *Contexts* (Fall 2022): 21–26.

Clark, Richard E. "Antagonism Between Achievement and Enjoyment in ATI Studies." *Educational Psychologist* 17, no. 2 (1982): 92–101.

Consuela, Francis. *Conversations with Octavia Butler.* Jackson: University Press of Mississippi, 2009.

Cooper, Graham, and John Sweller. "Effects of Schema Acquisition and Rule Automation on Mathematical Problem-Solving Transfer." *Journal of Educational Psychology* 79, no. 4 (1987): 347–62.

Cornelius, Adam, dir. *Ecstasy of Order: The Tetris Masters.* 2021.

Cowan, Nelson. "The Magical Number 4 in Short-Term Memory: A Reconsideration of Mental Storage Capacity." *Behavioral and Brain Sciences* 24, no. 1 (2001): 87–114.

Cowen, Tyler. "Learn Like an Athlete, Knowledge Workers Should Train." *Marginal Revolution*, July 12, 2019. Accessed June 28, 2023. https://marginalrevolution.com/marginalrevolution/2019/07/learn-like-an-athlete-knowledge-workers-should-train.html.

Craske, Michelle G., Michael Treanor, Christopher C. Conway, Tomislav Zbozinek, and Bram Vervliet. "Maximizing Exposure Therapy: An Inhibitory Learning Approach." *Behavioral Research and Therapy* 58 (2014): 10–23.

Crowley, Roger. *The Guns of Constantinople.* July 30, 2007. Accessed June 27, 2023. https://www.historynet.com/the-guns-of-constantinople/.

Csikszentmihalyi, Mihalyi. "Creativity and Genius: A Systems Perspective." In *Genius and the Mind*, by Andrew Steptoe, 39–66. New York: Oxford University Press, 1988.

Da Vinci, Leonardo. *Leonardo's Notebooks: Writing and Art of the Great Master.* Edited by H. Anna Suh. New York: Black Dog & Leventhal, 2013.

Davis, Martin, Yuri Matijasevič, and Julia Robinson. "Hilbert's Tenth Problem. Diophantine Equations: Positive Aspects of a Negative Solution." American Mathematical Society, 1976.

Davis, Miles, and Quincy Troupe. *Miles: The Autobiography.* New York: Simon & Schuster, 1989.

Davis, Richard. "Creativity in Neurosurgical Publications." *Neurosurgery* 20, no. 4 (1987): 652–63.

De Groot, Adrianus Dingeman. *Het denken van den schaker* (Thought and choice in chess). Amsterdam: N.V. Noord-Hollandsche Uitgevers Maatschappij, 1946.

DeKeyser, Robert. "Beyond Explicit Rule Learning: Automatizing Second Language Morphosyntax." *Studies in Second Language Acquisition* 19, no. 2 (1997): 195–221.

Dempster, Frank N. "The Spacing Effect: A Case Study in the Failure to Apply the Results of Psychological Research." *American Psychologist* 43, no. 8 (1988): 627.

Dethier, Dylan. "What Tiger Woods' First-Ever TV Appearance (at Age 2!) Really Taught Us." *Golf*, March 24, 2020. Accessed June 27, 2023. https://golf.com/news/tiger-woods-youtube-project-first-tv-appearance/.

Dewey, John. *Democracy and Education.* New York: Macmillan, 1916.

Diamond, Jared. *Guns, Germs, and Steel: The Fates of Human Societies.* New York: Norton, 1997.

DiSessa, Andrea A. "Unlearning Aristotelian Physics: A Study of Knowledge-Based Learning." *Cognitive Science* 6, no. 1 (1982): 37–75.

Duncker, Karl. "On Problem Solving." *Psychological Monographs* 58, no. 5 (1945): i–113.

Eden, Scott. "Stroke of Madness." ESPN, January 13, 2013. Accessed June 27, 2023. https://www.espn.com/golf/story/_/id/8865487/tiger-woods-reinvents-golf-swing-third-career-espn-magazine.

Edison Innovation Foundation. "Famous Quotes by Thomas Edison." 2020. Accessed June 27, 2023. https://www.thomasedison.org/edison-quotes.

Efland, Arthur D. *A History of Art Education.* New York: Teachers College Press, 1990.

Egan, Dennis, and Barry Schwartz. "Chunking in Recall of Symbolic Drawings." *Memory & Cognition* 7 (1979): 149–58.

Eglington, Luke, and Sean Kang. "Interleaved Presentation Benefits Science Category Learning." *Journal of Applied Research in Memory and Cognition* 6, no. 4 (2017): 475–85.

Einstein, Albert. "Physics and Reality." Translated by Jean Piccard. *Journal of the Franklin Institute* 221, no. 3 (1936): 349–82.

Engelmann, Siegfried, and Douglas Carnine. *Theory of Instruction: Principles and Applications.* New York: Irvington, 1982.

Ericsson, K. Anders. *Development of Professional Expertise: Toward Measurement of Expert Performance and Design of Optimal Learning Environments.* Cambridge: Cambridge University Press, 2009.

Ericsson, K. Anders, and Walter Kintsch. "Long-Term Working Memory." *Psychological Review* 102, no. 2 (1995): 211–45.

Ericsson, K. Anders, and Robert Pool. *Peak: Secrets from the New Science of Expertise.* Houghton Mifflin Harcourt, 2016.

Ericsson, K. Anders, and Jacqui Smith. *Toward a General Theory of Expertise: Prospects and Limits.* Cambridge: Cambridge University Press, 1991.

Ericsson, K. Anders, Ralf T. Krampe, and Clemens Tesch-Römer. "The Role of Deliberate Practice in the Acquisition of Expert Performance." *Psychological Review* 100, no. 3 (1993): 363.

Fabiani, Monica, Jean Buckley, Gabriele Gratton, Michael G. H. Coles, Emanuel Donchin, and Robert Logie. "The Training of Complex Task Performance." *Acta Psychologica* 71, no. 1–3 (1989): 259–99.

Farndale, Nigel. "Magnus Carlsen: Grandmaster Flash." *Guardian*, October 19, 2013. Accessed June 26, 2023. https://www.theguardian.com/sport/2013/oct/19/magnus -carlsen-chess-grandmaster.

Federal Trade Commission. "Lumosity to Pay $2 Million to Settle FTC Deceptive Advertising Charges for Its 'Brain Training' Program." Press release, January 5, 2016. Accessed June 26, 2023. https://www.ftc.gov/news-events/news/press-releases /2016/01/lumosity-pay-2-million-settle-ftc-deceptive-advertising-charges-its-brain -training-program.

———. "[Proposed] Stipulated Final Judgment and Order for Permanent Injunction and Other Equitable Relief." January 8, 2016. Accessed June 26, 2023. https://www.ftc .gov/system/files/documents/cases/160105lumoslabsstip.pdf.

Fenton, Charles Andrew. *The Apprenticeship of Ernest Hemingway.* New York: Farrar, Straus & Young, 1954.

Feske, Ulrike, and Dianne L. Chambless. "Cognitive Behavioral versus Exposure Only Treatment for Social Phobia: A Meta-Analysis." *Behavior Therapy* 26, no. 4 (1995): 695–720.

Feynman, Richard. *"Surely You're Joking, Mr. Feynman!" Adventures of a Curious Character.* New York: Norton, 1985.

"Feynman: Knowing versus Understanding." Video, YouTube, May 17, 2012. Accessed June 27, 2023. https://www.youtube.com/watch?v=NM-zWTU7X-k.

Fitts, Paul Morris, and Michael Posner. *Human Performance.* Belmont, CA: Brooks/ Cole, 1967.

Foa, Edna, Constance Dancu, Elizabeth Hembree, Lisa Jaycox, Elizabeth Meadows, and Gordon P. Street. "A Comparison of Exposure Therapy, Stress Inoculation Training, and Their Combination for Reducing Posttraumatic Stress Disorder in Female Assault Victims." *Journal of Consulting and Clinical Psychology* 67, no. 2 (1999): 194–200.

Fong, Geoffrey, David Krantz, and Richard Nisbett. "The Effects of Statistical Training on Thinking About Everyday Problems." *Cognitive Psychology* 18 (1986): 253–92.

Free to Choose. Performed by Milton Friedman, 1980.

Gaming Historian. *The Story of Tetris.* February 2, 2018. Accessed June 26, 2023. https://www.youtube.com/watch?v=_fQtxKmgJC8.

Gao, Yuan, Renae Low, Putai Jin, and John Sweller. "Effects of Speaker Variability on Learning Foreign-Accented English for EFL Learners." *Journal of Educational Psychology* 105, no. 3 (2013): 649.

Gardener, Howard. *The Unschooled Mind: How Children Think and How Schools Should Teach.* New York: Basic Books, 1991.

Ghofrani, Hossein, Ian Osterloh, and Friedrich Grimminger. "Sildenafil: From Angina to Erectile Dysfunction to Pulmonary Hypertension and Beyond." *Nature Reviews Drug Discovery* 5, no. 8 (2006): 689–702.

Gick, Mary, and Keith Holyoak. "Analogical Problem Solving." *Cognitive Psychology* 12 (1980): 306–55.

Girma, Haben. *Haben: The Deafblind Woman Who Conquered Harvard Law.* New York: Twelve, 2019.

Glogger-Frey, Inga, Corrina Fleischer, Lisa Grüny, Julian Kappich, and Alexander Renkl. "Inventing a Solution and Studying a Worked Solution Prepare Differently for Learning from Direct Instruction." *Learning and Instruction* 39 (2015): 72–87.

Goldsmith, Jeffrey. "This Is Your Brain on Tetris." *Wired*, May 1, 1994. Accessed June 26, 2023. https://www.wired.com/1994/05/tetris-2/.

Goldstone, Robert. "Isolated and Interrelated Concepts." *Memory & Cognition* 24 (1996): 608–28.

Gould, Robert A., Susan Buckminster, Mark H. Pollack, Michael W. Otto, and Liang Yap. "Cognitive-Behavioral and Pharmacological Treatment for Social Phobia: A Meta-Analysis." *Clinical Psychology: Science and Practice* 4, no. 4 (1997): 291–306.

Gould, Robert A., Michael W. Otto, and Mark H. Pollack. "A Meta-Analysis of Treatment Outcome for Panic Disorder." *Clinical Psychology Review* 15, no. 8 (1995): 819–44.

Gould, Robert A., Michael W. Otto, Mark H. Pollack, and Liang Yap. "Cognitive Behavioral and Pharmacological Treatment of Generalized Anxiety Disorder: A Preliminary Meta-Analysis." *Behavior Therapy* 28, no. 2 (1997): 285–305.

Green, John. "Why Are Humans Suddenly Getting Better at Tetris?" Video, YouTube, October 18, 2018. Accessed June 26, 2023. https://www.youtube.com/watch?v=twS0SrDg-fc.

Greenwald, Morgan. "30 Life-Changing Inventions That Were Totally Accidental." *BestLife*, September 25, 2018. Accessed June 27, 2023. https://bestlifeonline.com/acidental-inventions/.

Grice, H. P. "Logic and Conversation." In *Speech Acts*, by Peter Cole and Jerry L. Morgan, 41–58. Leiden: Brill, 1975.

Grove, William, and Paul Meehl. "Comparative Efficiency of Informal (Subjective, Impressionistic) and Formal (Mechanical, Algorithmic) Prediction Procedures: The Clinical-Statistical Controversy." *Psychology, Public Policy, and Law* 2 (1996): 293–323.

Guskey, Thomas R. *Implementing Mastery Learning, 3rd ed.* Thousand Oaks, CA: Corwin, 2023.

Haier, Richard, Sherif Karama, Leonard Leyba, and Rex E Jung. "MRI Assessment of Cortical Thickness and Functional Activity Changes in Adolescent Girls Following Three Months of Practice on a Visual-Spatial Task." *BMC Research Notes* 2, no. 174 (2009): 174.

Harmon, Claude "Butch," Jr., and Steve Eubanks. *The Pro: Lessons from My Father About Golf and Life.* New York: Crown, 2006.

Hatala, Rose, Lee Brooks, and Geoffrey Norman. "Practice Makes Perfect: The Critical Role of Mixed Practice in the Acquistion of ECG Interpretation Skills." *Advances in Health Sciences Education* 8 (2003): 17–26.

Hatano, Giyoo, and Kayoko Inagaki. "Two Courses of Expertise." *Child Development and Education in Japan* (1986): 262–72.

Hattie, John. *Visible Learning: A Synthesis of Over 800 Meta-Analyses Relating to Achievement.* New York: Routledge, 2008.

Hayes, John. "Cognitive Processes in Creativity." In *Handbook of Creativity*, edited by J. A. Glover, R. R. Ronning, and C. R. Reynolds, 135–45. New York: Plenum, 1989.

Heckman, James J., John Eric Humphries, and Tim Kautz. *The Myth of Achievement Tests: The GED and the Role of Character in American Life.* Chicago: University of Chicago Press, 2013.

Henderson, Laura. "Semaglutide: A Medical Expert's Guide." myBMI, January 23, 2023. https://my-bmi.co.uk/medical-therapy/history-of-semaglutide.

Hendon Mob. "Norway All Time Money List." June 26, 2023. Accessed June 27, 2023. https://pokerdb.thehendonmob.com/ranking/209/.

Henrich, Joseph. *The Secret of Our Success.* Princeton, NJ: Princeton University Press, 2015.

Hermann, Dorothy. *Helen Keller: A Life.* New York: Knopf, 1998.

Herrmann, Esther, Josep Call, María Victoria Hernàndez-Lloreda, Brian Hare, and Michael Tomasello. "Humans Have Evolved Specialized Skills of Social Cognition: The Cultural Intelligence Hypothesis." *Science* 317, no. 5843 (2007): 1360–66.

Heydenreich, Ludwig Heinrich. "Leonardo da Vinci: Italian Artist, Engineer, Scientist." *Britannica*, June 14, 2023. Accessed June 27, 2023. https://www.britannica.com/biography/Leonardo-da-Vinci.

Hirsch, E. D. *Cultural Literacy: What Every American Needs to Know.* New York: Vintage, 1988.

History.com. "Thomas Edison." November 9, 2009. Accessed June 27, 2023. https://www.history.com/topics/inventions/thomas-edison.

Hodge, Frederick Arthur. *John Locke and Formal Discipline.* Lynchburg, VA: Bell, 1911.

Hofmann, Stefan G. "Cognitive Processes During Fear Acquisition and Extinction in Animals and Humans: Implications for Exposure Therapy and Anxiety Disorders." *Clinical Psychology Review* 28, no. 2 (2008): 199–210.

Hofmann, Stefan G., and Gordon J. G. Asmundson. "Acceptance and Mindfulness-Based Therapy: New Wave or Old Hat?" *Clinical Psychology Review* 28, no. 1 (2008): 1–16.

Holmes, Oliver Wendell, Jr. *The Essential Holmes*. Edited by Richard A. Posner. Chicago: University of Chicago Press, 1992.

Howes, Anton. "Age of Invention: Upstream, Downstream." Age of Invention, January 21, 2021. Accessed June 27, 2023. https://www.ageofinvention.xyz/p/age-of-invention-upstream-downstream.

Imir, Zvon. "Annette Obrestad Poker Journey: The 18-Year-Old Poker Queen of Europe." My Poker Coaching. Accessed June 27, 2023. https://www.mypokercoaching.com/annette-obrestad/.

Isaacson, Walter. *Einstein: His Life and Universe*. New York: Simon & Schuster, 2007.

Jacobs, John, Carolyn Prince, Robert Hays, and Eduardo Salas. "A Meta-Analysis of the Flight Simulator Training Research." Naval Training Systems Center, Human Factors Division, August 1990.

James, William. *The Principles of Psychology*. Vol. 2. New York: Henry Holt, 1890.

Janis, Irving. *Air War and Emotional Stress: Psychological Studies of Bombing and Civilian Defense*. New York: McGraw-Hill, 1951.

Jarodzka, Halszka, Thomas Balslev, Marcus Nyström Kenneth Holmqvist, Katharina Scheiter, Peter Gerjets, and Berit Eika. "Conveying Clinical Reasoning Based on Visual Observation via Eye-Movement Modelling Examples." *Instructional Science* 40 (2012): 813–827.

Jimoyiannis, Athanassios, and Vassilis Komis. "Computer Simulations in Physics Teaching and Learning: A Case Study on Students' Understanding of Trajectory Motion." *Computers & Education* 36, no. 2 (2001): 183–204.

Jones, Jeffrey M. "Americans Reading Fewer Books Than in Past." Gallup, January 10, 2022. Accessed June 26, 2023. https://news.gallup.com/poll/388541/americans-reading-fewer-books-past.aspx.

Josephson, Matthew. *Edison: A Biography*. New York: McGraw-Hill, 1959.

Judd, Charles Hubbard. "The Relation of Special Training and General Intelligence." *Educational Review* 36 (1908): 28–42.

Juel, Connie, and Diane Roper-Schneider. "The Influence of Basal Readers on First Grade Reading." *Reading Research Quarterly* 20 (1985): 134–52.

Kahneman, Daniel. "Don't Blink! The Hazards of Overconfidence." *New York Times*, October 19, 2011. Accessed June 27, 2023. https://www.nytimes.com/2011/10/23/magazine/dont-blink-the-hazards-of-confidence.html.

———. *Thinking, Fast and Slow*. New York: Farrar, Straus & Giroux, 2011.

Kahneman, Daniel, and Gary Klein. "Conditions for Intuitive Expertise: A Failure to Disagree." *American Psychologist* 64, no. 6 (2009): 515.

Kahneman, Daniel, Amos Tversky, and P. Slovic. "Judgements of and by Representativeness." In *Judgement Under Uncertainty: Heuristics and Biases*. Cambridge: Cambridge University Press, 1982.

Kalyuga, Slava. "Cognitive Load Theory: How Many Types of Load Does It Really Need?" *Educational Psychology Review* 23, no. 1 (2011): 19.

———. "Expertise Reversal Effect and Its Implications for Learner-Tailored Instruction." *Educational Psychology Review* 19 (2007): 509–39.

Kang, Sean, and Harold Pashler. "Learning Painting Styles: Spacing Is Advantageous When It Promotes Discriminative Contrast." *Applied Cognitive Psychology* 26, no. 1 (2012): 97–103.

Kanigel, Robert. *Apprentice to Genius: The Making of a Scientific Dynasty.* Baltimore: Johns Hopkins University Press, 1993.

Kapur, Manu. "Productive Failure." *Cognition and Instruction* 26 (2008): 379–424.

Karpicke, Jeffrey. "Metacognitive Control and Strategy Selection: Deciding to Practice Retrieval During Learning." *Journal of Experimental Psychology: General* 138, no. 4 (2009): 469.

Karpicke, Jeffrey, and Janelle Blunt. "Retrieval Practice Produces More Learning Than Elaborative Studying with Concept Mapping." *Science* 331, no. 6018 (2011): 772–75.

Keller, Helen. *The Story of My Life.* New York: Doubleday, Page, 1903.

Kelly, Kevin. "103 Bits of Advice I Wish I Had Known." Technium, April 28, 2022. Accessed June 26, 2023. https://kk.org/thetechnium/103-bits-of-advice-i-wish-i-had-known/.

Kiersz, Andy. "Any Rubik's Cube Can Be Solved in 20 Moves, but It Took Over 30 Years for Anyone to Figure That Out." *Business Insider*, January 18, 2019. Accessed June 26, 2023. https://www.businessinsider.com/rubiks-cube-gods-number-steps-to-solve-any-cube-2019-1.

Kiger, Patrick J. "How Nixon's WWII Poker Game Helped Bankroll His First Run for Congress." History.com, February 19, 2019. Accessed June 27, 2023. https://www.history.com/news/richard-nixon-campaign-funds-wwii-poker.

Kintsch, Walter. *Comprehension: A Paradigm for Cognition.* Cambridge: Cambridge University Press, 1998.

Kirschner, Paul A. "Epistemology or Pedagogy, That Is The Question." In *Constructivist Instruction: Success or Failure?*, by Sigmund Tobias and Thomas Duffy, 144–58. New York: Routledge, 2009.

Kirschner, Paul, John Sweller, and Richard E. Clark. "Why Minimal Guidance During Instruction Does Not Work: An Analysis of the Failure of Constructivist, Discovery, Problem-Based, Experiential, and Inquiry-Based Teaching." *Educational Psychologist* 41, no. 2 (2006): 75–86.

Klahr, David. *Exploring Science: The Cognition and Development of Discovery Processes.* Cambridge, MA: MIT Press, 2000.

Klahr, David, and Milena Nigam. "The Equivalence of Learning Paths in Early Science Instruction: Effects of Direct Instruction and Discovery Learning." *Psychological Science* 15, no. 10 (2004): 661–67.

Klein, Gary A., Roberta Calderwood, and Anne Clinton-Cirocco. "Rapid Decision Making on the Fire Ground." *Proceedings of the Human Factors Society Annual Meeting* 30, no. 6 (1986): 576–80.

Klein, Gary, Steve Wolf, Laura Militello, and Caroline Zsambok. "Characteristics of Skilled Option Generation in Chess." *Organizational Behavior and Human Decision Processes* 62, no. 1 (1995): 63–69.

Kleiner, Morris M., and Evgeny S. Vorotnikov. "At What Cost? State and National Estimates of the Economic Costs of Occupational Licensing." Institute for Justice, 2018.

Kluger, Avraham, and Angelo DeNisi. "The Effects of Feedback Interventions on Performance: A Historical Review, a Meta-Analysis, and a Preliminary Feedback Intervention Theory." *Psychological Bulletin* 119, no. 2 (1996): 254–84.

Kornell, Nate, and Robert Bjork. "Learning Concepts and Categories: Is Spacing the 'Enemy of Induction'?" *Psychological Science* 19, no. 6 (2008): 585–92.

Kubricht, James R., Keith Holyoak, and Hongjing Lu. "Intuitive Physics: Current Research and Controversies." *Trends in Cognitive Science* 21, no. 10 (2017): 749–59.

Langley, Pat, Herbert A. Simon, Gary L. Bradshaw, and Jan M. Zytkow. *Scientific Discovery: Computational Explorations of the Creative Processes.* Cambridge, MA: MIT Press, 1987.

Lave, Jean, and Etienne Wenger. *Situated Learning: Legitimate, Peripheral Participation.* Cambridge: Cambridge University Press, 1991.

LeDoux, Joseph. *Anxious: Using the Brain to Understand and Treat Fear and Anxiety.* New York: Penguin Books, 2015.

LeFevre, Jo-Anne, and Peter Dixon. "Do Written Instructions Need Examples?" *Cognition and Instruction* 3, no. 1 (1986): 1–30.

Likourezos, Vicki, Slava Kalyuga, and John Sweller. "The Variability Effect: When Instructional Variability Is Advantageous." *Educational Psychology Review* 31 (2019): 479–97.

Lintern, Gavan, Stanley Roscoe, and Jonathan Sivier. "Display Principles, Control Dynamics, and Environmental Factors in Pilot Training and Transfer." *Journal of Human Factors and Ergonomics Society* 32, no. 3 (1990): 299–317.

Locke, John. *Some Thoughts Concerning Education.* London, 1693.

Logan, Gordon. "Toward an Instance Theory of Automatization." *Psychological Review* 95, no. 4 (1988): 492–527.

Luchins, Abraham. "Mechanization in Problem Solving: The Effect of Einstellung." *Psychological Monographs* 45, no. 6 (1942): i–95.

Maddox, Brenda. *Rosalind Franklin: The Dark Lady of DNA.* New York: Harper Perennial, 2003.

Magill, Richard, and Kellie Hall. "A Review of the Contextual Interference Effect in Motor Acquisition." *Human Movement Science* 9, no. 3–5 (1990): 241–89.

Magyar, Màrton. *The 50 Greatest Stories in Poker History.* Las Vegas, NV: Huntington Press, 2021.

Marcus, Gary, Steven Pinker, Michael Ullman, Michelle Hollander, T. John Rosen, Fei Xu, and Harald Clahsen. "Overregularization in Language Acquisition." *Monographs of the Society for Research in Child Development* (1992): i–178.

Marks, Isaac. *Fears, Phobias, and Rituals: Panic, Anxiety and Their Disorders.* Oxford: Oxford University Press, 1987.

Marrow, Alfred. *The Practical Theorist: The Life and Work of Kurt Lewin.* New York: Basic Books, 1969.

Masters, Rich, and Jon Maxwell. "The Theory of Reinvestment." *International Review of Sport and Exercise Psychology* 1, no. 2 (2008): 160–83.

Matlen, Bryan, and David Klahr. "Sequential Effects of High and Low Instructional Guidance on Children's Acquisition of Experimentation Skills: Is It All in the Timing?" *Instructional Science* 41 (2013): 621–34.

Matthews, Karen, Robert Helmreich, and William Beane. "Pattern A, Achievement Striving, and Scientific Merit: Does Pattern A Help or Hinder?" *Journal of Personality and Social Psychology* 39, no. 5 (1980): 962.

Mavin, Timothy J., and Patrick S. Murray. "The Development of Airline Pilot Skills Through Simulated Practice." In *Learning Through Practice: Models, Traditions, Orientations and Approaches,* edited by Stephen Billet. Dordrecht, Netherlands: Springer, 2010.

Mayer, Richard. "Should There Be a Three-Strikes Rule Against Pure Discovery Learning?" *American Psychologist* 59, no. 1 (2004): 14–19.

McClelland, James, David E. Rumelhart, and PDP Research Group. *Parallel Distributed Processing.* Cambridge, MA: MIT Press, 1986.

McKenna, David. "Robert Smith-Barry: The Man Who Taught the World to Fly." BBC, February 23, 2013. Accessed June 27, 2023. https://www.bbc.co.uk/news/uk-england-21321362.

McNamara, Danielle, and Walter Kintsch. "Learning from Texts: Effects of Prior Knowledge and Text Coherence." *Discourse Processes* 22, no. 3 (1996): 247–88.

Meehl, Paul. *Clinical versus Statistical Prediction: A Theoretical Analysis and Review of the Evidence.* Minneapolis: University of Minnesota Press, 1954.

Meikeljohn, Alexander. "Is Mental Training a Myth?" *Educational Review* 37 (1908): 126–41.

Melby-Lervag, Monica, Thomas S. Redick, and Charles Hulme. "Working Memory Training Does Not Improve Performance on Measures of Intelligence or Other Measures of 'Far Transfer': Evidence from a Meta-Analytic Review." *Perspectives on Psychological Science* 11, no. 4 (2016): 512–34.

Mercier, Hugo, and Dan Sperber. *The Enigma of Reason.* Cambridge, MA: Harvard University Press, 2017.

Merriënboer, Jeroen Van, and Fred Paas. "Automation and Schema Acquisition in Learning Elementary Computer Programming: Implications for the Design of Practice." *Computers in Human Behavior* 6 (1990): 273–89.

Merriënboer, Jeroen van, Marcel de Croock, and Otto Jelsma. "The Transfer Paradox: Effects of Contextual Interference on Retention and Transfer Performance of a Complex Cognitive Skill." *Perceptual and Motor Skills* 84 (1997): 784–86.

Merton, Robert. "Singletons and Multiples in Scientific Discovery: A Chapter in the Sociology of Science." *Proceedings of the American Philosophical Society* 105, no. 5 (1961): 470–86.

Miller, George A. "The Magical Number Seven, Plus or Minus Two: Some Limits on Our Capacity for Processing Information." *Psychological Review* 63, no. 2 (1956): 81–97.

Mineka, Susan, and Richard Zinbarg. "A Contemporary Learning Theory Perspective on the Etiology of Anxiety Disorders: It's Not What You Thought It Was." *American Psychologist* 61, no. 1 (2006): 10–26.

Morley, Robert Michael. "Earning Their Wings: British Pilot Training 1912–1918." MA thesis, University of Saskatchewan, 2006.

Moshman, David, and Molly Geil. "Collaborative Reasoning: Evidence for Collective Rationality." *Thinking & Reasoning* 4, no. 3 (1998): 231–48.

Mowrer, O. Hobart. *Learning Theory and Behavior.* New York: John Wiley, 1960.

Nakata, Tatsuya, and Yuichi Suzuki. "Mixed Grammar Exercises Facilitates Long-Term Retention: Effects of Blocking, Interleaving, and Increasing Practice." *Modern Language Journal* 103, no. 3 (2019): 629–47.

Naylor, James C., and George E. Briggs. "Effects of Task Complexity and Task Organization on the Relative Efficiency of Part and Whole Training Methods." *Journal of Experimental Psychology* 65, no. 3 (1963): 217–24.

Negreanu, Daniel. "Daniel Negreanu Teaches Poker." MasterClass, October 2020. Accessed June 27, 2023. https://www.masterclass.com/classes/daniel-negreanu -teaches-poker.

Neisser, Ulric. *Cognition and Reality: Principles and Implications of Cognitive Psychology.* San Francisco: W. H. Freeman, 1976.

Newell, Allen, and Herbert Simon. *Human Problem Solving.* Englewood Cliffs, NJ: Prentice-Hall, 1972.

Newman, William R., and Lawrence Principe. *Alchemy Tried in Fire: Starkey, Boyle, and the Fate of Helmontian Chymistry.* Chicago: University of Chicago Press, 2002.

Newport, Cal. *Deep Work: Rules for Focused Success in a Distracted World.* New York: Grand Central, 2016.

Noack, Hannes, Martin Lövdén, Florian Schmiedek, and Ulman Lindenberger. "Cognitive Plasticity in Adulthood and Old Age: Gauging the Generality of Cognitive Intervention Effects." *Restorative Neurology and Neuroscience* 27 (2009): 435–53.

NSC Injury Facts. "Deaths by Transportation Mode." 2023. Accessed June 27, 2023. https:// injuryfacts.nsc.org/home-and-community/safety-topics/deaths-by-transportation -mode/.

Obrestad, Annette. "My Story." Video, YouTube, October 13, 2018. Accessed June 27, 2023. https://www.youtube.com/watch?v=mk-0CmsIVFg.

Ogburn, William, and Dorothy Thomas. "Are Inventions Inevitable? A Note on Social Evolution." *Political Science Quarterly* 37, no. 1 (1922): 83–98.

Owen, Adrain M., Adam Hampshire, Jessica A. Grahn, Robert Stenton, Said Dajani, Alistair S. Burns, Robert J. Howard, and Clive G. Ballard. "Putting Brain Training to the Test." *Nature* 465, no. 7299 (2010): 775–78.

Owen, Elizabeth, and John Sweller. "What Do Students Learn While Solving Mathematics Problems?" *Journal of Educational Psychology* 77, no. 3 (1985): 272–84.

Owens, Thomas. *Bebop: The Music and Its Players.* Oxford: Oxford University Press, 1996.

Oxford Reference. "Zone of Proximal Development." Accessed June 26, 2023. https://www.oxfordreference.com/display/10.1093/oi/authority.20110803133528287 ;jsessionid=77DCED74A08B38309BD994609A081496.

Pan, Steven, Jahan Tajran, Jarrett Lovelett, Jessica Osuna, and Timothy Rickard. "Does Interleaved Practice Enhance Foreign Language Learning? The Effects of Training Schedule on Spanish Verb Conjugation Skills." *Journal of Educational Psychology* 111, no. 7 (2019): 1172.

Panter-Downes, Mollie. *London War Notes.* New York: Farrar, Straus & Giroux, 1971.

Patel, Vimla, and Guy Groen. "Developmental Accounts of the Transition from Medical Student to Doctor: Some Problems and Suggestions." *Medical Education* 25, no. 6 (1991): 527–35.

Pauling, Linus. Interview by Robert Richter of WGBH-Boston in *Linus Pauling, Crusading Scientist,* video, 1977.

Piaget, Jean. "Piaget's Theory." In *Carmichael's Manual of Child Psychology,* vol. 1, edited by Paul H. Mussen. New York: Wiley, 1970.

Pinker, Steven, and Arthur Morey. *The Language Instinct: How the Mind Creates Language.* New York: William Morrow, 1994.

Planck, Max. *Scientific Autobiography and Other Papers.* New York: Philosophical Library, 1949.

Plato. *Phaedrus,* in *Complete Works,* edited by J. M. Cooper. Indianapolis: Hackett, 1997.

Plato. *Plato's Republic.* Translated by Benjamin Jowett. Altenmünster, Germany: Jazzybee Verlag Jürgen Beck, n.d.

Pogrebin, Robin, and Scott Reyburn. "Leonardo da Vinci Painting Sells for $450.3 Million, Shattering Auction Highs." *New York Times,* November 15, 2017. Accessed June 26, 2023. https://www.nytimes.com/2017/11/15/arts/design/leonardo-da-vinci -salvator-mundi-christies-auction.html.

Poincaré, Henri. *The Foundations of Science: Science and Hypothesis, the Value of Science, Science and Method.* New York: Science Press, 1913.

PokerListings. "About Chris Moneymaker." 2011. Accessed June 27, 2023. https:// web.archive.org/web/20110822203101/http://www.pokerlistings.com/poker-player _chris-moneymaker.

———. "Best Poker Moments—Annette Obrestad Shares Secrets of Blind Online Poker Win." Video, YouTube, November 11, 2021. Accessed June 27, 2023. https:// www.youtube.com/watch?v=ROE0uB51E0w.

Polanyi, Michael. *The Tacit Dimension.* Garden City, NY: Doubleday, 1966.

Price, Derek J. de Solla. *Little Science, Big Science.* New York: Columbia University Press, 1963.

Principe, Lawrence. *The Secrets of Alchemy.* Chicago: University of Chicago Press, 2012.

Quetelet, Adolphe. *A Treatise on Man and the Development of His Faculties.* Edinburgh, 1842.

Quote Investigator. "Can't Somebody Bring Me a One-Handed Economist?" April 10, 2019. Accessed June 27, 2023. https://quoteinvestigator.com/2019/04/10/one-handed/.

———. "It Is Better to Know Nothing Than to Know What Ain't So?" May 30, 2015. Accessed June 27, 2023. https://quoteinvestigator.com/2015/05/30/better-know/.

Rachman, Stanley J. *Fear and Courage.* San Francisco: W. H. Freeman, 1990.

Ramnerö, Jonas. "Exposure Therapy for Anxiety Disorders: Is There Room for Cognitive Interventions?" In *Exposure Therapy: Rethinking the Model, Refining the Method,* edited by Peter Neudeck and Hans-Ulrich Wittchen, 275–97. New York: Springer, 2012.

Rantanen, Esa M., and Donald A. Talleur. "Incremental Transfer and Cost Effectiveness of Ground-Based Flight Trainers in University Aviation Programs." *Proceedings of the Human Factors and Ergonomics Society Annual Meeting* (2005): 764–68.

Rawlings, Bruce S. "After a Decade of Tool Innovation, What Comes Next?" *Child Development Perspectives* 16, no. 2 (2022): 118–24.

Reed, Stephen K., Alexandra Dempster, and Michael Ettinger. "Usefulness of Analogous Solutions for Solving Algebra Word Problems." *Journal of Experimental Psychology: Learning, Memory, and Cognition* 11, no. 1 (1985): 106–25.

Reijnoudt, Jan, and Niek Sterk. *Tragedie Op Tenerife.* Kampen, Netherlands: Kok, 2002.

Ritchie, Stuart. *Intelligence: All That Matters.* London: Quercus, 2016.

Ritchie, Stuart J., Timothy C. Bates, and Robert Plomin. "Does Learning to Read Improve Intelligence? A Longitudinal Multivariate Analysis of Identical Twins from Age 7 to 16." *Child Development* 86, no. 1 (2015): 23–36.

Roediger, Henry L., III, and Andrew C. Butler. "The Critical Role of Retrieval Practice in Long-Term Retention." *Trends in Cognitive Science* 15, no. 1 (2011): 20–27.

Roscoe, Stanley. "Incremental Transfer Effectiveness." *Human Factors* 13, no. 6 (1971): 561–67.

Rosenshine, Barak, and Robert Stevens. "Teaching Functions." In *Handbook of Research on Teaching,* 3rd ed., edited by M. C. Wittrock, 376–91. New York: Macmillan, 1986.

Rowland, Christopher. "The Effect of Testing versus Restudy on Retention: A Meta-Analytic Review of the Testing Effect." *Psychological Bulletin* 140, no. 6 (2014): 1432–63.

Saelee, Joseph. "First Ever Level 34 in NES Tetris." Video, YouTube, February 15, 2020. Accessed June 26, 2023. https://www.youtube.com/watch?v=rWMUYBinriw.

———. "284 Lines (Full Video)." Video, YouTube, February 15, 2020. Accessed June 26, 2023. https://www.youtube.com/watch?v=L7SRuMG6AJc.

Saigh, Philip A. "Pre- and Postinvasion Anxiety in Lebanon." *Behavior Therapy* 15, no. 2 (1984): 185–90.

Sala, Giovanni, and Fernand Gobet. "Does Far Transfer Exist? Negative Evidence from Chess, Music, and Working Memory Training." *Current Directions in Psychological Science* 26, no. 6 (2017): 515–20.

Schonbrun, Zach. "A New Generation Stacks Up Championships in an Old Game: Tetris." *New York Times*, December 28, 2021. Accessed June 26, 2023. https://www.nytimes.com/2021/12/28/sports/tetris-game.html.

Schwartz, Daniel, and Taylor Martin. "Inventing to Prepare for Future Learning: The Hidden Efficiency of Encouraging Original Student Production in Statistics Instruction." *Cognition and Instruction* 22, no. 2 (2004): 129–84.

Seligman, Martin. "Phobias and Preparedness." *Behavior Therapy* 2, no. 3 (1971): 307–20.

Shaw, George Bernard. *The Doctor's Dilemma.* First presented 1906.

Shea, John, and Robyn Morgan. "Contextual Interference Effects on the Acquisition, Retention, and Transfer of a Motor Skill." *Journal of Experimental Psychology: Human Learning and Memory* 5, no. 2 (1979): 179.

Siegel, Paul, and Richard Warren. "Less Is Still More: Maintenance of the Very Brief Exposure Effect 1 Year Later." *Emotion* 13, no. 2 (2013): 338–44.

Siegler, Robert S. *Emerging Minds: The Process of Change in Children's Thinking.* Oxford: Oxford University Press, 1998.

Simon, Herbert. *Administrative Behavior.* New York: Macmillan, 1947.

———. "How Managers Express Their Creativity." *Engineering Management International* 4 (1986): 71–76.

———. "What Is an 'Explanation' of Behavior?" *Psychological Science* 3, no. 3 (1992): 150–61.

Simonton, Dean. *Greatness: Who Makes History and Why.* New York: Guilford Press, 1994.

Singh, Simon. *Fermat's Last Theorem.* London: Fourth Estate, 1997.

Singley, Mark, and John Anderson. *The Transfer of Cognitive Skill.* Cambridge, MA: Harvard University Press, 1989.

Sinha, Tanmay, and Manu Kapur. "When Problem Solving Followed by Instruction Works: Evidence for Productive Failure." *Review of Educational Research* 91, no. 5 (2021): 761–98.

Skinner, Burrhus Frederic. "A Case History in Scientific Method." *American Psychologist* 11, no. 5 (1956): 221.

Souriau, Paul. *Théorie de l'Invention.* Paris: Hachette, 1881.

Spaeth, Edmund B., Jr. "What a Lawyer Needs to Learn." In *Tacit Knowledge in Professional Practice: Researcher and Practitioner Perspectives*, edited by Robert J. Sternberg and Joseph A. Horvath, 38–57. Mahwah, NJ: Lawrence Erlbaum, 1999.

Stanovich, Keith. "Matthew Effects in Reading: Some Consequences of Individual Differences in the Acquisition of Literacy." *International Literacy Association* 21, no. 4 (1986): 360–407.

Sternberg, Robert J., and James C. Kaufman, eds. *The Cambridge Handbook of Creativity.* Cambridge: Cambridge University Press, 1999.

Stokes, A. B. "War Strains and Mental Health." *Journal of Nervous and Mental Disease* 101, no. 3 (1945): 215–19.

Swain, Merrill. "Communicative Competence: Some Roles for Comprehensible Input and Comprehensible Output in Its Development." In *Input in Second Language Acquisition,* edited by Susan M. Gass and Carolyn G. Madden. New York: Newbury House, 1985.

Sweller, John. "Story of a Research Program." *Education Review* 23 (2016).

Sweller, John, and Matt Levine. "Effects of Goal Specificity on Means-Ends Analysis and Learning." *Journal of Experimental Psychology: Learning, Memory and Cognition* 8, no. 5 (1982): 463–74.

Sweller, John, Robert Mawer, and Walter Howe. "Consequences of History-Cued and Means-End Strategies in Problem Solving." *American Journal of Psychology* 95, no. 3 (1982): 455–83.

Sweller, John, Robert F. Mawer, and Mark R. Ward. "Development of Expertise in Mathematical Problem Solving." *Journal of Experimental Psychology: General* 112, no. 4 (1983): 639–61.

Tetlock, Philip. *Expert Political Judgment: How Good Is It? How Can We Know?* Princeton, NJ: Princeton University Press, 2006.

Tetlock, Philip, and Dan Gardener. *Superforecasting: The Art and Science of Prediction.* Toronto: Signal, 2015.

Thaden-Koch, Thomas C., Robert Dufresne, and Jose Mestre. "Coordination of Knowledge in Judging Animated Motion." *Physical Review Special Topics: Physics Education Research* 2, no. 2 (2006).

Thorndike, Edward. *Educational Psychology.* New York: Lemke & Buechner, 1903.

———. "The Effect of Changed Data upon Reasoning." *Journal of Experimental Psychology* 5, no. 1 (1922): 33.

———. *Human Learning.* New York: Century, 1931.

———. "Mental Discipline in High School Studies." *Journal of Educational Psychology* 15, no. 1 (1924): 1.

———. *The Principles of Teaching: Based on Psychology.* New York: A.G. Seiler, 1906.

Titmuss, Richard. *Problems of Social Policy.* London: His Majesty's Stationery Office, 1950.

Tricot, André, and John Sweller. "Domain-Specific Knowledge and Why Teaching Generic Skills Does Not Work." *Educational Psychology Review* 26, no. 2 (2014): 265–83.

Twain, Mark. *Life as I Find It.* Edited by Charles Neider. New York: Harper & Row, 1977.

US Air Force. "Link Trainer." May 13, 2022. Accessed June 27, 2023. https://web .archive.org/web/20120124230852/http://www.nationalmuseum.af.mil/factsheets /factsheet_print.asp?fsID=3371.

US Department of Education. National Center for Education Statistics. "Adult Literacy in the United States." September 17, 2019. Accessed June 26, 2023. https:// web.archive.org/web/20200730223012/https:/nces.ed.gov/datapoints/2019179.asp.

———. "What PIAAC Measures." 2019. Accessed June 26, 2023. https://nces.ed.gov /surveys/piaac/measure.asp.

Van Etten, Michelle, and Steven Taylor. "Comparative Efficacy of Treatments for Post-Traumatic Stress Disorder: A Meta-Analysis." *Clinical Psychology and Psychotherapy* 5, no. 3 (1998): 126–44.

VanLengen, Craig A. "Does Instruction in Computer Programming Improve Problem-Solving Ability?" *CIS Educator Forum* 2, no. 2 (1990): 11–15.

Vernon, Philip. "Psychological Effects of Air-Raids." *Journal of Abnormal and Social Psychology* 36, no. 4 (1941): 457.

Vervliet, Bram, Michelle G. Craske, and Dirk Hermans. "Fear Extinction and Relapse: State of the Art." *Annual Review of Clinical Psychology* 9 (2013): 215–48.

Voss, James F., Jeffrey Blais, Mary L. Means, Terry R. Greene, and Ellen Ahwesh. "Informal Reasoning and Subject Matter Knowledge in the Solving of Economics Problems by Naive and Novice Individuals." *Cognition and Instruction* 3, no. 4 (1986): 269–302.

Walk That Bass. "Bebop Explained." May 24, 2019. Accessed June 27, 2023. https:// www.youtube.com/watch?v=gEwWjJ7c0u4.

Watrin, Luc, Gizem Hülür, and Oliver Wilhelm. "Training Working Memory for Two Years—No Evidence of Latent Transfer to Intelligence." *Journal of Experimental Psychology: Learning, Memory and Cognition* 48, no. 5 (2022): 717–33.

Watson, James. *The Double Helix.* New York: Atheneum, 1968.

Wenger, Etienne. *Communities of Practice: Learning, Meaning, and Identity.* Cambridge: Cambridge University Press, 1999.

Wertheimer, Max. *Productive Thinking.* New York: Harper, 1959.

White, Lynn, Jr. *Medieval Technology and Social Change.* Oxford: Clarendon Press, 1962.

Whitehead, Alfred North. *The Aims of Education.* New York: Macmillan, 1929.

Wickens, Christopher D., Shaun Hutchins, Thomas Carolan, and John Cumming. "Effectiveness of Part-Task Training and Increasing-Difficulty Training Strategies: A Meta-Analysis Approach." *Human Factors: The Journal of the Human Factors and Ergonomics Society* 55, no. 2 (2012): 461–70.

Wieman, Carl, and Katherine Perkins. "Transforming Physics Education." *Physics Today* 58, no. 11 (2005): 36.

Wightman, D. C., and G. Lintern. "Part-Task Training of Tracking in Manual Control." Naval Training Equipment Center, 1984.

Willingham, Daniel T., Elizabeth M. Hughes, and David G. Dobolyi. "The Scientific Status of Learning Styles Theories." *Teaching of Psychology* 42, no. 3 (2015): 266–71.

Wise, John A., V. David Hopkin, and Daniel J. Garland. *Handbook of Aviation Human Factors.* 2nd ed. Boca Raton, FL: CRC Press, 2010.

Wolitzky-Taylor, Kate B., Jonathan D. Horowitz, Mark B. Powers, and Michael J. Telch. "Psychological Approaches in the Treatment of Specific Phobias: A Meta-Analysis." *Clinical Psychology Review* 28, no. 6 (2008): 1021–37.

Wolpe, Joseph. *Psychotherapy by Reciprocal Inhibition.* Stanford, CA: Stanford University Press, 1958.

Woodworth, Robert, and Edward Thorndike. "The Influence of Improvement in One Mental Function upon the Efficiency of Other Functions." *Psychological Review* 8, no. 3 (1901): 247.

World Series of Poker. "2007 World Series of Poker Europe." September 2007. Accessed June 27, 2023. https://web.archive.org/web/20080417044214/http://www.worldseriesofpoker.com/tourney/updates_pn.asp?tourneyID=3572&groupid=316.

Wulf, Gabriele, and Charles Shea. "Principles Derived from the Study of Simple Skills Do Not Generalize to Complex Skill Learning." *Psychonomic Bulletin & Review* 9, no. 2 (2002): 185–211.

Wulf, Gabriele, Barbara Lauterbach, and Tonya Toole. "The Learning Advantages of an External Focus of Attention in Golf." *Research Quarterly for Exercise and Sport* 70, no. 2 (1999): 120–26.

Yong, Ed. "The Real Wisdom of the Crowds." *National Geographic,* January 31, 2013. Accessed June 27, 2023. https://www.nationalgeographic.com/science/article/the-real-wisdom-of-the-crowds.

Zsambok, Caroline, and Gary Klein. *Naturalistic Decision Making.* Mahwah, NJ: Erlbaum, 1997.

Zuckerman, Harriet. *Scientific Elite: Nobel Laureates in the United States.* New Brunswick, NJ: Transaction, 1977.

INDEX

ABOUT THE AUTHOR

SCOTT H. YOUNG is the *Wall Street Journal* bestselling author of *Ultra-learning*, a podcast host, a computer programmer, and an avid reader. Since 2006, he has published weekly essays to help people learn and think better. His work has been featured in the *New York Times*, *Pocket*, and *Business Insider*; on the BBC; and at TEDx, among other outlets. He doesn't promise to have all the answers, just a place to start. He lives in Vancouver, Canada.

BY THE SAME AUTHOR

Learn a new skill, stay relevant and adapt to
whatever the workplace throws your way. Ultralearning
is the essential guide to future-proofing your career
and maximizing your competitive advantage
through self-education.

Available in paperback, ebook and audiobook

ORDER YOUR COPY NOW